The James Bond Songs

The James Bond Songs

Pop Anthems of Late Capitalism

ADRIAN DAUB

AND

CHARLES KRONENGOLD

OXFORD
UNIVERSITY PRESS

Oxford University Press is a department of the University of
Oxford. It furthers the University's objective of excellence in research,
scholarship, and education by publishing worldwide.

Oxford   New York
Auckland   Cape Town   Dar es Salaam   Hong Kong   Karachi
Kuala Lumpur   Madrid   Melbourne   Mexico City   Nairobi
New Delhi   Shanghai   Taipei   Toronto

With offices in
Argentina   Austria   Brazil   Chile   Czech Republic   France   Greece
Guatemala   Hungary   Italy   Japan   Poland   Portugal   Singapore
South Korea   Switzerland   Thailand   Turkey   Ukraine   Vietnam

Oxford is a registered trademark of Oxford University Press
in the UK and certain other countries.

Published in the United States of America by
Oxford University Press
198 Madison Avenue, New York, NY 10016

Library of Congress Cataloging-in-Publication Data
Daub, Adrian, author.
The James Bond songs : pop anthems of late capitalism / Adrian Daub and Charles Kronengold.
pages cm
Includes bibliographical references and index.
ISBN 978–0–19–023452–2 (hardcover : alk. paper)
1. Motion picture music—History and criticism.   2. James Bond films—History and criticism.
3. Bond, James (Fictitious character)
I. Kronengold, Charles (Charles Stewart), author.   II. Title.
ML2075.D36 2015
781.5'42—dc23

9 8 7 6 5 4 3 2 1
Printed in the United States of America
on acid-free paper

CONTENTS

LIST OF FIGURES

The James Bond Songs

Introduction

James Bond and the End(s) of the Pop Song

The James Bond films have a loyal audience; maybe you're part of it. Their songs do not. They hardly represent the heights of popular music. So why have we written a book about them? Partly because they keep getting pushed out into cultural space as if you cared—since 1965 there have been at least thirty songs, and at least forty compilations of those songs, pressed in over a dozen countries. But mostly we wanted to write this book because we think the Bond songs say something about what's happened to pop music since the early 1960s, and what's happened to us as listeners to pop.

Over this fifty-year span, the process of making and hearing pop songs has been turned upside-down. Pop records have been produced under vastly different technological and institutional regimes for an ever-widening range of audiences who are being addressed in all sorts of ways. A pop song from 2014 might be unrecognizable as such to a listener transported from 1964. Or not; pop music of the post–rock and roll era has also managed to preserve older themes and pre-rock musical aesthetics. The Bond songs fascinate us for precisely the way they engage this dynamic of change and stasis. They both reveal and conceal pop's many transformations while grasping a singular strand of pop-music tradition in a viselike grip that even Jaws and his fellow Bond heavies would admire.

A Bond song begins in a kind of no man's land. It's neither part of the narrative nor entirely independent from it. What these songs are actually "about" can be surprisingly difficult to parse. And together these songs form a canon unlike any other. The songs themselves are interesting artifacts, of course. Some have aged better than others, but none has aged all that well. Some may inspire nostalgia, depending on your age. Others may leave you dumbfounded, certain you've never heard them before in your life, even though you're pretty sure you caught the movie once on TNT. In this they're like many other film songs. But their status as a canon can direct our hearings and rehearings in particular ways, especially because they press on the pop song's sore spots: uncertainties about its addressees, demands that it sound both "familiar" and "new" (and the instability of these two aesthetic categories), and stubborn questions about whether pop music actually has a purpose.

The songs that open the James Bond movies are commercial products, tie-ins to the films designed to sell movie tickets and, ideally, storm the pop charts. Everybody knows they may be quickly forgotten afterward (quick: who sang "All Time High"?). But that's the price to pay for having a song with a mission. Bond songs have to both conform to contemporary top-40 hits in important respects (you don't want them to sound too weird for radio play) and be sufficiently different from top-40 songs in order to be recognizable as part of the brand. These songs are assemblages of particular features intended to do a specific job. There may not be a formula, but there's list of ingredients, a sense of proportion, and so on. While other pop songs may try to make us forget that they likewise have jobs to do, Bond songs really can't and won't. But for all that, these records are not particularly slick. They stick out on the charts even when they climb them. And once these songs have been edged out of the spotlight, the charts seem a less strange, far more boring place. The Bond songs may sound a little like the songs above and below them on the charts, but they are also substantially different. They're awkward and lumbering pop chimeras, beholden to conventions pop abandoned decades ago. Just the idea of a big Hollywood studio hiring a quintessentially eighties flash-in-the-pan like the band a-ha to ape a hybrid musical idiom created (and already belated) in the early sixties is in itself so wonderfully strange that we felt it deserved a book.

When you listen to the songs that open the Bond movies (and a handful of others that run over the closing credits), you realize that they weren't "of their moment" even when they were first recorded. James Bond was a creation of the fifties and became an emblem of the early sixties—and his development was arrested there. The gadgets and babes kept up with the times (and an interesting book could be written about the changing tastes reflected in the curves of the Bond girls), but the songs remained resolutely stuck in time. At least partly: the blaring brass, orchestral textures, and murder-ballad-style texts remained fixtures well into the 1990s. But each Bond song nevertheless brought those well-worn textures into dialogue with the music of its moment, and thus with the hopes, anxieties, and politics of that moment.

That dialogue was central to the job these songs had to do in the films they opened. For all the constraints the increasingly formulaic Bond universe placed on these songs, their job consisted of getting the audience into a headspace in which, say, the 60s and the 80s could coexist. The lights would dim in a 1983 theater, and the opening sequence would feature the boxy cars and boxier coats of the era. Then the silhouetted strippers would start gyrating, the song would come on, and in a weird way the movie told you that you were now in two places at once. The song said this through its instrumentation, its lyrics, its voice. The visuals of the opening sequence would tout the timeless values of the series' universe—diamonds, guns, and T & A—but the song would talk about time and history. It would try to sound like 1964's iconic "Goldfinger" in some way, it would acknowledge its own failure to do so in some way, and it would present a voice (perhaps familiar, perhaps unknown) to hold up to all the other voices that had come before.

Every Bond song establishes a relation between Shirley Bassey's "Goldfinger" and the year of its film's release—differently, depending on the sensibilities, age, and styles of the artists involved, as well as the particularities of that year's top-40 pop. And as the Bond songs accumulate, each new song has to piece out its relation to more and more musical stuff. If you're composing a Bond song the first step is to listen to the old ones; what what you hear will influence how you understand the exact nature of your job. And of course there's always a chance you'll mishear the older songs, misunderstand the tradition, or forget to account for a few of the Bond songs that bear upon yours. That's part of the risk—an unusual one in pop music. In tracing the history of the Bond songs, you trace pop music's own sense of its history. Pop, which often thrives on being of-the-moment and disposable, usually doesn't want to concern its audience too much with its own provenance, often preferring to pretend it doesn't have any. The performers knew, of course, and some savvy listeners might too. But they weren't who the record was for. Bond songs, by contrast, are for people who know the Bond songs.

Self-reflexivity forced itself upon Bond singers far more urgently and obviously than it impinged on their non-Bond work. There they could strategically forget, something that the Bond songs made impossible from the first. Almost from the beginning the Bond songs registered the tensions between older and newer aesthetic practices, technological regimes, and modes of distribution. There never was a moment when they weren't strange and a little out of time. Even Bassey, the queen of the Bond song herself, had most of her non-Bond success in Vegas—another bauble of 60s kitsch preserved in time, like a fly in amber, by the glacial grind of capitalism while the world around it moved on.

To see how inimical this untimeliness is to the way pop music usually works, consider the following. Classical music has gods: you ascend to heaven and you are one more of the elect. You do not displace someone else—the ascension of Brahms and Wagner didn't displace Mozart and Beethoven. But pop stars, and to a lesser extent the songs that make them temporarily famous, always exist under the threat of being disposable and local; that's why we have *kings* of pop. They ascend the throne; they throw some orgies and command some minions; and lackeys put their faces on any piece of merchandise big enough to carry it. But all the while there are pretenders and would-be assassins waiting in the wings. Then you get forced off the throne, or you expire on a Las Vegas toilet, and suddenly someone else is walking around in your vestments and hogging your throne. You die, you lose your cachet, you get charged with some sex crimes, and suddenly Neverland belongs to the bank and your crown passes on to someone else.

In all these respects, the Bond song is unusual pop. A new Bond song never displaces the last one. Unlike the top-20 acts that often depend on their audience forgetting that their music had a history (aided no doubt by the fact that some fans are so young that they simply don't remember any of it), Bond songs forced some of pop's most business-as-usual crooners, belters, hacks, and scribblers—some of the most shameless purveyors of disposable tunes—to insert themselves into a lineage, to grapple with all the artists who had played this particular game, without *any* hope of replacing them or outdoing them. Bond songs are about the early sixties, yes, but they're also about how their own moment differs from the sixties. Over the decades they've found many ways of measuring that difference.

Pop music is supposed to be portable, to travel well. It's supposed to sound good on different continents, in different contexts, to wildly different audiences who probably hear wildly different things. It should sound good on a stereo system, through headphones, on a cheap transistor radio, banged out on a piano, or intoned by a six-year-old. It should be intelligible even if it's heard only in part, even if you only catch a few phrases wafting through the windows of a passing car. Above all, a pop record is supposed to make us forget that it can change as it grows old—as we grow old. The moment you realize you've aged out of the target window for a particular kind of pop music is when you recognize a song as a cover and no one else around you does. It can be embarrassing to possess memories that everyone else is too young for. And it can be worse when you feel you can't shake pop's memories of its own history: it's even more embarrassing when you listen to a pop song and hear *other people's* memories. The James Bond songs are precisely the kind of pop music that makes you feel old.

They're also pop music that makes you feel like a dirty old man. When Bassey was recording "Diamonds Are Forever" in 1971, composer John Barry supposedly tried to coax a more lively performance from the singer by telling her to imagine she was serenading a penis. Barry probably wasn't aware of it, but he was carrying on a tradition started by Ian Fleming himself: in the Bond novels, too, there are moments where all plausible deniability is cast aside and the sexual subtext of the spy story is turned simply into text. In the novel *The Man with the Golden Gun* (1965), Bond prepares his hunt for the killer Francisco "Pistols" Scaramanga by reading a dossier drawn up by MI6. There he comes across a psychologist's opinion that "in the Freudian thesis, [Scaramanga's] 'arm's length' would become the length of the masculine organ." While Bond doesn't encounter this dossier in the 1974 film version, he doesn't have to: the song spells it all out for you.

The songs tell us that whatever else the movies purport to be about—guns, subs, nukes, launch codes—they are really all about sex. If you've ever seen a Bond film this won't come as a shock to you, but it is nevertheless remarkable that the songs are the only place (beyond the Bond girls' salacious names) where the films ever flat-out admit this fact. The song was where the movies abandoned the nudge nudge wink wink ethos of double entendre and hoary pun; it's where from the beginning they left behind the sexual mores of the years when James Bond was President Kennedy's Cape Cod beach reading, and said flat out what was what. And they did so in a female voice.

For a long stretch, between Tom Jones's "Thunderball" and Chris Cornell's "You Know My Name" (for the *Casino Royale* reboot in 2006), the Bond song was almost exclusively a feminine domain, and it was the domain of a particular kind of femininity. The singers were frequently nonwhite (Shirley Bassey, Gladys Knight, Patti LaBelle, Tina Turner) and they were sexually ambiguous—female voices are as ubiquitous in the Bond songs as they are absent from the Bond films. The song was where the film's sexual politics were turned on their head: "the news is that I am in control," k.d. lang intones in her song for *Tomorrow Never Dies* (1997). It only makes explicit what had been obvious for decades. Within the confines of the Bond song the world of James Bond is reimagined. Where in the films women are whimpering airheads or seductive sexpots, the women who "speak" in the songs (and the women who sang the songs) were decidedly different. The songs held up a funhouse mirror to the world of the Bond film proper, as though they spoke, with palpable trepidation, of a world in which (gasp!) women controlled the hero's destiny, in which they had him in their power, in which they knew far more than he did.

But if most of the singers of the Bond songs' heyday were women, they were carefully kept apart from the Bond movies' other female stars, the Bond girls. Shirley Bassey lent her voice to three Bond songs, and she is identified with the series more than anyone besides Sean Connery. She never had a cameo in any of the films she put her stamp on. The one exception, Madonna's brief cameo in 2002's *Die Another Day* (as well as Sheena Easton's appearance in the song sequence of *For Your Eyes Only*), was a calculated breach of decorum. You just didn't introduce your Bond girls to your Bond singers. Their relationship was implicitly adversarial: Shirley Bassey herself assumes the role of a woman hurt by Auric Goldfinger in her signature song, but she evinces precious little sympathy for those who follow her into Goldfinger's trap. In a stretch of songs from the Brosnan years (most famous among them is 1995's "GoldenEye"), the singer seems to impersonate something like James Bond's stalker girlfriend—but that stalker girlfriend turns out to be the film's villain instead. Those songs thus set up the movie that follows as a struggle between the Bond girls' desire for the superspy and the much more powerful and destructive desire that motivated the film's baddies—the object of which, it turned out, was once again Bond himself.

This book traces some of the musical and lyrical conceits that have allowed James Bond to remain not just a box-office draw, but an intermittent chart-topper with his own "best of" as well. It will be a story of adaptation and tradition that is rather unusual in pop music. At the same time it is the story of shifting mores and audience interests—reflected, and to some extent transformed, by the Bond song. It is a story of a billion-dollar franchise that reserved the right to open each movie with a pretty perverse bit of musical nostalgia—and to talk about sex and violence, desire and destruction, hedonism and accumulation, and what connects them, with a frankness neither Fleming's books nor the films ever managed.

POP WITH A TRADITION, OR *THE BEST OF JAMES BOND*

We realized this group of songs was worth studying when we considered the oddness of a common thrift-store find, *The Best of James Bond*, first released in 1992. Various iterations of this album turn up on CD, LP, and cassette. It's amusing that there is such a thing and that it bears this title. Let that sink in for a moment: *The Best* of a man who is neither songwriter or performer nor, for that matter, real—a fictional character who doesn't even sing. And what do these compilations pull together? There are albums that are of their moment, that matter primarily because of their umbilical connection to a particular point in time. They show the state of the art, or anticipate where music was heading; they provide the definitive statement on a decade, a genre, an event. *The Best of James Bond* does no such thing. It simply compiles a set of songs recorded decades apart, written by a large group of accomplished but unabashedly commercial composers and lyricists, and typically sung by washed-up or not-quite stars.

That this flotsam exists as a compilation is itself puzzling and significant. It speaks to the way these songs were and still are intended to be appreciated. *The Best of James Bond* is not some promotional item or kitschy curio (unlike the original soundtrack albums the songs initially appear on). It's a fairly solid seller that continues to be updated with new songs and rereleased. A competing product, *Best of Bond . . . James Bond*, works similarly, sometimes throwing in some instrumental numbers along with the songs. It too exists in many versions. These albums were preceded by *James Bond Greatest Hits*, an early-eighties product that, like the others, compiled all the extant Bond songs. Linking these songs together brings out their similarities as well as their differences. These compilations also provide an easy way to map the Bond songs onto the trajectory of post-1950s top-40 pop. The Bond songs can start to seem like a coherent body of work—which papers over the fact that they're not meant to be unified by makers, style, artistic impulse, mood, subject matter, or anything else that's supposed to guide the curation of long-playing albums.

But in what sense are these musical numbers the "greatest" or "best" of James Bond? Best at what? Remember, these albums include the *entirety* of the title songs, and sometimes the instrumental themes as well. A compilation normally edits, and its omissions often speak louder than what it takes aboard. These albums vacuum it all up, independent of any judgment of quality, relevance, or coherence. Some of the songs have had an impact on their own, a few ("You Only Live Twice," for instance) probably less than they should have. Many others seem to have gone into torpor as soon as they left the pop charts, until the moment a Bond compilation kissed them awake. A few, like Lulu's "The Man with the Golden Gun," came nowhere near the charts in the first place; the most you can say is that they were essentially written to be on this kind of compilation twenty years in the future.

So why not call these albums *The Complete James Bond*? Record companies have often stoked the desires of completists; there would be no shame in wanting *all* of James Bond. So why "best"? Is it just that songs are "better" than low-profile instrumental cues—that the idea behind these compilations is to simply get rid of the chaff? These albums certainly function that way, culling most of the songs (and sometimes the main instrumental themes) from the original soundtracks.

We think there's a deeper sense in which the Bond songs represent the "best" of this fictional character; it derives from something fundamental about what pop records are good for. We should note, first, that these songs mostly *aren't* the best of their artists, moments, kinds, or styles. Usually they don't find their way onto other compilations. Their composers, lyricists, and performers knew what they were getting into. In writing or singing a Bond song, these artists accepted a musical idiom and an ideology that would make the song a strange fit for their own "best of" collections. Instead it would leave the song orphaned until such a point that the song and its peers could be collected in an album of their own. You're supposed to judge these songs not by reference to the artist's other output, or by other songs popular or influential the year they came out; it's with reference to the other Bond songs.

And these records are not "best" because they generate their singers' finest performances. Making songs for this canon puts the Bond-song vocalists in a funny position, and it shows. Consider what the Bond songs ask of their singers. A Bond-song artist must give up something of her artistic autonomy. She dispels the illusion that she's singing because she's inspired. For three minutes or so she has to adjust her basic aesthetic in order to play a narrowly defined role, make a little money, and gain a certain sort of publicity, even if that publicity is entirely in the shadow of the film's promotion. And a lot more is asked of her: as part of the job she signs up for, she needs to grasp, participate in, and help perpetuate the mysterious tradition we described earlier.

The Bond singer is asked to squeeze her specific sound, style, and history into a pretty narrow set of gestures and practices that she has to make her own, but from which she's not supposed to depart in any major way. Often we're aware of the struggle this requires: we can get an odd feeling of intimacy watching this familiar (or unfamiliar) singer doing this weird thing on such a big stage. Especially if we know her other work, we can sense how hard it is for her to find a place for herself in an increasingly crowded network of singers, songwriters, instrumentalists, producers, engineers, songs, films, musical themes, poetic devices, and cinematic effects. We may be excited for certain favorite artists of ours to be picked for the next Bond song, but it seems a little anxiety on our favorite artist's behalf is also called for.

Two things hold this network together. One is the coherence of the Bond brand. This concerns not just plots and motifs (danger, diamonds, gold, guns), but also an overall feel—a kind of lushness that's somewhere between intoxicating and suffocating, a kind of nihilism that nevertheless wears its heart on its sleeve. It's a coherence established over decades, in a joint effort among directors, producers, composers, set designers, actors. and others. This network of people, songs, and films depends equally on a second element: a belief in the power and efficacy of the decaying-but-inexhaustible pop song.

This is why a collection of all the Bond songs on a CD can be billed as the "best of." *All* the Bond songs are "best" in the sense that songs do a better job of branding than anything else does: better than a single bloody image, better than the revolving door of stars, better than Fleming's novels, better than the films themselves. The Bond brand can't be captured entirely visually, or narratively, or verbally, or through an actor's accent or the sound of a revolver: there's something more. And a Bond song can get at that "more" because it works verbally and nonverbally, directly and indirectly; it targets both collective memory and what you personally remember. And it interpellates us more *gently* than any other Bond-brand element, because in addition to functioning as a Bond song, it can also be heard as just a song—an ordinary, competently made pop record. Something that can sneak up on us while driving in our car, listening to the radio. Unlike most other elements of James Bond's universe, the songs are more firmly rooted in *our* world than in *his*. We recognize the theme songs, but he probably wouldn't.

Bond songs are effective branding mechanisms partly because of this gentleness: a Bond song never really burns a mark onto anyone's hide. It delineates the main character relatively softly—we never get a lyric like, "They say that cat Shaft is a bad mother." Its gestures toward the narrative are always oblique. And most importantly a Bond song is never just about the brand: it has enough other stuff going on that it can make us momentarily forget why it has been brought into existence. A Bond song can effectively fulfill its main responsibility precisely because, like any pop record, it takes many aims, effects, tendencies, values, rhythms, and—let us never forget—the work of many hands, and makes them part of a single entity.

The Bond-song tradition is founded in the unshakable belief that there is a peculiar power to the pop song. A two- to four-minute pop record can encapsulate the ideas of a particular cultural, historical, and technological moment, along with the tensions between these ideas. A song can say (and *not* say) something about a character, a singer, a genre, an era, a place—and about you and "us." Heard start to finish, a song creates a bounded moment of measured time, *its* time, in a way that heightens *your* experience of thoughts, sensations, moods, and memories. (No other branding mechanism, including advertising music, can quite accomplish these effects.) And the Bond films are content to let us abide with their theme songs and the weird soap-bubble universes they conjure for two or three minutes. Their plots take a break, the visuals go into some kind of free-associative territory of dancing silhouettes and bubbling water, and we're left alone with the credits and the songs, but really mostly the songs. Left to experience them, respond to them, fail to respond to them. It's a rare bit of generosity in the hyperefficient world of mainstream film.

As such, *The Best of James Bond* establishes new modes of connection between brand, film, song, style, culture, and history. Don't ask this of *Bugs Bunny's Greatest Hits* or *Sesame Street Gold! The Best of Sesame Street*, even if you think those albums are of better quality. Of course there are albums collecting the musical output of the Muppets or *The Simpsons*, but those are about the funny voices, and they hail from the world *of* the Muppets or *of* Springfield. They don't speak about our world. The Bond-song compilations display their characteristic mix of songness and Bondness, and they walk a tightrope between his world and ours. Which is why they're more than novelty items. Bond songs are introduced into historic time, they age, and they gradually add to a tradition and a canon. This tradition—this shared way of experiencing and judging these songs—thrives on what pop songs are best at (even when they aren't very good). Our book is an attempt to take this rather unusual tradition seriously.

THE BOND SOUND

The Bond songs sounded antiquated from the first—all the passage of time has done is to make their untimeliness noticeable to even the most casual listener. Monty Norman's James Bond theme was part of a bumper crop of incredibly catchy theme songs that mixed big-band jazz and traditional soundtrack composition starting in the mid-1950s: recall Henry Mancini's theme for the *Peter Gunn* television series (1958) and Lalo Schifrin's theme for the CBS series *Mission: Impossible* (1966). They too were diffused into pop culture, spawning covers, appropriations, and parodies. They too remain instantly recognizable. But they are artifacts of a certain era; no one seriously tries to update or continue their legacy in some fashion every two or three years.

No story of the songs we will be discussing in this book would be complete unless the songs are contextualized as part of a larger Bond sound, with its own ties to time and its passage. By "Bond sound" we don't mean any one style, or any one set of musical motifs, but rather a repertory of themes, motifs, sounds, styles, and aesthetic practices—sometimes obvious and recognizable, sometimes harder to pinpoint. One example: when Hal Needham's ensemble comedy *The Cannonball Run* (1981) has Roger Moore appear as Seymour Goldfarb Jr., heir to a girdle fortune, who fancies himself a superspy, composer Al Capps constantly alludes to the James Bond theme, without ever actually plagiarizing it. This is the magic of the Bond sound.

That sound is largely the creation of John Barry. The iconic Bond theme itself was written by Monty Norman, but Barry not only arranged it for his band, the John Barry Seven, as heard in the very mod credit sequence for *Dr. No*, he added the gun-barrel fanfare with the surf-guitar riff for the next Bond adventure. These musical gestures have opened nearly every Bond film since *From Russia with Love*. The sound of early Bond seems very modish to modern ears: trebly electric guitars, big-band brass, throaty belting. But in fact Barry took Norman's theme, which was far more specific to its moment, and gave it a makeover in a style that was already in decline at the time.

Barry came of age right before rock and roll hit British shores. He's part of the first generation of film-music composers who emerged after—and out of—rhythm and blues and rock and roll. Originally a trumpet player, he had wanted to focus on jazz arranging when he saw an opportunity to take a band on the road while accompanying visiting American rock and roll singers. The John Barry Seven became well known in the U.K. through frequent touring (which after a time Barry himself stopped participating in), recordings, and appearances on TV. Barry took a synthetic approach to rock and roll. He studied rock and roll records and performances and recreated them as a musical arranger—as part of a mix that also included jazz, pop, and classical elements. At the time this approach was called "progressive" because it showed how rock and roll could embrace more "sophisticated" styles. But in retrospect it shows how old-fashioned Barry's style really was: he created intensity through orchestration rather than amplification or vigorous playing; he never lost his tendency toward big-band jazz aesthetics. And he was never willing to allow a song to sustain itself on just a groove: he always had to add a melody, to compose, to orchestrate.

When he took over composing duties from Norman on *From Russia with Love*, Barry tweaked the James Bond sound in a way that ensured that it could (and would) be recycled by every subsequent film. Monty Norman's score for *Dr. No* had been closely tied in with the Jamaican theme of the film, with calypso numbers and original songs by Jamaican artists. Barry moved the scores into a hybrid space, combining the big-band stylings of Norman's creation with string-heavy pseudo-classical arrangements in the mold of Golden Age Hollywood. Most famous in this respect is the secondary Bond theme, "007," first introduced in *From Russia with Love* and frequently alluded to thereafter. It's less recognizable than the James Bond theme, but it sounds an awful lot like Barry's more classical-sounding scores of the 70s, 80s, and even the 90s.

It was this hybrid sound that would create Bond's sonic legacy. However instantly the surf-guitar riffs and the big-band brass arrangements sounded like relics, the orchestral sound to which Barry married them in *From Russia with Love* read and still reads as timeless to moviegoing audiences. We accept their kinds of melodies as somehow outside of time. They end up in Cincinnati Pops recordings, marching band concerts, and fireworks shows on the Fourth of July. Barry's work integrated a 50s novelty sound into the line that runs from Central European transplants like Franz Waxman and Erich Wolfgang Korngold via John Williams and

Jerry Goldsmith to James Horner and James Newton Howard. And the strange thing about this musical style is that it sounds instantly "classic."

Whether Barry intended this or not, his score for *From Russia with Love* combined something that sounded instantly dated with something that sounded instantly timeless, something you couldn't *help* but place in a particular moment, and something else you just couldn't place. This hybridity has made the Bond sound so enduring: Lalo Schifrin's famous 1966 theme for *Mission: Impossible* is an instant throwback, and when it plays in a movie starring Tom Cruise it's a citation. Not so with James Bond. There's just enough timelessness in those arrangements for the music to sound like it's not out of joint with its time, and just enough modishness for it to say something new rather than quoting something we've heard twenty times before.

But specific—and quotable—features of Barry's compositional style too are key to the Bond sound. Perhaps the most essential single feature of the Bond sound is a brief, repeated musical motif that first appears in Barry's arrangement of the James Bond theme: the rising and falling chromatic line that goes from the fifth scale degree to the lowered sixth to the raised sixth and back down. (In the Bond theme's key of E minor it's B-C-C♯-C.) This motif may be part of Norman's original conception of the theme song; it's certainly in keeping with the theme's style and melodic materials. But Barry runs with it. He appears to think about it the way classical music people think about Wagner's "*Tristan* chord": as an emblem of everything chromatic harmony can signify—longing, irresolution, instability, tension, psychological intensity, not to mention sexual desire—and all it can musically accomplish. He reuses Norman's theme with a different intention, and the other Bond composers follow his use, not Norman's.

When Paul Epworth, the composer of the 2012 Bond song "Skyfall," said he'd discovered "the modal structure or the chord that seemed to always unify" the Bond songs, he likely had this particular chromatic musical motif in mind. It's telling that Epworth took himself to have discovered some kind of ready-made "structure." But he was really only importing a motif that belongs to two worlds at once. Because Barry hears

Monty Norman's melody in two ways: as a jazz-derived blue-note motif, and as something far more like classical music of the Romantic period, closer to the kind of chromatic voice-leading we find in the work of late-nineteenth-century composers like Wagner and Bruckner. The jazz elements hail from big-band music (probably via Mancini et al.): note, for instance, the raised sixth degree, which derives from the blues scale. Barry hears both of these in Norman's theme. And why wouldn't he—both big-band jazz and late Romantic music were mainstays in postwar film scores, especially for Barry's generation. But Epworth hears only the classical part, and "Skyfall" is pretty much the least jazzy thing to ever open a Bond film. Another thing Epworth fails to register is how the principal Bond motif appears in what is called an "inner" voice. Placed lower than the main melody, but above the bass line, it can easily go unnoticed. It's not meant to occupy the foreground; it has to be listened for.

At the same time, Epworth, geeking out over "the modal structure" of the Bond songs, has it right in one respect. The Bond motifs appear on the commercial sheet-music versions: this says they're essential to the song and not an arrangement touch added at a later stage, something that could be there or not. For all their traditional focus on voice/melody, and participation in the economies of the record, something about Barry's Bond songs wants to be puzzled out at the piano or, better, pored over as sheet music. It's the odd harmonic progressions, the convoluted, jagged melodic contours, the disconnect between a vocal melody and the surprising harmonies beneath it, and, especially, the many allusions to earlier Bond songs and scores. Epworth may not be that great at listening to the canon, but it's almost as if he's read his way through it, because the song he ended up writing for Adele replicates one of the features that the need for citation imposes on the Bond song: "Skyfall" moves very slowly and deliberately. Like generations of Bond singers before her, Adele has to adapt to a glacial pace so that the citations have all the time they need to be grasped by the (too few) Bond geeks who are out there listening for them.

As music for both ear and eye, Barry's style had crystallized well before his first Bond songs. Songs Barry composed for his Seven band

and other artists already reveal the snaking melodies, "modern" harmonies, and "crime-jazz" blue-notes that define his Bond-song approach. Pre-Bond songs like "Bees Knees," "Christella," and "The Menace" make clear—through both recordings and sheet music—that Barry was fully in control of his convoluted, hybrid style during the brief moment when it was actually kind of in fashion. His facility in putting this blend of jazz, classical, and pop into what was still considered rock and roll constitutes something of an achievement. It also makes it unsurprising that the rock-derived elements were the first thing to drop out of his style. Barry seemed more at home with full orchestra than with electric instruments, more comfortable working in melody and harmony than in texture and rhythm. Of course, that's not where music wanted to go during the years Barry, or people aping Barry, wrote Bond songs, and the fascinating aesthetic distinctiveness of the Bond song at least in part is simply a result of Barry being deaf to rock-derived elements. The Bond songs were from the first on a collision course with music history.

At the same time, Barry's sound is the product of many hands. That's what saved the Bond songs from being mere aesthetic curios. The people behind the Bond sound were professional enough to understand they needed to go with the times in some ways, and to grapple even with the sounds they didn't want to include (or, as time wore on, couldn't include) on their records. For instance, though you've probably never heard of him, Vic Flick is as essential to the Bond sound as Barry. It's him playing that trebly guitar on all those credit sequences for at least seven films, from *Dr. No* through 1989's *License to Kill*. His big break came working with Barry's Seven in 1957, when the group went on tour with Paul Anka, but it was on records especially that he was able to make a mark. It's his style of guitar playing—and often his very guitar-parts themselves—that feed into genres like skiffle and, a bit later, surf. Flick's sound represented both old and new ways of playing and producing the electric guitar: old because it didn't overdrive the amp to produce distortion, and because it drew on traditional playing techniques, but new because it relied on a specific kind of instrument, and specific ways of miking, amplifying, and processing the guitar. Most importantly Vic Flick had a recognizable *sound*, and it was a sound that thrived in the recording studio. Even Barry's old-school approach, which focused on melody and harmony—musical elements that could be made visible on sheet music—still required the sonic materiality that musicians like Flick were there to provide. Instrumentalists like Flick became as essential to post–rock and roll pop as the singers, composers, and lyricists, because they provided its textures; they provided what made it different from earlier pop. The electric guitar was uniquely important in post–rock and roll pop: an electric guitar can cut through a texture, so it can always be noticed if you want it to be, and of course it's a principal signifier of rock and roll itself. Barry's collaborators thus made sure that the Bond sound went with the times, even if it seldom came close to actually capturing the musical zeitgeist. As a result, Bond sounds like someone's slightly outdated idea of modern.

But one of the biggest contributors to the Bond sound is someone you don't actually hear. Sidney Margo was a session violinist. He may be playing violin on some of the soundtracks. But he's important because he got into a lucrative sideline that enterprising and well-connected studio musicians sometimes try to tap into: he became a contractor for studio sessions, finding and hiring the musicians to play on particular dates. Margo had no trouble finding good orchestral musicians. But choosing rhythm-section players was a bit more difficult—and increasingly important in an era when even most pop records were expected to have a solid groove produced by drums, electric bass, and some combination of keyboard(s) and guitar(s). Margo couldn't or wouldn't assemble rhythm sections that performed at the level of their U.S. counterparts. It's notable that, with the exception of "Goldfinger," none of the Barry-led Bond songs did well on the U.S. singles charts. Until the poor U.S. pop-chart performance of a-ha's "The Living Daylights," *every* commercial dud among the Bond songs had one of Barry's rhythm sections partly to blame. Barry never got this memo. The more important rhythm sections became to the music topping the charts—soul, hard rock, funk, disco—the more he buried himself in the orchestra.

The Bond sound as synthesized by Barry and his cronies remained a constant for the series. Barry himself wrote the scores for a grand total of eleven Bond films—his last assignment was 1987's *The Living Daylights*. There were a few attempts to modernize the sound in the 1970s (bringing in George Martin, Marvin Hamlisch, and Bill Conti for *Live and Let Die, The Spy Who Loved Me*, and *For Your Eyes Only*, respectively), but this was frequently done by discofying or funkifying the preexisting motifs—in other words, treating Monty Norman's theme the way "Night on Disco Mountain" treats Musorgsky. Michael Kamen's score for *License to Kill* and the scores for the Pierce Brosnan movies after *GoldenEye*, as well as the first few Daniel Craig movies, were utterly faithful in aping Barry's style. Like Thomas Newman, who took the reins when his frequent collaborator Sam Mendes was handed the franchise, Kamen and Arnold were content to polish the silver and update the sound only sparingly. This unique amalgam made for the Bond sound's longevity, but it would be hard to argue that it didn't also become something of a straitjacket. Bond never sounded so superannuated that fans demanded a different sound; but by the same token he was never allowed to sound entirely new either. The only time the producers made an attempt at updating the scores of the Bond movies, fan criticism was harsh. They had hired frequent Luc Besson collaborator Eric Serra to write a heavily percussive and synthesized score for Pierce Brosnan's first outing as Bond, 1995's *GoldenEye*, but the score was so controversial among the producers that they rescored several important scenes with another composer's work that incorporated the old themes more overtly.

So the Bond sound could give the impression of being universal and modish at the same time. In a funny way this made James Bond an even more sterling paladin for the West and for capitalism: he combined the timelessness of a diamond with the modishness of an iPad. The Bond scores transport the viewer back in time and give her the feeling she's plugged into her own historical moment—the same way that Bond's gadgets marry the MVPs of the SkyMall catalog with futuristic features like lasers and car remote control.

If the Bond score managed the peculiar alchemy of staying current and timeless, the Bond song was probably the painting up in the attic aging in its stead. The elements that gelled so effortlessly in the scores soon grated against each other in the songs. The awkwardness the scores avoided, the songs were forced to enact. What seemed effortless and even elegant in the scores was rendered grotesque by generations of crooners trying their hand at more or less successful impressions of Shirley Bassey.

This was because, for at least the first twenty years, the Bond songs were usually composed by the same man who wrote the score. Mostly that meant Barry, but Hamlisch and Conti kept up the tradition. That connection was finally broken in the early 70s, only to be reestablished by David Arnold for a brief spell in the 90s. The fact that the song was always connected to the motivic material of the score restricted what exactly could happen musically in the song. It also made for a style of songwriting that wasn't widely practiced any more, a style that was in fact on its way out when Barry collaborated with Leslie Bricusse and Anthony Newley on *Goldfinger* in 1964.

BOND IN CONTEXT: POP AFTER ROCK AND ROLL, HOLLYWOOD AFTER THE STUDIO SYSTEM

Throughout this book we try to remember that the Bond songs are pop *records* and not just pop *songs*. This is a crucial distinction in Anglo-American popular music. Songs can be performed by many different people in many different ways; what's essential about them can normally be written down and rendered as sheet music. Records, by contrast, contain actual *sounds*, including sounds that *can't* be written down. These sounds are essential to a pop record, even if the pop song it presents could be presented some other way. Where the written-out song could be called a map, or a scheme, or a script, the record is actually a primary text.

Historically this distinction has meant a lot. Sheet music projects a set of musical values that defines mainstream pop in the Tin Pan Alley era and after. Chief among these values is the sense that the voice performs whatever is *particular* to the song while the accompaniment can be reduced to its chord changes (and perhaps a rhythmic figure) without any significant loss of information. The stylized piano parts of Tin Pan Alley sheet music shift an even greater weight onto the vocal melody and the lyrics. But once records start to outsell sheet music, we find an increasing emphasis on grooves and on what is called *feel*, we hear musical arrangements becoming more and more assertive across a range of styles, and we see the emergence of record production as a creative realm alongside songwriting, performance, and arrangement. The rhythm section and percussion instruments play a greatly enhanced role—and not merely a rhythmic role, but textural, melodic/harmonic, formal, and generic.

The Bond films emerged at a moment when record production was becoming more assertive and tensions between the song and the record were coming to the fore. Changing production practices from the fifties into the seventies worked toward clearer differentiation of elements in a mix, and thus supported a more heterogeneous collection of materials. Beginning in the sixties this added up to a new kind of musical discourse, in which smaller musical objects—a dissonant brass chord, an electric-guitar twang, a simple piano-accompaniment figure—started to resemble objets trouvés. A sense of *particles* constituting the musical discourse, and of *objects* in the stereo field, could make a recorded song feel like an *assemblage*. As such these records embodied multiple sets of values: different genres, different modes of continuity, different sorts of comportment. These changes had effects even on pop records, like Barry's Bond songs, that sought to emphasize pop music's traditional aesthetic values.

What *is* the pop song, exactly, in the post–rock and roll era? What becomes of it when it has to contend with rock, soul, and hip hop and a parade of other aesthetic, cultural, and technological shifts? It has chased after teens, tweens, grownups, and little kids, sometimes all at once. It has been shaped by the tenacity of its sheet-music roots, the emergence of the album as the dominant commodity form, a major record-industry boom and bust, the digital turn, and questions about whether and how music will persist as a commodity. Listeners curate them in different ways. And all the while, nobody can say what pop songs are for: they have no point, no reason for existing, other than to *be popular*. A pop song doesn't have the clear function of dance music or the clear meanings of gospel. Pop music has never been given the mandate to speak for a subculture, as rock and roll, punk, and hip hop have. It doesn't usually trade on its deep connection to tradition, as the blues and country do.

But the Bond songs are special pop songs because of course they do have a raison d'etre. The end of the studio system in Hollywood brought a renewed reliance on theme songs designed as singles. The Bond songs were part of that. The Bond music became important in promoting the first outing, *Dr. No* (1961), because Fleming was reluctant to attach Bond's name to many product tie-ins, and because Sean Connery was a complete unknown at the time. The songs are effects of the decay of the studio system and the new and different demands (on merchandising, publicity, etc.) placed on each element of production in the wake of the old system. At the same time, the Bond films are far from New Hollywood (or Nouvelle Vague) auteurism. The songs featured in the films of Jean-Luc Godard, Jacques Demy, or François Truffaut spring from a curatorial impulse—their point is to inflect the aesthetic impact of the film. (Or imagine the final scene of Mike Nichols's *The Graduate* without "The Sound of Silence"!) The Bond songs never get to inflect anything—they are meant to provide one more part of the whole, saying the same thing, promoting the same message. Lucky for us (and lucky for you given that you've invested in this book) they didn't always succeed. Instead, they always said more and less than they were supposed to, and they were by far the most unruly part of the Bond series when it came to defending and glamorizing the economic and political order Bond was sworn to defend.

THE BOND SONGS AND LATE CAPITALISM

The Keynesian economist Joan Robinson noted drily that "modern capitalism has no purpose except to keep the show going." As the West has transitioned from making things to consuming them, and accumulating debt to pay for them, the show and keeping it going have become far more important than any actual product. Our labor now goes into putting on the show: it is a labor of stirring, maintaining, and circulating affect. As

Michael Hardt and Antonio Negri have put it, affective labor "produces ideas, symbols, codes, texts, linguistic figures, images." And, they point out, such labor is often invisible—it can be harder to spot, easier to forget about, more easily mystified as "art." As pop records have become huge productions with so many hands on deck, have they not come to resemble a factory of affect? There, the affective laborer performs his or her little tasks: making his or her Scottish accent part of the song, playing a drum fill on a special electronic percussion instrument most people haven't heard, engineering the sound of a string section in a way that says Abbey Road Studios. But in the new millennium, capitalism is no longer about making things. And a pop record is precisely the sort of artisanal "thing" that seems so old-fashioned today: a bunch of middle-aged professionals banging out a product over a conference table.

This has put a unique pressure on the Bond songs. They are love songs for capitalism. But capitalism is the very thing that's making them less and less possible. They understand their aesthetic effort in the studio and on stage as a kind of analogue for the job James Bond does out there in the field and on screen. Their job isn't just to beat back the commies, or to blandly assert the superiority of capitalism. It's to make capitalism's superiority accessible to our affects: you see James Bond stride into the room in his three-piece suit, you see him order a vodka martini, you hear that music and you know, you just know, that ours is the best of all possible economic regimes. But that consensus has also evolved over the sixty years that James Bond has been with us. He still looks ravishing defending the West, but the West has changed, and the world around it has changed. And it fell to the songs, far more than to the films around them, to register those changes.

Because those changes also affected the making of pop records. The Bond songs started out being all things to all people—just jazzy enough to pass muster, but not too obviously "ethnic" to freak out the squares; sardonic about sex, violence, and luxury but not to a point that it came off as political; sexy and a little louche, but always careful to drape its meanings in a polite veil of double entendre. In straining for this kind of universality, the Bond songs have come under a lot of pressure. They seek to inspire and assert a commonness and sharedness that rarely still exists in our fragmented pop culture. The collective aesthetic experiences their love songs seek to instill are made impossible by the very object they're singing love songs for. Those three minutes of ritualized nothingness, where we sit in hushed silence while a singer we don't much care for offers nonsensical lyrics, and strange silhouetted ladies do a circus routine off guns and diamonds, are a kind of church service. And the songs we hear on *The Best of James Bond* are its hymns or perhaps better its anthems. Because we're supposed to feel jubilant, not meek, when we hear them; we're supposed to belt them out with a hell-yeah kind of pride.

In the subtitle to this book, we call these songs "anthems" of capitalism, but in many respects these songs are never as "anthemic" as they would like to be. Sure, you can jubilantly belt out the chorus to "Live and Let Die," but the song makes clear that when you do, you're issuing a correction—you're negating an earlier statement "you" made about living and letting live. It's as though "We are the Champions" included a line that pointed out that you just recently sang "oh, we're totally gonna lose, and we probably shouldn't keep fighting till the end." Or think of Carly Simon's "Nobody Does It Better"—in the version of the song that appears on records, she closes out the number with a big outchorus, but in the film version the song whimpers to a close. Precisely because they are the work of many hands, the Bond songs are so readily retooled for use in the movies that the big, the bold, the fist-pumpy can always be drained from them. The anthems they want to offer they can't.

The Bond films have always registered capitalism's problems along with its promise. The mobility of capital across national boundaries was what enabled its bad guys to buy giant lasers and construct hollowed-out volcano lairs. The resultant weakness of supranational organizations (how many times does the UN show up in a Bond film, and how often is NATO mentioned?) was what made MI6 the go-to policeman of Bond's universe. Again and again the bad guys could succeed because public goods were handed to private individuals. It was hard to look at Jill Masterson's body petrified in gold over the opening credits for *Goldfinger* and not read it as some kind of warning. Of course, the Bond films had a ready-made answer to such global challenges: the show must go on. The kind of capitalism embodied by the Auric Goldfingers and Ernst Stavro Blofelds of the world was both an excess of capitalism and its negation—the *Austin Powers* movies got a lot of mileage out of the fact that the schemes the villains spend their money on are always uneconomical and offer a truly awful return on investment. They sink their money into space stations and underwater lairs, and then demand sums that will barely have them recouping their losses; or they just try to destroy the very economy that made them so obscenely rich.

The songs registered the same worries, even as they celebrated the very mode of production that allowed them to exist in the first place. But they had to somehow cope with the fact that the world around them was changing, that capitalism was entering some stage of lateness, that it really no longer either deserved or even enabled the kinds of anthems they wanted to write for it. They could cope with those changes—except by changing. Pop records were changing, Bond songs not really. Filmmaking was changing, Bond films not really. Capitalism was changing, Bond's view of it not really. Pop has always avoided talking about capitalism, or about any unpleasant topic, for that matter, by changing the subject, by offering another fizzy, spontaneous, of-the-moment concoction sung by a twenty-year-old who had been a nobody three years prior and would be in rehab three years hence. But the Bond songs by contrast are pop obsessed with their tradition, with their history; they were forced to respond to a changing landscape by giving the same prefab answer for a half-century. Ultimately, the Bond songs offer a unique lens into how we late capitalists dream. By putting them on the couch, we put ourselves on the couch.

SKYFALL
Adele

"At Skyfall"

The Bond Song, Repression, and Repetition

And though we are not now that strength which in old days
Moved earth and heaven; that which we are, we are.
                    —ALFRED LORD TENNYSON, *"Ulysses"*

In telling the story of the Bond songs, there is really no better place to start than at the end. That is because our task—listening to fifty years' worth of songs, sampling, comparing, decoding—is also the task of every new Bond song. Each of them is an act of listening, of remembering; but just as much of mishearing, forgetting, repressing. And the songs have gradually become aware of this fact. Adele's "Skyfall" wants to uncover what has been forgotten, to work through what has been repressed. She wants to look back over fifty years of songs and distill a kind of essence from them. And of course to turn that essence into a platinum-selling record.

The movie *Skyfall* made repetition and its difficulties one of its main themes. It's about latent content and the sometimes violent process of bringing it to light. But it's also a movie that isn't content to be "just" a continuation of the Bond tradition. It decides to put Bond on the couch—it wants to offer a kind of quintessence of the Bond character, not just put him through the paces once more. And Adele's title song wants to do the same; it tries to play Sigmund Freud for the Bond songs, all fifty years of them. It does so with gestures that both hearken back to a fifty-year tradition of Bond openers and attempt to move beyond them. Its means of doing so feel modern in a way that most Bond songs do not.

But it must be said that nothing new emerges in the film. What novelty *Skyfall* promises turns out in the end to be prologue—not to a new Bond, but to the familiar Bond of old. The new beginning is really a prequel to the Connery Bond films. More generally, the film doesn't significantly rewrite the Bond character or his origin story, but it makes explicit things that previously were only alluded to or tacitly understood. Bond nerds knew that Bond was an orphan, as indeed were most agents with double-0 status, but how the death of his parents affected him was never spelled out, nor the fact that M became something of a parental substitute.

Skyfall takes things that went without saying and puts them on screen. Fleming fans know that the author called his mother "M," but it's Javier Bardem's villain Raoul Silva who makes the link explicit, calling Judi Dench "Mommy." The Bond movies long repressed the fact that there was something odd about tiny Britain saving the day film after film, with the world's actual superpowers every time unable to do so. *Skyfall* has M invoke a line from Tennyson's poem "Ulysses" during a hearing in Whitehall: "We are not now that strength which in old days / Moved earth and heaven; that which we are, we are." That the Bond fantasy compensates for Britain's increasingly bruised and shaky self-confidence hasn't exactly been a secret (Simon Winder's very fun *The Man Who Saved Britain* devotes nearly three-hundred pages to the idea). But *Skyfall* feels the need to make that function explicit.

The same goes for the song. Adele self-consciously hews to formula, and if one can fault her song for anything it is that it doesn't actually do much to tweak that formula. The song's producer and co-composer Paul Epworth explained that his research for the song consisted of watching the classic Bond films looking for the "musical code" of "the" Bond song. Epworth not only appropriates John Barry's favorite Bond-theme motif, he also draws on the chord progressions he gleaned from his study of the

Bond-song canon. His borrowings are minute and precisely targeted: one short accompaniment pattern to signal the piano part of "Live and Let Die," one spiky minor-9th brass chord to capture Barry's horn arrangements, one note on a trebly electric guitar to recall the original Bond theme's guitar riff. "Skyfall" does the Bond sound at the subatomic level. It's a Bond song for the age of the genome: it isn't content to repeat the gestures and flourishes of the Bond formula, it has to sequence its very DNA.

Still, the film's opening title sequence makes a few connections that had previously been obvious only to the more Freudian of Bond-song fans. Consider the word "Skyfall" itself. It's in a long line of Bond titles (usually proper names) that make little or no sense: we don't know what a "Skyfall" is any more than we know what an "Octopussy" or a "Moonraker" are. But for once the movie itself acknowledges that the title doesn't make any sense. The word first occurs in the film during a therapy session: an analyst asks Bond to play an association game, but Bond walks out when the word "Skyfall" comes up. The enigmatic title of both song and film becomes the central mystery of the film's plot, and the fact that it is introduced in therapy makes it clear that the mystery lies in Bond's own psyche, not in some island hideout or atop an alpine peak.

No, "Skyfall," as the film's viewer soon finds out, is the Bond family estate, a place containing all of James Bond's assorted childhood traumas, which he conveniently and somewhat needlessly blows to hell in the film's climactic shootout. The opening title sequence takes the title at its word: it has no more of a clue what "Skyfall" is than the viewer does, but it hears "Skyfall" and begins to free-associate, presenting dreamlike images with a Bond figure constantly falling (see Fig. 1.1). Beneath every floor, every ground yawns another bottomless pit; behind every surface, a bewildering depth of field. In some sense it's an allegory for the way we encounter Adele's song: a shiny surface littered with clues, a song to be figured out, to be penetrated, rather than just enjoyed.

Even Bond's own face, Bond's skin, Bond's shadow turn into just another surface behind which roils another seemingly limitless cosmos. "Our world is not more transparent now," M asserts, in what may count as one of the film's thesis statements. Perhaps she should have said our world is more

Figure 1.1 Bond skyfalling—opening image of the title sequence for *Skyfall* (2012).

opaque now because it is so transparent. That at least is the sense we get from *Skyfall*'s title sequence: the surface will not hold. Even by the standard of the Bond films' title sequences, which were always triumphs of visual effects trickery, *Skyfall*'s credit sequence is an orgy of computer-generated imagery: plants, locations, objects, everything morphs into everything else. Nothing lingers long enough to hold our attention. Thanks to the magic of computer-generated imagery and the magic of pop psychology, where once our gaze might have stopped nothing opposes it now.

It's all laid out quite plainly in the song and the visuals that accompany it. But Bond spends the better part of the movie running away from the clarity and transparency of it. He is a creature of shadow and invisibility, whose surfaces are supposed to be respected rather than penetrated. This in an age in which a terrorist can expose agents' identities by posting a clip to YouTube. "Skyfall," the word and the piece of music, is the last bit of resistance in a world in which everything has become oppressively transparent. All Bond can do is refuse to associate the word with anything. He has to walk out.

Walking out on an analyst is a tradition as old, if not older, than actually seeing an analyst. Sigmund Freud, for one, was puzzled for much of his career as to why people would abandon a "talking cure," and with characteristic self-confidence Freud always assumed that the fault rested with the patient rather than the doctor. In *Beyond the Pleasure Principle* Freud suggested that patients who jumped ship were suffering from a "compulsion to repeat": "They struggle to break off the unfinished treatment, they know how to re-create the feeling of being disdained, how to force the physician to adopt brusque speech and a chilling manner towards them. . . . Nothing of all this could ever have afforded any pleasure; . . . The act is repeated in spite of everything; a powerful compulsion insists on it."

Repetition is also the name of the game in Adele's song. The word "Skyfall" recurs about as often as you'd expect in a James Bond song, which is to say she repeats it a lot. Adele has a way of slurring into the word, especially in the line concluding "at Skyfall," to the point that it sometimes sounds like a slip of the tongue. In the film, James Bond's trip with M to the titular family estate makes little logical sense. Why shanghai M to a remote area where the considerable resources of the British secret service can do nothing to help her? Bond and M seem caught in a kind of folie à deux, a compulsion to return to an origin—an origin that for one of them means death and for the other means a rebirth of sorts.

There is something dreamlike about the certitude with which Bond and M make their way to Scotland. The song ambles into the word "Skyfall" with the same dreamy logic. Asking why "Skyfall" pops up in the lyrics, asking why Bond and M go to Skyfall, is beside the point. They just have to. Just like Adele has to adhere to certain conventions if she wants to make a Bond song: Paul Epworth can try to reduce the Bond song to a "code," but really it is no such thing. Repeating the Bond formula is compulsory, but one does it almost as though in a dream.

Looking back, we can recognize this somnambulism in many of the James Bond songs, and what may have seemed illogical the on first (or second or third) time you listen turns out to be its own kind of logic, the logic of dreams. The songs' seemingly nonsensical lyrics resemble the word association game Bond plays with his analyst. The way Bond, in silhouette, walks or falls or runs toward something he seemingly can't reach, or runs away from something he can't evade, had something dreamlike about it all along. But no Bond film before *Skyfall* makes that explicit.

In the lyrics to Madonna's "Die Another Day," released a decade before "Skyfall," there is the line, "Sigmund Freud, analyze this." Madonna makes it sound like a taunt rather than a plea. There is nothing here to analyze; it's all surface. She's not giving away the game, there's no big reveal here, only a nodding acknowledgment that, yes, this is what it has been about all along. Adele follows in Madonna's footsteps. Her song acquires a tic all too familiar from previous Bond songs—the incessant repetition of a barely sensible word or phrase—and finally makes explicit what lies behind that eternal recurrence: the repetition compulsion of a neurotic subject, namely Bond. The structure of the Bond song, in other words, is that of Bond's own psyche. When the screen goes dark and the busty silhouettes commence their titillating ministry, we are glimpsing the mind of James Bond. We linger in his dreams and traumas.

Or so "Skyfall" thinks. Adele's song and the way it's presented in the film propose a theory of what it is we're watching when the dancing silhouettes take over: is it the musical sequence Bond sees in his head, his Technicolor dreams when he goes to sleep after a day of shooting and screwing? *Skyfall* isn't the first Bond film to propose a theory as to what the credit sequence actually *is*, but it is probably the most direct in its theorizing.

Goldfinger's opening projects scenes from the film onto the golden limbs of petrified Jill Masterson (see Fig. 1.2). It was an allegory of cinema. The film seems to treat the sequence as an acknowledgment of film's integration into the capitalism it wants to critique. The very substance Shirley Bassey warns us about, with increasing panic, forms the screen on which cinema can perform its magic. Goldfinger's love of gold, and the moviegoer's desire for the images projected onto Masterson's lifeless body, aren't really that different. What's coming is coming; the opening sequence knows it can't change the phenomenon it warns about.

The analogous sequence in *Skyfall* is different. It is possessed of a mania for depth: no sparkling lustrous surface will hold its interest for long, it has to penetrate ever deeper. As the sequence opens, Bond sinks to the bottom of a river, but the bottom opens up and swallows him (see Fig. 1.3). Under every surface is another chasm. Of course, it's not clear that

Figure 1.2 The female body as projection surface—the iconic title sequence for *Goldfinger* (1964).

Figure 1.3 The surface cannot hold—James Bond's descent in the title sequence for *Skyfall*.

gaining greater depth actually gives us greater clarity: the sequence starts with Bond's gun coming to rest at the bottom of a body of water, and as the camera begins its obsessive forward motion, the underwater plants change into the trees around the family plot at Skyfall (see Figs. 1.4 and 1.5). We could say that this is a clarification: we're moving toward something more meaningful about Bond than some undulating plants.

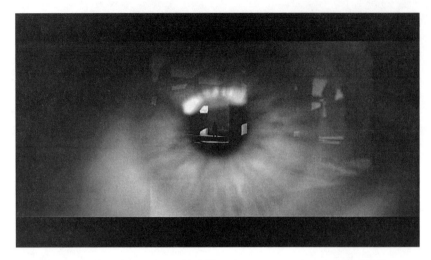

Figure 1.4 Dissolves dominate in *Skyfall*'s title sequence—here James Bond's eye turns into a shadowy underground cavern.

Figure 1.5 The family graveyard at Skyfall.

But the sequence can't stop itself, can't tarry with any one set of objects it happens upon. A tombstone turns into the house that gives the film its title—if anything, this reverses our general sense of what lies "behind" what. Bond's eye turns into a subterranean cavern where he battles his own shadows (see Fig. 1.4). Guns turn into flora, which turns back into knives (see Fig. 1.5). When we get to Bond's heart, the blood vessels turn into burning targets, which turn into dancing drag-ons, and eventually back into the family plot at Skyfall, and we realize we've come full circle. The title sequence's visuals know what the song and the movie don't always realize: that going deeper doesn't always yield deeper knowledge, that part of zooming in and digging down is knowing when to stop.

THE BOND SONG AS REPETITION COMPULSION

As Freud knew, coming face to face with recovered unconscious mate-rial can be exciting, and in that excitement there's a danger that we'll stop digging. We've figured out what "really" lurks behind our symp-toms, and we clap our hands elated at a job well done, when in reality there is another layer underneath, and another layer underneath that, and the digging will never really end. Late in his career, Freud chas-tised fellow psychoanalysts who would say, when faced with a former patient who was clearly not well, "His analysis is not finished" or "He was never analyzed to the end." Freud suggested that the "end" implied in this judgment doesn't really exist, though even capable analysts and smart patients may convince themselves otherwise. In a way, "Skyfall" is beset by this very problem.

In interviews, Epworth referred to the "eureka" moment when he fig-ured out "the modal structure or the chord that always seemed to unify" the Bond songs. *Skyfall*'s credit sequence likewise thinks it has grasped the very nature of the Bond song. And to some extent that's correct, of course. The sonic materiality of the song is reassuringly retro. Its full, smooth string and brass arrangements and tamped-down bass and drums signal the soundworld of "Diamonds Are Forever" with the "Live and Let Die" piano thrown in. And like those early-70s Bond songs, "Skyfall" tries to reach back even further, toward pre-rock pop—toward an ide-alized golden age of songwriting when what really mattered were the written-out melody, harmony, and lyrics. Epworth was surely keen-eyed in his analysis. But at some point he stopped digging, and his attempt at a

Bond-song analysis can itself be analyzed for the memories it dredges up and the things it represses.

Because Epworth gets the Bond song only partly right. "Skyfall" overshoots the mark in its analytic endeavor; it misremembers and mishears. Its initial two-measure chord-succession—a ponderous C minor/A♭ major/F minor progression that stalls right when we'd expect it to drive to a V chord on G major—is actually flatter and simpler than anything else in the Bond-song canon. Its melodic sequences are even more deliberate than Barry's, making the song's unfolding feel very predictable. And "Skyfall" completely neglects the odd moments of low-modernist punchiness and the fumbling attempts at up-to-date styles that are just as much a part of the Bond sound as droning horns and threatening chord progressions.

So "Skyfall" isn't so much a summation or meta–Bond song, it is just like any other Bond song. Epworth wants to be Freud in his armchair, or perhaps better, wants his *song* to be Freud in his armchair, with fifty years' worth of Bond songs begging for analysis on the couch. But in the end, Epworth mishears: in attempting to recollect and then repeat the Bond song "as such," he picks up on some aspects, not others, and remembers some features while neglecting others. He acts, in other words, like any one of us when we put on headphones and listen to our favorite song—fanboy, not Freud.

Consider for instance the incredibly bare-bones piano part that delivers the simple three-chord sequence underpinning the intro section and most of the verse. Both *Skyfall* the movie and title song are obsessed with the idea that analysis means stripping down. The film's MI6 moves from its newfangled hi-tech building into a World War II–era bunker; the film's Q, usually the purveyor of invisible cars and exploding pens, this time gives Bond only one gift: an ordinary-looking pistol. And instead of the usual exploding jumbo jets, the film's climax features Bond and a villain and a burning house. *Skyfall* is obsessed with reduction, concentration, getting to the "code," to use Epworth's phrase, underneath or behind the surface occurrences. What it actually *does* looks quite different, of course: Epworth's DNA image is striking, but going through earlier songs to find things that you can use in your own song isn't actually anything special—it's what every pop songwriter has done!

Still, it remains significant that Epworth, and by extension the song he wrote for Adele, *meant* to do so much more: both want to push through to whatever lies behind the surface of the Bond song, to penetrate to its deeper genetic code. The simplified piano accompaniment is an attempt to do exactly that. Adele had gone to that well before (although without Epworth guiding her) in her mega-hit "Someone Like You," but however effective the piano might have been for that song, it's an odd fit for a Bond song. Epworth strips away too much; he digs right past the quintessence of the Bond song (which is, after all, not exactly a sparse genre) and just keeps burrowing, convinced that a truer essence must lie further below. What he finds, ultimately—the "musical code" of the Bond song—is the not-so-secret oscillation between lowered and raised sixth-degrees of the scale: the familiar G/A♭/A/A♭ pattern that has become perhaps the most characteristic Bond-sound motif.

"Skyfall" is a reduction that overshoots, partly because it misremembers what Bond songs actually sound like. And, tellingly, it misses its mark because it takes the Bond song to stand in for the pure pop song as such (which indeed can be stripped down in the way Epworth envisions): a construction that can be reduced to its lyrics, melody, and harmony with no loss of information. But the Bond song is a supremely anomalous kind of pop song, and always has been.

What does "Skyfall" get wrong? For one thing, it feels incredibly long even though the version in the film concludes in less than four minutes, and even though the tempo isn't unusually slow. This, and the emphasis on the piano part, gives the song its Barry-on-steroids ponderousness. There is something almost funereal about the pace, especially for the whole measures when the F-minor chord just sits there, not wanting to go either this way or that. The repetitions slow things down even before the chorus sets in and echoes each line, further ratcheting down the tension. The deliberately weak chord progression renders even the quoted Bond-motif fairly inert. The "code" Epworth claimed to have sequenced really consists of little beyond the repetition of a title and a lot of major/minor inflections in the vein of the old Monty Norman theme.

There is, in short, little luster, no swagger, no sex in this arrangement. Which is well enough. None of this means that "Skyfall" is a bad song—just that the project of providing a code, an analysis, a summa of the Bond song seems doomed from the start. Epworth seems to have identified mournfulness as one of the features of the Bond-song canon. In keeping with the trauma theme of *Skyfall* he understands the Bond song as essentially a mourning song. That certainly captures *some* of what Bond songs are about, but "Skyfall" develops a kind of analytic tunnel vision, completely forgetting what else is part of the Bond formula: sadistic glee, lustiness, swagger, bravado, menace, not to mention the tongue-in-cheek attitude that often governs the songs' mix of sex and violence.

It's not surprising that Epworth wasn't able to transport all of that into his "code" of the Bond song. It's hard to imagine what the resulting song would have sounded like, and in all likelihood it wouldn't have sounded great. But it's interesting that Epworth's and Adele's archaeological dig into Bond's unconscious yields such one-sided results. The two *think* they're getting at the quintessence of the Bond sound, but what they're digging up is merely a single aspect of the thing they're trying to remember. Like a patient who strides out of a session with his analyst, confident that whatever bauble analysis has unearthed that day will be the key to *everything*, to his past and future, Adele and Epworth fetishize one aspect of the Bond song (Aha! It's a mourning song!) and believe that now, truly, they must have mastered the "code."

In fact, what they take to be a moment of remembrance, of anamnesis even, turns out to be that most twenty-first century of operations: Epworth isn't decoding the Bond-song canon, he's sampling it. Like Vanilla Ice stealing the bassline of "Under Pressure," Epworth is picking out a particular moment or aspect of the thing he's trying to unearth, and then putting it to use in his own creation. The song is an attempt to *not* repeat, to not give in to the repetition-compulsion it claims lies at the heart of its own predecessors. It wants to provide the discourse that would puncture that repetition, make it visible, maybe make the compulsion treatable.

This is where *Skyfall*, both song and movie, betray their own unconscious: they're entirely obsessed with eureka moments, dramatic reveals, big summations, complete rewritings, that turn out to not amount to that much on closer inspection. Director Sam Mendes can't seem to find a way of just making another James Bond film; it has to be the *summa* of the James Bond film, its future and its past, its alpha and omega. Adele's song works the same way: the song is terrified of being just another song in a series. Instead of being another entry in James Bond's dream diary, it wants to be the psychoanalysis of that diary.

Adele was the perfect carrier of that analysis. A massively successful singer, she had what few Bond singers before had: camp cred and a large gay following. Here too, "Skyfall" isn't content to let this roil under the surface, it has to drag it into the light, point to things, and make them obvious as they can be. Susan Sontag once offered the definition that camp is art that *appears* serious, and that certainly takes itself seriously, but at the same time "cannot be taken altogether seriously because it is 'too much.'" That pretty well fits the Bond song, which traffics in muchness and has never met a self-serious turn of phrase or portentous instrumentation it didn't like. And it's hard to imagine that among the decades' worth of craftsmen, crackpots, and genuine artists who wrote these things, there were none who were aware of the Bond song's camp status. "Skyfall" is a place where once again a thing that goes without saying is elevated from subtext to text.

But there's another thing Sontag knew: camp is hard to do intentionally. It easily comes off as condescending and insulting—or just plain silly. "Skyfall" is a pretty good Bond song, and an even better pop song, because it doesn't think it's above camp, above the Bond song. Adele's song is best in those moments when it betrays a willingness to stop digging, without any sense of triumph or declaration of an end (to the series, to analysis, to the canon). In these moments it is fine being one in a line, another beautiful, meaningless, nonsensical dream with no more smarts about itself than any of its dummy forebears.

And there are plenty of such moments, like the incessant turn to Monty Norman's theme, and the insane build from a simple piano opening to the gospel-choir-with-Vivaldi-concerto close. Or moments when the song admits that, yes, it is one of many, and another shall follow. Think of its obviously ironic first line: fifty years into the franchise, opening its most successful entry ever, the song announces rather improbably that "this is the end." Or think of the moments when Adele imports her own vocal mannerisms, her strange pronunciation (who says "tall" that way?), into the performance. At those moments, she's acknowledging Shirley Bassey, not trying to outdo her. At those moments she's joining Bassey on stage at the Sands, not forcing her onto the analyst's couch. At those moments she abandons all pretentiousness, but instead is about Tin Pan Alley, about keeping them happy and getting the job done. At those moments the song's self-awareness doesn't get in the way of making new blunders, new slips, new mistakes.

BEING EXPLICIT

The central idea of "Skyfall," that the song sequences that open the Bond films are representations of the hero's unconscious, isn't that surprising. If anything, part of James Bond's maddening charm has always been how the psychic investments that attach to him are so incredibly easy to see through. The Bond adventures are wish fulfillment! Really, you think? Its guns may be phallic symbols! Thank you, Dr. Freud, but the books already spell that out explicitly. Ian Fleming would often call his mother "M" in his letters? Not really surprising, if you are at all familiar with the Bond stories. But the moment of explicitness, the sudden eagerness with which latent content is rendered conscious in *Skyfall*, is still striking. It's a secret everyone was in on for the better part of fifty years—why bother spilling it now?

For an answer, consider again the film's plot, especially the strange drive up north. One doesn't have to be a psychoanalyst to think that this is what Freud would have called a "parapraxis," that is, a slip-up or "symptomatic action." Freud introduced the term in his book *The Psychopathology of Everyday Life*, and Bond may have wanted to consult it before jetting off to Skyfall. Instead, Javier Bardem's villain Raoul Silva shoots up a government hearing and Bond finds no better response than to retrieve the iconic Aston Martin and set off on a road trip north. As in the cases of misremembering, linguistic slips, and accidental actions that Freud collects in his book, it is clear what they *mean* to do: save M, defend themselves against Silva, retreat from combat. But it's not clear how their actual move makes any of that happen.

The move doesn't make logical sense, but it makes analytic sense: Silva is part of the Empire's defense system that has turned on the Empire. Bond seems to conclude that all of the Empire's defense systems are liable to turn on M as well, that anything that is supposed to protect M can be used against her. Only by going back to the origin, to a place of vulnerability, can the potentially destructive power of these defense mechanisms be overcome. This is the Freudian picture of the psyche, where it isn't so much the unconscious that produces psychological symptoms (our ego is far too bossy to allow that), but rather the way in which our ego checks and thwarts that unconscious. When we have psychological problems it is not our unconscious, but rather our defense from it, that turns against us.

Saying that Freud would have a field day with James Bond isn't exactly novel. And it's also not what *Skyfall* is saying. After all, the trip to the physical place Skyfall is the second such trip Bond makes—the first is with his analyst in the word association game. The film is proposing that the trip up north is no longer a tactical move on Bond's part. He has recognized Silva as a psychic entity and decides that he needs to psychoanalyze him out of existence. *Skyfall* is not the first movie in which Bond is forced to recognize that his job is to some extent a collection of neurotic symptoms. But it's the first in which Bond realizes that this makes introspection a weapon in his arsenal. Of course, it doesn't make it more than that – introspection is not an end in itself for a man like James Bond, it is a means to an end. Bond returns to his origin point to blow it up in an insane shootout, to ensure he'll never have to deal with his past again.

That is the moment Adele's song celebrates. "This is the end," the song begins, and in a certain way that's entirely accurate. The shootout at Skyfall is the end of the beginning of Bond. By the time it is over we realize that the Daniel Craig movies have all led up to the point at which we first met Sean Connery. Everything we know about the classic James Bond is now in place: M is a man, Miss Moneypenny is at her desk, Q is once again a young man. The death of Judi Dench's M is the moment the origin story ends and the real story of Bond can begin. Skyfall stands for everything Bond has to repress to be the stone-cold bastard we meet in the classic Bond films.

The song anticipates this structure. The first few lines suggest that they are going to explain *why* "this is the end," but all we get is a repetition of the first line: "This is the end . . . for this is the end." And even the chorus is a kind of ouroboros, a snake biting its own tail, rhyming "sky fall" with "Skyfall":

> Let the sky fall,
> When it crumbles,
> We will stand tall,
> Face it all,
> Together at Skyfall.

Between the two Skyfalls are two people, who "will stand tall, face it all." But who are they? The people who stand together at Skyfall in the film are Bond and M—and it seems likely that Adele's song is a song of mourning for M, even though we don't realize it when we hear it. When it plays in the film, after Bond's splashdown in an Anatolian river, we may think it's a mourning song for Bond—even though as always his watery burial, like all his watery burials, doesn't take. But since we don't know, the "we" hangs as a central mystery over what is already a fairly mysterious song. The identities of the two people "standing tall" "with your hand in my hand" remain as mysterious as the nature of their bond. Lines like "my loving arms keeping you from harm" make it sound maternal; at other moments it sounds romantic.

But the song rubs our faces in the question: Adele's song is careful to stick to Bond-song orthodoxy, but it diverges starkly on one single point. No previous Bond song had relied on a large group of backup singers. Surely, Paul Epworth noticed this fact in his survey of Bond songs, and yet he decided to violate this precept. Starting in the song's second chorus, Adele is accompanied by a full backup chorus in the manner of a gospel choir. This vocal arrangement places Adele in relation to a community—a new idea for the Bond song. The Bond song tends to rely on the heroic soloist, because it mirrors its solitary hero. The singer, like Bond, works alone, surrounded by the sumptuousness of the orchestra—an expensive line item in any music budget. The lavish orchestral textures of a Bond song, including those of "Skyfall," are about conspicuous consumption: they are the musical equivalent of waterproof cars and vodka martinis. But rarely does the sound of a community of voices ring out through this desert of bling. "Skyfall" creates a group of singers, and that includes the doubled vocal-tracks of Adele herself, which we hear earlier in the song. When "Skyfall" gives us more than the single solitary voice, it's telling us that its hero always has backup, its hero is always part of a "we." But the nature of that "we" is left tantalizingly open.

This is what makes the opening sequence, and the use of Adele's song in it, so clearly unique: the film insists on transparency, on making obvious what went without saying; the song's lyrics and its music reverse-engineer and reconstruct the Bond song in almost blinding clarity. But at the center of the song is a mystery, and the title "Skyfall" turns out to be a red herring. Skyfall is not the secret of the movie, it's not what Bond walks out on. It is the "we" in the song. Those two people hand-in-hand are the true mystery of Skyfall. And however much the song and the film are obsessed with explicating the implicit, this mystery they let lie.

BACK IN TIME

"I am become a name," Ulysses reflects in Tennyson's poem, and it's this line as much as any that is likely to have drawn screenwriters John Logan, Robert Wade, and Neal Purvis to the poem. *Skyfall* is a movie about names and what hides behind them, "Skyfall" being the central one. But in telling a story about names, *Skyfall* intends to put its finger on the essence of James Bond. He is, in essence, a name. Whenever Bond has started over, with a new actor, a new tone, a new aesthetic, he has been Bond in name only. The tagline for *GoldenEye* was: "You know the name. You know the number." A decade later, as Daniel Craig took over the mantle, the title song was "You Know My Name." And in "Skyfall," Adele intones, "you may have my number, you may know my name, but you never take my heart."

Time makes names of us all, and though James Bond has struggled mightily and agelessly against that fate, he has also always been the embodiment of the opposite idea—that becoming a name isn't perhaps the worst thing. The roving, penetrating gaze cast by the title sequence and by Adele's song, the gaze that wants to peep behind everything and that accepts no surface as just surface, may not be a good thing. "What we are, we are," M says, quoting Tennyson. *Skyfall* is the story of what lies behind the name "James Bond," beneath the surface of this deeply superficial man. But it investigates the space behind and beneath only to discard it. It visits Skyfall only to dare Silva to blow it up. In the end, we don't learn how James Bond became the man he is. We learn how he became the name he is, how he cast off all the signifieds that attached to it, and how he stashed them in a remote estate in Scotland and blew them to bits. James Bond begins *Skyfall* as James Bond, he ends it as "James Bond," a name and (thankfully, beautifully, miraculously) nothing more.

And in a way Adele's song, and the masterful opening sequence that accompanies it, defend the surface, prettiness, shallowness. Of course there are depths, but it's pointless to pry. There's not much to be gained by it, just more pretty shapes intimating depths that neither song nor title sequence actually manage to plumb. The song Epworth wrote for Adele is an invitation to linger, to tarry with the pretty surfaces and the bottom-less voices—to luxuriate in its seemingly nonsensical lyrics, surrender to its gyrating depthless dancers and two-dimensional harmonies. The following chapters will beat that very path into James Bond's musical past.

GOLDFINGER
Shirley Bassey

KISS KISS BANG BANG
Dionne Warwick

FROM RUSSIA WITH LOVE
Matt Monro

THUNDERBALL
Tom Jones

2

"A Golden Girl Knows"

The Ballads of James Bond

Matt Monro's "From Russia with Love" is technically the first Bond song, but chances are you've never heard it. That's because, although the movie has one of those mod title sequences we associate with Bond films, the title song doesn't actually appear in it. Instead it plays over the end credits. There's an orchestral arrangement of Monro's tune that plays for part of the opening credits, but like the one in *Dr. No* this credit sequence transitions into a different song, in this case the iconic Monty Norman theme, midway through.

The placement is instructive, because in many ways Norman's song reminds us how a theme song is *supposed* to behave, certainly in a film from 1963, but pretty much continuing until today. The Bond songs became the strange beasts they are by abandoning a lot of these features. Film songs don't usually stop the movie cold five to five ten minutes after it's started. Monro's song far more sensically sneaks into the film's final scene—the action is over, our hero has emerged victorious, and the luxuriant strings and delicate bolero rhythm are just the salve our sore ears need after two hours of action. The brass instruments are kept in check; Monro croons about Russia and love, rather than screeching out increasingly hysterical warnings about some ridiculously named heavy. His voice is pure pop, with no sense of a particular place or any other musical style. The most stylistically specific element is a tack-piano mimicking an Eastern European hammered dulcimer. Nothing stops this title song from being an ordinary pop record.

The song comes on as Bond and his girl, with the uncharacteristically nonridiculous name Tatiana Romanova, are taking a gondola across the canals of Venice (see Fig. 2.1). Gently, drifting in on a cushion of strings and horns, Monro's tune starts playing in the background. We've heard the song once before, wafting briefly from a radio, but this time it doesn't appear diegetically, meaning the characters don't hear it being played.

But they do talk over it, a fate that would never again befall a Bond song. After "From Russia with Love," Bond songs commanded sepulchral silence and religious devotion—the movie comes to a virtual halt in order for the song to start. By contrast, in *From Russia with Love* the song is introduced very much as a film song: this is how an end-credit song is

Figure 2.1 Bond and Tatiana Romanova celebrate the conclusion of a successful adventure; final scene of *From Russia with Love* (1963).

supposed to arrive. The fact that the characters can't hear it, but that we do, is a first nudge out of the film's world, as though a hypnotist were releasing us ever so gently from his spell. We hear Monro's lyrics invoke "From Russia with Love," and we remember that, huh, funny, that's the name of the film we've been watching.

This gesture is almost too successful, however, for Monro's song comes close to telling Bond and Tatiana that they're characters in a movie. No sooner has the song started that Tatiana suddenly interrupts their kisses because "we're being filmed." Lucky for the millions of voyeurs who depend on Tatiana's being filmed, and who may feel like they've been caught, it turns out she's referring to a couple of tourists training a camera on the lovers from a bridge, not to the massive big-budget film crew all around them (see Fig. 2.2).

As if that moment weren't strange enough, the voyeuristic tourists remind Bond of another important film within the film. Earlier in *From Russia with Love*, agents of SPECTRE have filmed Bond and Romanova making love, intending to use the film to blackmail Bond. He's gotten the film back, of course, and now he pulls the film roll from his pocket, throws it overboard, and waves it a mocking goodbye as the words "The End" appear (see Figs. 2.3 and 2.4).

Figure 2.2 "But James, we're being filmed."

Figure 2.3 The film's cinematic MacGuffin.

Figure 2.4 For about a second *From Russia with Love* really *is* the end . . .

That film roll (which, owing to the technology of the time, really does look like a miniature of the reels that commercial films were shot on) and the film *From Russia with Love* stand in a strange relationship to one another: the big film, the one we've been watching, depends on the small one for its plot. In this respect the little film reel is no different from the various launch codes, nukes, submarines, decoders, and so on that James Bond and other cinematic agents hunt in most of their adventures.

Alfred Hitchcock famously called this the MacGuffin, because, well, because any name works really. It's the object everyone in a spy story chases because without it there would be no story. What the object is becomes completely beside the point, as long as different people want it. What's interesting about the film reel is that it isn't a pure MacGuffin, however, because it embodies something that we viewers very much desire but cannot have. We may not care about launch codes and wouldn't know what to do with a decoder should one fall into our possession. But we'd most likely find a use for a reel of Sean Connery making love to Daniela Bianchi.

That is to say: the object that Bond discards right as we're told that this is "The End" is the thing that brings us to the theater. But it's also the missing reel that *by going missing* makes it possible for us to go to the theater and watch *From Russia with Love*. If the film really did feature a full James Bond sex-tape, we'd probably not go to see it, nor would anyone outside of the seediest portions of Times Square have let us in 1963. We go to the movies to watch attractive famous people prepare to have sex, and we go to the movies to not see them actually do so. Our *not* actually seeing them do it is just as important as the fiction that film characters have sex.

In a normal spy thriller we audience members have zero investment in the actual MacGuffin. We don't come to the theater for launch codes. The little tape Bond tosses into the Venetian canal, by contrast, is in some sense *our* MacGuffin. It's the thing that will have us coming back for more, it's what makes cinema a fundamentally serial enterprise. We watch Bond and Tatiana lock lips, and we know we won't get to the good stuff. But we get to sit down again next year in another darkened theater, and perhaps that time we'll get lucky!

The jettisoned reel is the opposite of the text declaring this "The End." What's on that reel is indeed the end-all of cinematic voyeurism, the always-deferred money shot that draws us in again and again. But precisely because it's withheld, this isn't in fact the end. There will be another adventure, another chance at that tape, another chance to be disappointed that it's missing yet again.

And indeed, as the credits start to roll and Monro's song takes over the soundtrack, the scene's finality is amended in a way that Bond viewers are most familiar with by now. We read: "Not quite the End. James Bond will return in the next Ian Fleming thriller 'Goldfinger'" (see Fig. 2.5). This was the first time a Bond movie had ended with this promise.

And it was a promise that was scored (and underscored) with a theme song. Even though "From Russia with Love" was not placed where succeeding Bond songs were placed, even though its integration into the movie hewed to established Hollywood models the Bond songs would soon abandon—in this one respect the Bond films established the role of their songs from the very first. Bond songs were about seriality—about the adventure that came before, about the adventure that would come after. Even for those twelve months between October 1963 (when *From Russia* was released) and September 1964 (when *Goldfinger* had its premiere at Leicester Square), when there was just one of these songs, the song was about repetition, about tradition, and about the series.

In that, they differed from the James Bond theme, which has been the source of so much musical (and extramusical) continuity for the series. But part of being in a *series* is that while some things remain the same,

Figure 2.5 ... but as Matt Monro's theme plays us out we're told that there's another one coming. The beginning of a Bond tradition.

others develop with time. The uses of the James Bond theme, with very minor exceptions, suggest not so much seriality as identity. And this theme arrives in a way that makes it feel new and natural each time. Whenever a new Bond is brought into the series, it's this little melody that convinces us that, yes, this man is not an impostor, he is the real James Bond. As atypical as Monro's tune would turn out to be for the Bond canon, it's already about the Bond canon. It acknowledges that more films and more songs will come—that they'll sound a little different, but still be Bond songs. The Monty Norman theme proclaims that there can be only one Bond theme.

But why the move to the *beginning* of the picture? What happens when the musical acknowledgment of seriality pretty much opens the film, rather than closes it with a winking acknowledgment that, yes, if this thing makes enough cash we'll probably crank out another? This seems like a trivial question but it goes to the core of how these puzzling songs effect their nontrivial reshaping of cinematic time and form. Because it turns out that by frontloading the moneymaking aspects of the film—the fact that you're seeing this because it's a James Bond picture and not one of the many knockoffs, parodies, and also-rans—the films actually tie their rather strange form to their overall theme: the films celebrate capitalism, and they do so by foregrounding the film itself as a capitalist endeavor. Not lofty ideas or liberal values will win against the Russkies: it'll rather be cool drinks, hot chicks, and awesome songs, and we'll all sit around and wait for two or three minutes while the Bond song runs up a big tab.

The powers of capitalism are so powerful in the James Bond movies that they can take on the most powerful thing of all: capitalism itself. As a freshman might put it after a bong hit: can capitalism create a stone so heavy capitalism itself can't move it? The Bond films think it can.

"From Russia with Love" isn't about that—it's hard to say what on earth that song *is* about. Nor does the music provide much help: Monro's quintessential film-song voice, the unassertive musical arrangement, and the low-profile bolero rhythm all mean that "From Russia" can pass as a typical title song. But the song that picked up where it left off, the one that picked up the reel Bond tossed from the Venice gondola, the one that started the decades-long relay race of Bond songs—*that* song is all about capitalism. Goldfinger, the man with the Midas touch: a song about a figure for capitalism run amok brought to you by a bunch of Marxists. And yet a song and movie about how the only cure for the excesses of capitalism is . . . more capitalism.

"GOLDFINGER" AS MURDER BALLAD

Monro's theme song pioneered the idea that a Bond song had to repeat the title phrase, and repeat it a lot, meaning be damned—a tradition the franchise would cling to with almost fetishistic fealty. It took the thought of asking professionals to write and record a song about an "Octopussy" for the series to (temporarily) shake it.

In almost every respect, it is "Goldfinger" rather than "From Russia with Love" that provided the matrix that Bond songs spent the next fifty years aping. That's as true for the song's narrative dimensions as for the music. Musically, "Goldfinger" became identical with James Bond in a way that "From Russia with Love" did not. Monro's song had been a characterless ballad whose most notable instrumental touch was a modified piano that stood in for a Hungarian cimbalom that (taking liberties from the zither you hear in *The Third Man*) was supposed to somehow signify Russia. "Goldfinger" brought in the screaming muted brass, which (along with the churning strings) would become the bread and butter for Bond songs going forward—although the screaming brass was of course also a key feature of Monty Norman's Bond theme, which *Goldfinger* references far more directly than Monro's song.

This continuity is undeniable, but it can hide how different "Goldfinger" is from the two dozen songs that would draw on it in the decades between *Thunderball* and *Skyfall*. If the music points forward, to decades of more or less derivative Bond songs, the lyrics highlight an ancestry that future Bond songs would pretty much leave behind. More clearly than the later songs, this song's text presents its audience with a morality tale, although the intention of the teller is left tantalizingly ambiguous. Bassey's song delivers an increasingly urgent warning against allowing the film's villain to ensnare the audience in his plots: "Goldfinger, the man with the Midas touch / beckons you to enter his web of sin / but don't go in."

In fact, while most of the James Bond songs that would follow "Goldfinger" have more or less identifiable addressees (sometimes the audience, often enough Bond himself), "Goldfinger" is alone in interpellating a very particular kind of listener: the singer wants to warn "pretty girls" who may be tempted by Auric Goldfinger's "golden words." Insofar as we take the warning seriously, we are addressed as though we were seducible young women; or we're addressed only if we *are* seducible young women. That means either the song turns us all into libertines, or it concerns a communication with a small subgroup of listeners to which the rest of us are mere spectators. There's a lesson being taught here, and we may worry with a gulp whether it might apply to us.

Although the song hides it mostly in the chorus, *Goldfinger* does tell a rather specific, albeit hypothetical, tale, that of an innocent young woman drawn in by Goldfinger's seductive allure against her better judgment, but lost before she realizes what has happened.

> Golden words he will pour in your ear,
> but his lies can't disguise what you fear.
> For a golden girl knows when he's kissed her.
> It's the kiss of death from Mr.
> Goldfinger.

It is worth pointing out the strange kind of knowledge imputed to this girl. She steps into Goldfinger's trap with eyes wide open (after all "his lies can't disguise" what she already fears), but her knowledge does little to mitigate her fate. And *fate* may well be the operative word here. In the universe of "Goldfinger," death is not so much the punishment for being seduced into the villain's world, one that could have been avoided with a bit more gumption or virtue; there is something altogether inescapable about the destiny laid out in the chorus. Why are we, or the "golden girls," being taught a lesson, if there's really nothing to be done about Goldfinger's trap? "Goldfinger" pretends to contain a warning, but really it luxuriates in the very seduction about which it would warn us. The injunction is simply an elaborate ruse to hide the pleasure of transgression.

For us who overhear this faux warning, the pleasure is embodied in Bassey's voice. *She*'s the seducer, the one pouring "golden words" in our collective ear. It doesn't matter if we try to turn away, as the song's amped-up coda makes abundantly clear. In his typical fashion Barry writes it all out, creates intensity through musical arrangement, and doesn't give his singer the opportunity to improvise. Instead he forces her into a series of repetitions: for the song's final thirty seconds, Bassey seemingly belts out nothing but "only gold" and "gold" as Barry's favorite Bond-theme motif brings the musical accompaniment to a boil. The whole thing achieves an almost overbearing affect. It's likely that when Monty Python spoofed the Bond-song format with the opening song to *Life of Brian* (1979), the ridiculous repetition of the name Brian is directly inspired by the over-the-top coda to Bassey's "Goldfinger."

But though the ending of "Goldfinger" is indeed faintly ludicrous, its intensity has a point. How are we to understand its collision of controlled pop-song aesthetics and dial-911 urgency? "Goldfinger" is otherwise a paragon of lyrical and compositional economy; singing "gold" again and again tells us there's something more, something looming just outside the frame. What is this intense repetition driving at? Are we to infer that the singer, whatever her relationship to Goldfinger, knows only too well that "he loves only gold," that she found out the hard way? While there's nothing to suggest outright that whoever is speaking in this song, whoever is addressing the "golden girls" tempted by Goldfinger's advances, has herself received the "kiss of death from Mr. Goldfinger," such a reading gives sense to the song's overflow of sound, meaning, and affect.

The singer's performance in "Goldfinger" should just be about Bassey getting paid to do x in service of y. That's exactly what Barry praised Tom Jones's performance of "Thunderball" for: Jones doesn't think too much, Barry suggested, he just belts out the song, and that's a good thing. But in "Goldfinger" there's something that exceeds the provision of work for hire. The exaggerated intensity ignites the film's central tensions between gender, labor, money, violence, and lived experience. It's easy to hear the song as rather brutally collapsing the distance between Bassey and the song's persona. In late-capitalist exchange, you don't just sell your affective labor, you're supposed to serve up your memories and experiences too.

It is clear, in any event, that the singer is not (or at least is no longer) one of the "pretty girls." In this respect, too, "Goldfinger" defined the Bond songs for at least twenty years: she is a seasoned veteran, a pro, certainly not an ingénue, though once upon a time she may have been one. Bassey's throaty alto telegraphs a kind of femininity altogether different than that of most women who cross Bond's path in the actual film. This is a configuration that remains intact in the Bond films well into the twenty-first century: in many Bond songs the female singer does not adopt the role of a Bond girl or of a woman that Bond and the villain might struggle over; but rather the role of a more mature woman dispensing advice or background knowledge to either the Bond girl or Bond himself. Over the decades these roles could vary: sometimes the singer was a deep-voiced femme fatale, sometimes a traumatized victim, frequently a mixture of the two. What the Bond girls lacked in experience, the Bond singers more than made up for.

This runs from Shirley Bassey, who dispenses wisdom to the Pussy Galores of the world, right down to Madonna, who not only sings the title song to *Die Another Day* but also appears in the movie as a downright maternal figure—a fencing instructor named Verity who tries to talk sense into Bond as his yearning for revenge threatens to get the better of his judgment.

Even if the intimations that the warning about "the man with the Midas touch" might well come from one who learned this lesson the hard way are just that, intimations, "Goldfinger" nevertheless clearly introduces a configuration that would come to structure the relationship between song and film in many Bonds to come (though certainly not all). The grizzled veteran who sings the opening song stands in clear contrast to the young, naïve, and less-than-competent sexpots that populate the Bond adventures from *Goldfinger* to *License to Kill* (1989).

"Goldfinger" in many respects set the scene for both the way the songs sounded in future Bond films and the way the songs managed to arrange James Bond's world. The demimondaine blowsiness of the vocals, the barely concealed admiration for whatever baddie our singer happens to be serenading—all of this the Bond songs were keen to preserve for decades to come. But if they *sounded* like they were of the same genre, later Bond songs, at least after "Thunderball," in fact departed significantly from the generic DNA of their key progenitor. In important respects "Goldfinger" is an altogether atypical Bond song.

A specific tale of a named criminal who preys on women. A tale presented as a word of caution to impressionable young women, but which seems to take a little too much pleasure in describing their seduction. A villain who operates almost as a stand-in for the blind forces of fate. Its narrative and mode of address mark "Goldfinger" as a murder ballad. It's not a bad choice of genre. Like Bond films, ballads are about repetition, about seriality, about a jump from villain to villain. You tell the one about The Death of Parcy Reed, then one of your listeners asks you about the terrible butchery in so-and-so. You chase the next ballad, the next tale of murder most foul, the next thrill the same way audiences chase the film-roll from Bond film to Bond film. Part of the fun in either case is that you know what's coming—if you've heard one ballad, watched one Bond movie, you've seen the blueprint for all.

You might not expect a song from a 1963 film to trace its lineage to a genre that was popular at eighteenth-century carnivals, but the murder ballads have never gone out of style. And a particular murder ballad was very much a fixture of the music of the early 60s. One of the most famous of these ballads is the ballad of Macheath, called Mack the Knife. The song "Mack the Knife" was written by the poet Bertolt Brecht and the composer Kurt Weill, husband of Lotte Lenya (who'd played the villain Rosa Klebb in *From Russia with Love*). Louis Armstrong revived interest in the English-language version around the beginning of 1956; following his hit single there were well over 400 recordings of the song between then and the composition of "Goldfinger." According to Bond lore, the Broccolis asked John Barry to follow the template of "Mack the Knife" in composing "Goldfinger," and you can hear Barry try in the song as we have it today.

"Mack the Knife" tells the story of a brutal killer who dispenses death with legendary efficiency—which the song has a hard time working up any outrage over. Not only does the song elevate Macheath into a figure of blind fate, it also explains why his native London does not catch up with Mackie and his nefarious deeds. As the famous opening lines have it: "The shark has pretty teeth, dear / and he keeps them pearly white. / just a jackknife has Macheath, babe / but he keeps it out of sight." Mackie's horrific deeds pose as nature, as something that just happens, as blind fate. It takes the murder balladeer to point out that what looks like a bizarre chain of accidents and random acts of violence are in truth all Mack's bloody trail.

Brecht and Weill present Mack the Knife as a kind of supervillain. In his own strange way, he brings order into the chaos of the London demimonde. What appeared to be indiscriminate violence, blind fate, turns out in the song's telling to have been one man's doing. Such are the villains of the early Bond songs as well: legendary bad guys whose fame is spread in cautionary ballads by brassy women at once horrified and enthralled by their "sin" and "lies." They bring death and destruction, sure, but they also bring a perverse sort of order to the world. Whereas the films present their villains as outwardly upstanding, albeit often mysterious, businessmen, the songs, or at least their singers, understand them as folkloric antiheroes. And the way the singer addresses us suggests that her audience is fully acquainted with them and their legend. We can imagine that perhaps the audience has requested the ballad of Goldfinger, the Moonraker, or the Man with the Golden Gun from Shirley Bassey in some seedy club off the Vegas Strip.

And that seems to be the point of these songs: unlike the movies, which require us to go through the motions of meeting yet another heavily accented debonair international businessman who is quite obviously a nefarious master criminal, with our master spy only slowly catching on, the songs function as initiations into an underworld in which a man like

Goldfinger is already a legend. There is a queasy sense of camaraderie here. The song treats us almost as Goldfinger's accomplices—after Shirley Bassey is done warning us, we can't know what we know and not be part of the underworld.

Being part of Bassey's audience means being a particular kind of person. This is significant, and it shows that however pop it was, "Goldfinger" still had one foot in a far older tradition. Pop songs after all are both more and less portable than traditional sung ballads. They are more portable in that we *don't* have to be a specific kind of person in a specific situation to hear and enjoy them. They are less portable in that they often rely on musical elements that don't travel well, that can't be transmitted via sheet music. A murder ballad was written down, or memorized, or passed along—and then someone else made the song her own. Or not really her own: no one owns ballads—to repeat ballads is not called covering them, it's just called singing them.

"Goldfinger" represents a midpoint between the murder ballad and the pop record. What makes the song memorable is not the lyrics or the melody—it's the piano-wire tension of Bassey's voice, the metallic shimmer of the recording, the reverberant thrum of the guitar and percussion, the fever pitch of the brass. But at the same time, the song *depends* on its being written down. Ballads typically have neat rhyme schemes and rhythm to help us remember. "Goldfinger" does not (unless rhyming "Midas touch" and "spider's touch" strikes you as latter-day Coleridge). Ballads often have a simple melody to guide the instrumentalists through the song—"Goldfinger" does not. What "Goldfinger" does have is an intricate fit between melody, harmony, and murder-ballad text that couldn't exist if Barry weren't putting pen to paper. "Goldfinger" maintains equilibrium between its status as a sheet-music ballad and its status as a sonic object.

Anthony Newley, who cowrote the song with Barry and Bricusse, actually recorded a version of the song that sounds a lot more like a traditional ballad. It's far more intimate, with spare instrumentation. Newley's voice sounds subdued—he's speaking to a few cognoscenti, not a roomful of concertgoers. Bassey's version retained some of that, but the way it dials the vocals and the brass to eleven, the way it's asking us to imagine a nightclub, but one the size of Caesar's Palace, shows the strain the sheer scale of the Bond aesthetic put on the ballad format. To be sure, "Goldfinger" committed fully to the murder-ballad genre, but it was just as fully committed to a totally different genre, namely the pop song. By the time the opening credits rolled for *Thunderball*, the murder-ballad connection was an empty husk, a mere gesture—Bond songs had turned into something else.

Even though so quickly discarded, this larval stage is nevertheless significant. Brecht and Weill's supervillain had a more overtly political function than the villains presented by the Bond movies. Their Macheath was a stand-in for capitalism, an entrepreneur of death who was, the song implies, no more or less worthy of praise than any other kind of entrepreneur. As Brecht famously put it, what's robbing a bank compared to running one? In a line so chilling the pair decided to leave it out of the English version, the balladeer recounts the story of a teenaged widow who finds herself raped by Mackie, presumably before being killed. "Mackie, what was your price?" the singer inquires—was it money, or the forcible sex? Sex, murder, money, it's all in a day's work for Macheath.

The "Mack the Knife" connection makes visible something that frequently gets lost in the Bond films. Almost all the villains over the last twenty-some films have been able to perpetrate their schemes thanks to their obscene wealth. They commingled sex, murder, and money in much the same way Brecht's Macheath does. Weill and Brecht thought Mackie's story spoke for itself—you almost couldn't hear it and miss the point. But somehow all the Bond songs *did* end up missing this specific point. The Bond films and the Bond songs are all about how capitalism has become a kind of fate, how extreme wealth enables invisible villains. Somehow, miraculously, the Bond movies, and their songs, fail to leverage this insight into a critique of capitalism.

The films can't really critique capitalist excess because in them Bond deploys the powers of capitalism (essentially sex, murder, and money again) against the excesses of that same system—the excessive wealth of a Blofeld or a Hugo Drax is checked by designer wristwatches and Aston

Martins. In this respect, the Bond films are utterly faithful to Fleming's books. In rereading the original novels, it is astonishing to see how many times Bond's unraveling of the villain's schemes involves simply winning a game of chance in a casino or a club—for instance, in *Casino Royale*, Bond must seize Le Chiffre's assets not by means of legal action or larceny, but rather through a game of bridge at a fancy casino. Money serves as bait for money to catch more money. The universe, once again symbolized by obscene amounts of cash, will right the imbalance obscene amounts of cash have created.

In the songs, things are more complicated. "Goldfinger" is the only song in fifty years that thematizes the villain's greed. The lyrics tell us that his seductions, his lies, his schemes are all in pursuit of gold. And the music, with the brasses' obscene metallic glare and Bassey's voice heightening the text's emphasis on "gold . . . gold . . . gold . . . only gold!," brings Auric Goldfinger and his riches into existence with far more presence and charisma than Gert Fröbe, the actor who plays him, ever could. With a singlemindedness that too is rare for the franchise, the whole song makes gold—as word, symbol, and substance—its singular focus, culminating in its protracted money-shot of a coda.

Six years later, Bassey would return to the franchise to serenade diamonds. But that song is about sex, relationships, men and women—everything except diamonds. "Goldfinger" wears its anticapitalist ancestry on its sleeve, but this legacy disappears from the Bond songs with astounding swiftness, and gets replaced by a system of meanings in which any mention of value refers ultimately back to sex or desire. "The Man with the Golden Gun" is pretty obviously about a penis. "Thunderball" talks about Monsieur Largo's needing more, "so he gives less," but it seems this has to do with women more than wealth. "GoldenEye" is about a voyeur. *After* "Goldfinger," gold was sex. *In* "Goldfinger," gold was gold.

This shift has to do with the legacy of Brecht and Lenya. Lenya is perhaps the only entirely unalluring woman to ever feature in the Bond series as either vixen or villain; and the song her husband's "Mack the Knife" inspired is unique in that it reduces sex to money, rather than the other way around. Later Bond songs (at least after "Thunderball") in some way repressed the Brecht/Lenya connection, and they did so musically. "Mack the Knife" may have wrought his fiendish influence more openly in the song's text, but there are traces of Brecht's aesthetics in the song's music as well.

Weill and Brecht had developed a specific kind of singing to go along with stories like Mack the Knife. Just as the song is so disturbing because it refuses to condemn or even comment on Mackie's actions, so the singer is supposed to keep affect out of his or her voice, making sure not to give the audience hints about how to feel. Bassey's reading of "Goldfinger" goes about it in the opposite way. Her every syllable drips with affect: every vowel-sound gets a tweak, whenever a word ends with a consonant it spouts a vapor-trail, each note seems deliberately placed. But the way Bassey's voice at times seems thick with glee over Goldfinger's dastardly exploits, while at others it seems likely she's been at the receiving end of at least some of them, and the way she manages to work herself into a real fury only by the song's end, do justice to the style in which "Mack the Knife" is meant to be sung.

Consider Bassey's voice: Shirley Bassey had a beautiful, deep voice, sonorous and rich. But this song never gives it a chance to relax and resonate, and the recording quality gives it an odd metallic buzziness. All the same Bassey turns in a remarkable performance. She maintains a sense of extreme emotional tension without letting us in on the melody's extreme difficulty. (And truly difficult it is: if you're in a karaoke bar and you hear the "Goldfinger" intro, run for the exits.) Bassey's performance is taut, controlled, refined, but it creates an oddly binary structure: there's "gold," and there's everything else. Which means we don't actually learn anything new about gold. This gives the song a surface texture that is, well, all about surface. The song shimmers, but, like the gold skin that covers Jill Masterson in the film's most iconic image, it's deliberately superficial, only skin deep.

It's for this reason that the opening titles use a technique the Bond films rarely returned to in the following decades: the golden faces and hands become screens on which images of Goldfinger, Pussy Galore, and

Figure 2.6 The title sequence to *Goldfinger* uses the characteristic posing female figures in an uncharacteristic way.

Bond are projected (see Fig. 2.6). Just like Masterson's gold coating, the song's surface sheen can seem suffocating. What menace there is in the story of "Goldfinger" comes not just from the fact that the singer seems at times far too pleased with the man she's supposedly warning us about, it also comes from the fact that the menace doesn't seem to register in her in ways that feel recognizable.

If the songs that followed "Goldfinger" abandoned describing the villains' wealth and started talking about seeking wealth as a way of talking about wanting sex, the opposite is true for the opening sequences. The objects of desire that drop out of the song lyrics seem to aggregate on screen as dislocated fetishes: the drifting guns, the floating diamonds. The screen is full of stuff we might want, with the nude silhouetted women jumping off of that stuff becoming almost an afterthought. The system of objects that disappears from the song lyrics themselves remain quite present in the title sequences.

But the opening visuals to which "Goldfinger" is set are entirely free of these disconnected objects. The image-track presents exactly one golden object: a woman's body, cinematically dismembered and parceled out into individual shots in a nod to censorship, but always identifiable. Desire and gold both attain a distinctly Bondian and distinctly capitalist hue in *Goldfinger*'s title sequence. Later songs tend instead to sing about desire and repress the fact that they're also singing about gold. The Brechtian DNA of "Goldfinger" doesn't allow that to happen.

"Goldfinger" was the song every other Bond song would try to sound like. By contrast, *Thunderball*, the movie that followed *Goldfinger* only a year later, introduced the visual scheme that every Bond film would try to imitate going forward. It's the iconic, instantly recognizable look of the Bond film's title sequence: gone were the rear projections, gone the subtle digs at capitalism. Instead we get female shapes diving through bubbling waters. The Brechtian DNA lives on, though, but the franchise has lost control of it. The ballad form, which had been so potent in helping "Goldfinger" walk a tightrope between an ode to and a warning about capitalism, turned against the franchise in the three different songs the producers commissioned to accompany the sequence.

WHO STRIKES LIKE *THUNDERBALL*? BALLAD AND POP SONG

The difference between the two opening sequences is as striking as its meaning is murky: The shiny, shimmering surface as a screen for projection of *Goldfinger* on the one hand (see Fig. 2.7), the all-enveloping, oceanic shapes of *Thunderball* on the other (see Fig. 2.8). One treats the (golden) female body as a projection screen, the other as negative space—whatever you project onto its blackness, you won't see it reflected back at you.

More than the opening for *Goldfinger*, the murky blues and the black silhouettes of *Thunderball* acknowledge the seriality of the Bond series. For us seasoned Bond viewers this is because every one of these things has substantially looked the same ever since. But it was also true for viewers who didn't have a half-century of Bond-film canon to pore over. Because the *Goldfinger*-opener is *specific*—we get shots of Gert Fröbe, of

Figure 2.7 The female body as screen.

Figure 2.8 The female body as a black spot on the screen—an aesthetic established by *Thunderball* (1965).

Honor Blackman, of Sean Connery, of a laser. The abstract image of the gold-covered Jill Masterson becomes a reflector for a pretty detailed preview of the narrative that is to follow.

Thunderball's opener moves in the opposite direction: it works *away* from the specific image that concludes the opening scene and moves toward incredibly abstract elements—water, bubbles, women (not identifiable women, just women as such), guns. There's something archetypal about what's being presented here—the movies of the 2000s (*Die Another Day* and *Skyfall* above all) made explicit that what these title sequences depict is probably a look into James Bond's subconscious, but that's been a pretty likely reading for these sequences all along.

As such, the main titles for *Thunderball* acknowledge that there is a James Bond adventure independent of the film we're seeing right now. We can abstract from this adventure toward the Bond adventure *in general*. There was one before and there will be one after, and they all emerge from this shapeless primordial ooze of limber-bodied silhouettes and bubbling water or magma. We're watching the franchise give birth to one of its offspring at the beginning of each Bond film—we're returning to the womb of the Bond franchise.

But all this pop-Freudianism covers up the one salient point about the Bond films' serialized nature that *Goldfinger* had dutifully foregrounded: the reason why yet another Bond film clambers from the primal soup is that there's more money to be made. As we saw in the previous chapter, the Bond movies of the 90s and early 2000s seemed to think of the franchise as a kind of repetition-compulsion—some inner destructive drive forces poor Bond to shoot and bang his way through another exotic locale every two years. But on some basic level that's just a romanticized or mystified version of what we all know is really the case—Bond does it because it's his job, and Albert Broccoli makes a movie about it every two years because it's made him filthy rich.

The psychological dimensions the opening visuals for *Thunderball* impute to the repetitiousness of the Bond franchise are a fib. "Goldfinger" had it right: it was all about gold. *Thunderball*'s opening visuals take its movie's political points (about capitalism, about the effects of money, about film's dependence on money) and render them psychological, that is to say natural. We're no longer to be *convinced* by Bond that capitalism, in spite of everything, is a pretty shiny thing, we're supposed to *accept* it the way we accept a diagnosis from our doctor.

Politically this may count as a suggestive "road not taken" scenario (What if the Bond films had maintained the far more ambivalent aesthetic of *Goldfinger*?), but as it turned out this little bit of dishonesty made the Bond songs much more interesting over the years. The songs still talked about money, diamonds, jobs, and so on, but they invested them with so much weight that some pretty glorious messes resulted. "Goldfinger" is a pretty straightforward song, as is "Mack the Knife." Starting with the three attempts at finding a song for *Thunderball*, things got messier—the songs wanted to say one thing but found themselves incapable of saying it, or in the worst case saying quite another.

Of course they *sounded* very much like "Goldfinger," but never as much as they wanted to. "Goldfinger" was a ballad, a ballad we, a louche audience of hard-living types ourselves, might hear in an off-the-Strip casino circa 1963. We know all about capitalism, but we also know it's a sham, that for every Howard Hughes there's a Goldfinger—or that every Howard Hughes *is* a Goldfinger. That specific scene breaks down with *Thunderball*.

"Goldfinger" established the Bond-song format, and it's amazing how quickly and decisively it did so. The aesthetic established by Bassey's song became a straitjacket almost instantly. When poor Johnny Cash submitted a song for the next film in the series, 1965's *Thunderball*, he assumed, entirely reasonably, that perhaps the next Bond song should crib from an entirely different musical vocabulary—so he wrote a pistolero-ballad with a backup chorus and blistering Western guitars.

The producers wanted none of it, and instead commissioned a song that sounded exactly like "Goldfinger"—from the singer of "Goldfinger." There's "don't mess with success," and then there's this. Of course, Bassey's version of "Mr. Kiss Kiss Bang Bang" didn't end up being used in the film, nor did Dionne Warwick's more canonical rendition of the same song. But that was, if anything, because the song, which was otherwise slavish in sticking to the ground that "Goldfinger" had trod before, departed from it in exactly one way, and that way doomed it: it didn't mention the word "Thunderball."

So the producers turned to Tom Jones to sing a song that would incorporate the title, and John Barry obligingly wrote another song with another set of lyrics. This one is all about "Thunderball," a word it repeats again and again, and it's equally slavish in aping the sound established by "Goldfinger."

Given that they were both intended as clones of "Goldfinger," the two songs aren't that different. But the way they repeatedly tried and failed to recapture the essence of that earlier song—first Bassey took a crack at it, then Warwick, then Jones—signified something about the way that the ground had shifted underneath the Bond song almost immediately after it had made its first grand entrance.

For whatever the songs are trying to do, it isn't working this time around. That isn't to say that either of the songs Barry wrote for *Thunderball* is bad or uninteresting. But the gestures that went down so naturally when Bassey belted her way through "Goldfinger" suddenly seem much harder to replicate—like a tightrope walker who in midair starts thinking about where her feet go, rather than just putting them there.

Take the instrumentation for example: both of the "Thunderball" songs are, if anything, even more orchestral than "Goldfinger." "Goldfinger" had combined a big-band arrangement with relatively light, darting strings. "Mr. Kiss Kiss Bang Bang" and "Thunderball" sound like they have an entire symphony orchestra backing the singer. The songs are basically extensions of the motion picture score, picking up not just on melodic material, but even on timbres and instrumentation. The songs are trying so hard to be more "Goldfinger" than "Goldfinger." It gets a bit tiring.

Most importantly, however, both songs remain in the ballad-mode established by "Goldfinger." They each introduce a "he" and explore "his" exploits—and those of either "Thunderball" or "Mr. Kiss Kiss Bang Bang" don't seem to diverge that much from those of "the man with the Midas touch." Pretty girls, cool stuff, and violence: those are the mainstays of the Bond ballads. But both songs seem to suffer from a serious identity crisis when it comes to their balladry. Remember, a ballad lives off a fairly stable set of identifications. They have an implied speaker (the storyteller who relates the story for some reason), an implied audience (people to whom the story is supposed to matter for some reason), and a subject (whose story is supposed to matter to both teller and audience). All of these were quite stable in "Goldfinger": there's a story of reception, who we are to hear the song and why we're hearing it, even though it's fictional of course.

All the attempts to make a "Goldfinger" clone for *Thunderball* have trouble with these identifications. The songwriters, producers, and everyone who has written about the film all assure us that "Mr. Kiss Kiss Bang Bang" is about James Bond. The identity of "Thunderball" is more of an open question, but most commentators agree it's about his antagonist Emilio Largo. It's good there's a consensus on these two songs, because on our own we might not be able to figure out who's who. Compare the following sets of lyrics:

He's tall and he's dark.	He always runs while others walk.
And like a shark, he looks for trouble.	He acts while other men just talk.
That's why the zero's double.	He looks at this world, and wants it all.
Mr. Kiss Kiss Bang Bang.	So he strikes, like Thunderball.
He's suave and he's smooth.	He knows the meaning of success.
And he can soothe you like vanilla.	His needs are more, so he gives less.
The gentleman's a killer.	They call him the winner who takes all.
Mr. Kiss Kiss Bang Bang.	And he strikes, like Thunderball.

They both seem to be about the same person—a woman-devouring, self-obsessed, murderous sociopath. They both obsessively reference the James Bond theme. And yet one of them is supposed to be about our hero, the other about the villain. If anything, "Mr. Kiss Kiss Bang Bang" makes Bond sounds a little worse than "Thunderball" does Largo—note that the "shark" line and the gentleman-killer line draw on the vocabulary of "Mack the Knife." One of them is supposed to be a murder ballad, the other is supposed to be the opposite of that (a hero's ballad, perhaps)—but they both end up making their subjects sound like Mack the Knife.

The songs' fealty to the themes that audiences had come to associate with Bond also creates problems for the kind of communication these songs want to set up with their audience. Both incorporate the Bond theme compulsively. In one of the songs it's supposedly as the leitmotif for the character the song is about; in the other it's to . . . reference the man who will kill the person being described? Reassure us that Bond is on the case? Tell us we're encountering the man described in the context of a Bond movie? Why that theme is there, and what it's supposed to mean to whom, is incredibly hard to decipher.

Both songs retain the ballad mode that "Goldfinger" had used, and if anything their music strengthens the connection to the "Mack the Knife"–style murder ballad. "Mr. Kiss Kiss Bang Bang" is in 3/4 time, which isn't an everyday thing on the pop charts—it's the kind of waltz-parody that Weill and Brecht often served up in their collaborations. The same goes for the singing style, at least in the first recorded version of the song (that is to say, the one by Shirley Bassey): Bassey's voice is talky, mostly free of vibrato. She declaims more than she sings, a style that hearkens back to Brecht and Weill's *Threepenny Opera*, to cabaret-style singing, and of course to "Goldfinger."

But this makes it all the more awkward that the relatively clear scene of reception imagined by the lyrics and text-setting for "Goldfinger" have all but evaporated in "Mr. Kiss Kiss Bang Bang" and "Thunderball." "Goldfinger" was a song sung by a demimondaine muse, a seedy woman in a seedy club. She knows Goldfinger, and most likely her listeners do too. Who is sitting in a cabaret listening to the exploits of James Bond? Are these listeners the same people who'd enjoy the thrilling tale of Emilio Largo's success at womanizing, violence, and world-domination? There are pretty traditional modes of staging lurking behind "Goldfinger"—the same can't be said for "Thunderball" and "Kiss Kiss"!

These two songs, and the way they can't settle on what story of themselves to tell, preserve the theatricality of "Goldfinger" but without actually imagining a specific theatrical setting for it. There is something free-floating about these songs, and it cuts to the very heart of the Bond series' take on capitalism: "Goldfinger" imported a Marxist aesthetic because it wanted to talk about capitalists as murderers, only to then offer more capitalism as the cure for the evils of capitalism. The two songs Barry wrote for *Thunderball* do the opposite: together they assert the fundamental equivalence of the secret agent and his antagonist. Neither is any more violent, misogynistic, or murderous than the other.

Both songs are ballads that lack a clear speaker, a clear addressee, and even a clear subject—the nature of everything they address seems to be in flux. The kind of theatricality on which the Brecht and Weill collaborations rested—in which intellectuals taught working-class audiences about the evils of capitalism—has vanished, even the debased Vegas Strip–version proffered by "Goldfinger." Maybe that's because capitalism itself has changed, but more likely it is because capitalism is, during this period, in the process of changing what a song is—and changing how we relate to a song.

Because the pop song doesn't usually have a kind of scene of reception in mind the way Bassey's "Goldfinger" does. As a murder ballad, "Mack the Knife" was supposed to tell a certain group of people some definite things. "Mr. Kiss Kiss Bang Bang" and "Thunderball," while using the same format as "Goldfinger," can no longer do that. In this they are prototypical pop songs. Pop is portable; you can enjoy it across the globe in a variety of settings, you can misunderstand it and still have fun with it. The two songs for *Thunderball*—both of which could be serenading either hero or villain, for an audience of either heroes or villains—can work either as a warning or as a celebration.

A mode of address has been lost in that one year from *Goldfinger* to *Thunderball*. The very sameness of "Goldfinger" and "Thunderball" places this shift in sharp relief—it reveals the advancing shadow that late capitalism was beginning to cast on the work of making a pop song. Both "Goldfinger" and "Thunderball" end with a long-held high note in the voice: Bassey sings "gold" and Jones sings "-ball." In Bassey's case: she does her job, nothing to be said. But Jones's high note was quickly associated with a story about him holding the note until he fainted in the studio. Late capitalism needs this silly story. A pop singer's affective labor had always been as important as his sound itself, but now you had to be able to *sell* that affective labor—soon you'd be *branding* it. From now on the Bond songs would not just test out what capitalism sounded like, they would also test out how capitalism influenced what a pop song sounded like, and how capitalism influenced who we were as a pop song's listeners.

YOU ONLY LIVE TWICE
Nancy Sinatra

THE LOOK OF LOVE
Dusty Springfield

3

"You Only Live Twice"

James Bond and (His) Age

James Bond is an artifact of a certain era, but that does not mean he reflects a stable set of attitudes or ideas somehow *of* that era. *Casino Royale*, the first of Fleming's Bond novels, was published in April 1953; the last of the iconic Connery films was released on New Year's Eve, 1971. Between the anti-colonial upheavals of the 1950s and the social unrest of the 1960s, the world into which Bond first emerged and the world in which he became a superstar underwent a series of dramatic and frequently convulsive transformations. British possessions that Bond visited in the early books were independent countries by the time Sean Connery's Bond arrived at Kingston airport to take up arms against *Dr. No.* And Japan and Germany, two countries the books' Bond regards with suspicion, played an entirely different role on the world stage by the time the movies came out.

What's striking, however, is how little of what roiled the planet during those decades appears in either Fleming's globe-spanning adventures or the films they inspired. For a world constantly threatened by nuke-wielding madmen, the world of James Bond seems surprisingly stable, even placid—a place where men, women, baccarat, booze, and guns are what they are and what they've always been. Decolonization, Labour Party politics, changing attitudes toward women—these appear in the margins of the Bond books, but they are always somewhere else. Wherever Bond is, the mores and structures of the 50s miraculously still hold sway. The movies are even quainter in that regard—their geopolitical fantasyland is deliberately free of geopolitics. Even in the first Bond movie, *Dr. No*, the script removed all the books' scenes that find Bond interacting with the colonial bureaucracy—for the simple reason that Jamaica was gaining full independence from Britain while the film was being written and shot.

Within the escapist universe created by the films, this was not surprising and probably not altogether unwelcome on the part of the audience. But one place where this stasis became perhaps too noticeable to remain pleasurable was in the songs that opened the Bond films. The revolutions of the fifties and sixties unfolded also through the medium of popular culture, and here was one place where the non-place beyond history and geography mapped out by the Bond films became glaringly, even gratingly, out-of-joint with its time. James Bond sounded temporally unmoored—his signature theme had the screaming brass and guitar riffs of a big band number, and the songs were sung by performers born well before the war. The strides soul, rock, and associated genres would make during the 60s left nary a trace in the Bond films' sonic vocabulary.

You Only Live Twice is different. The book differs from the other books, the song differs from the earlier Bond songs, and together they constitute the Bond series' first moment of self-consciousness about the tense relationship between Bond's world and our own. By its very theme—living twice, whatever that might mean—the book, the film, and Nancy Sinatra's iconic song acknowledge, for once, that the relative stability of the James Bond universe is an artificially stable simulacrum built over a roiling geopolitical reality, a world that has started to look, think, and *sound* very different from what has gone before.

LIVING TWICE

How do you live twice? What does it mean to say "you only live twice"? For thirty years the original of this phrase—the opt-out mantra "you only live once"—had worried sociologists and theologians. To assert it meant you didn't give a shit about the meaning of your life *or* the fabric of society. In Fritz Lang's 1937 film *You Only Live Once*, the title phrase becomes an ironic commentary on a world that never gives you a second chance. But by the mid-sixties there seemed little point to challenging this sentiment, which had become a pervasive advertising cliché. An invitation to "live a little" or "treat yourself" drowned out lingering concerns over whatever (a)moral principle this phrase embodied. The phrase is the ancestor of "the motto" YOLO, which the rapper Drake popularized in his 2011 song of the same name.

What a sixties Bond story inherits, then, is a tentative consumerism and its toothless critique. So Fleming ups the ante. "You only live twice" is a beguiling phrase, but ultimately hard to parse. Book, film, and song each interpret it differently; each ground it differently in their respective stories. But a funny thing happened as the phrase transitioned from novel title to film title to song title: the song provides an interpretation of the novel much more than of the film. *Singing* the phrase, in a slow caress of two chords that don't want to go anywhere, not only poses a riddle but suspends us in a moment when the sixties, the Bond world and *our* world can all float free. Together, the three artifacts bearing the name *You Only Live Twice* tell a story about James Bond in the 1960s, and a story about the 1960s tout court.

The novel *You Only Live Twice*, published in March 1964, five months before Fleming's death, presents the title phrase as part of a quotation, albeit one that may be fictional or is presented as fictional in the novel. The book's front matter quotes a haiku-like poem and attributes it to the Japanese poet Basho (1644–1694):

> You only live twice:
> Once when you are born
> And once when you look death in the face.

It certainly isn't a haiku in English (the last line is a few syllables too long), but that could be chalked up to the translation. Except that in the book this poem by Basho is presented as the work of none other than Commander James Bond. Bond's Japanese host, the Oxford-educated head of Japan's secret service, Tiger Tanaka, introduces him to the concept of the haiku and the person of Basho. He quotes a few poems, none of which seem to do anything for his guest—who then drops a haiku of his own. Tiger translates the text into Japanese and decides that the syllables just can't work out in Japanese and the text is therefore not a haiku.

Later in the novel, as Bond bids farewell to Tanaka to go on a deadly mission, he quotes himself inventing Basho: "As Basho said, or as Basho almost said: 'You only live twice.'" There is an element of cultural imperialism at work here: the British agent treats the great poet as a type, rather than an individual genius, and his work as a linguistic trick that can be emulated without much reflection. The distance between the twenty syllables Bond composes and the ones Basho might have composed is vast, but Bond seems to think the "almost" just concerns the extra three syllables.

At the same time, the way the poem either turns Bond's on-the-fly composition into an "actual" Basho poem, or else presents a (bastardized) version of a Basho poem as James Bond's invention, fits well with the book's overarching theme, which is about self-reinvention. Throughout *You Only Live Twice*, people reinvent themselves with amazing ease and speed, to the point of absurdity. Ernst Stavro Blofeld has reinvented himself (yet again) as Guntram Shatterhand, botanist extraordinaire, and Bond himself undergoes a series of rebirths so quick and far-fetched that they feel like full-fledged identity crises. After a bath in some dye and some careful grooming by his Japanese benefactors, Bond not only looks Japanese (a conceit the movie version of *You Only Live Twice* struggled mightily to reproduce on film), he even passes muster before his worst enemy. Confronted with the man who has twice foiled his most ingenious schemes, Blofeld cannot recognize Bond behind his disguise as a local Japanese miner.

After destroying Blofeld's lair, Bond falls seemingly to his death in the ocean. But he is rescued by the pearl-diving ingénue Kissy Suzuki, who has fallen in love with him. Bond has lost all memory and regains very little of it, although he picks up Japanese at lightning speed and learns to dive for abalone with great ease. As the book ends, Bond is living as Kissy's husband in a small fishing community, when the word "Vladivostok" stirs memories of his former life. Reinvention is easy and almost absurdly quick in *You Only Live Twice*. Note that the Bond of the films is not so much a quick study, but rather knows how to do most things already (piloting a plane or space shuttle, snowboarding). Fleming's Bond picks up new skills all the time, but usually they are not as far afield (speaking Japanese and abalone fishing) as in this novel, and he never picks them up quite this quickly.

The readiness with which skill sets, cultural knowledge, and identities are assumed and discarded seems to be part of the point. The "only" in the book's title is a red herring—the book is all about living twice, and what that might mean. The ease with which Bond picks up and sheds identities in *You Only Live Twice* has something adolescent about it; the ease with which he acquires skills most people have from childhood on is downright infantile. Yet at the same time the Bond of *You Only Live Twice* is emphatically middle-aged. The beginning of the novel finds Bond, still grieving over the death of his wife Tracy in *On Her Majesty's Secret Service*, in a park feeding the pigeons. Preoccupied with "the state of your health, the state of the weather, the wonders of nature," at "the threshold of middle age," forgetful and diffident—it's a picture of an agent at the onset of senescence.

But if living more than once is the defiant theme of this Bond novel, the definitiveness of "twice" puts the entire novel under a strange kind of scrutiny. When exactly does James Bond's second life start? When does he "look death in the face"? Is it when Kissy Suzuki's guileless beauty starts erasing his memory of Tracy? Or was it when Tracy died in the first place? Is it when he comes across Blofeld/Shatterhand's picture and realizes who he is up against? Is it when he comes face to face with Blofeld? When Blofeld tries to torture him to death? Or when he falls into the Sea of Japan from a helium balloon? Or is it the novel's final line, when Bond turns away from Kissy Suzuki and her oriental ways, and back toward his first life in the West? There is so much looking death in the face in *You Only Live Twice*, and there are so many rebirths—which one, then, is the second one, the one that seems to really count?

This ambiguity haunts the novel, and it clearly inspired Leslie Bricusse's lyrics for the film's title song. Its title shadows the novel as a command: you *must* be reborn, you *must* be different, you *must* give it one more shot. But this command somehow fails to actually attach itself to any of the crises Bond experiences in the novel. Bond, who composes the haiku, and who seems to be reflecting on his own experience in it, won't let on at what point he takes himself to be starting a new life. And Fleming's plotting is perhaps too inexpert to build up to a single identifiable climax. But whether by design or by accident, the title is so effective precisely because we don't quite know what it refers to. It hovers over the book's proceedings and casts them in a certain light, without ever allowing us to sit back and tell ourselves that now, surely, Bond has looked death in the face and is ready to live the second of his two lives. The book's plot concerns an existence looking for that incisive break, but that break turns out to be harder to spot than we would expect.

In that respect at least, Fleming's book and Fleming's phrase acknowledge and anticipate the way the decade was to unfold: there is a demand for transcendence but a difficulty in bringing that transcendence to bear on everyday life, to square the moment when everything looks different from the way things have always been. For however much its mind is stuck in the 50s, in other words, *You Only Live Twice* possesses a peculiarly 60s temporality: the way the reader or Bond himself looks at Bond's life is the way the decade looked up from a burnt bra, a love-in, a blown-up brownstone and expected to see the world somehow transformed for the simple fact of it. Nancy Sinatra's song makes this gaze its central topic.

DOUBLE-AGENT DOUBLE-AGED

If the temporality of rebirth tethers the novel's 007 more closely to the 60s than the plots of the earlier Bond novels, its theme also gets at a strange contradiction at the very heart of the Bond character. For lack of a better word, James Bond is "double-aged." And this double-agedness started mattering more in an era when political, social, and aesthetic fault lines often coincided with generational divisions. Neither Bond's general disposition nor the quandaries he faces are ciphers for the travails of adolescence—at least until he was remade in Batman's image in the Daniel Craig outings, Bond's methods are never too unorthodox, Bond is never too inexperienced, Bond is never too close to a case—or whatever tropes books and movies habitually throw at young characters.

If anything, Bond struggles with the perils of superannuation. In the novels M seems habitually tempted to retire him—his confrontation with Dr. No is intended as that, and in a much more cynical attempt to retire his former star agent, M sends him on a suicide mission after the "Man with the Golden Gun." The movies pick up on this theme, and frequently have Bond confront the specter of his own superfluity or (in the post-1989 movies) even that of his entire craft. Bond's travails, in other words, are those of middle management—older men are constantly tempted to replace him with younger men. His methods and preferences find M's approval, but they push him to the edge of being outdated. At least in the novels, the women he picks up, like Honeychile Rider in *Dr. No*, or Kissy Suzuki in *You Only Live Twice*, are drawn to him as something of a daddy-replacement, and when he talks down to them, it is in paternal rather than sexist tones.

This becomes quite clear in a particularly absurd plot development in *You Only Live Twice*. In the novel, Kissy Suzuki, full-breasted, ebullient, and twenty-three, falls in love with Bond because he reminds her of David Niven, whom she met while working as an extra in a Hollywood movie. Fleming intended this as an inside joke: Fleming knew Niven personally and had modeled Bond's appearance on the actor, and had in fact wanted to cast him as Bond. But the hat tip turns out to be unintentionally revealing. By the time *You Only Live Twice* hit bookstores David Niven was a good-looking fifty-four- year-old (as was Fleming himself, not coincidentally), and had stopped appearing in heartthrob roles and graduated to self-effacing comedies years ago. Plus the 1967 film had to contend with the image of a midde-aged Niven actually playing Sir James Bond in the big-budget spoof *Casino Royale*, which had opened about two months earlier. The idea of a young Japanese girl having a David Niven fetish in 1964 seems so laughably absurd, it's got its own article in *The Onion*: "Asian Teen Has Sweaty Middle-Aged-Man Fetish," in which the actor Paul Giamatti is the unlikely recipient of schoolgirl adulation.

No matter who is carrying the Walther PPK, whether he's wearing a sexy boxer-brief Speedo or a terrible toupee, they are never truly youthful, and they aren't intended to appeal to the adolescent in every viewer or reader. James Bond appeals to the curmudgeon who insists on "his" drink at "his" club—could we imagine Wolverine, for instance, being prissy enough to insist that the ice in his drink be shaken not stirred? The sheer number of geopolitical crises Fleming's Bond solves around the bridge or baccarat table says a lot about which age bracket these books targeted. When *You Only Live Twice* was published in 1964, the British critic Cyril Connolly called it "reactionary, sentimental, square"—words that weren't just true for the novel, but for its hero too.

At the same time, Bond is of course an unabashedly adolescent fantasy—never more so than in *You Only Live Twice*, with its yen for reinvention and rebirth. Bond exists in two times of life at once. He shoots and has sex like a young man, but with attitudes that, even in the 50s and 60s, felt a little grandfatherly; and he projects virility and a sense of European superiority, all the while constantly nostalgic for an age of European dominance that he (supposedly in his mid- to late thirties by 1964) never actually witnessed. His hard-edged cynicism and uncaring sadism are at times that of the "blunt weapon" Judi Dench's M describes in *Casino Royale* (2006), but at others resemble that of a man who has grown old doing the same job for much too long. The title *You Only Live Twice* thus spills the beans on one of James Bond's dirty little secrets—James Bond lives a double life, even within his fictional world he is fictitious. But the musical idiom in which the song spills those beans also points out why this double-agedness mattered in a different way by 1967.

In an entertainment field increasingly saturated with youth culture, the Bond series was steadfast in refusing to give in to its tropes. In the Bond films, there are no counterculture surrogates of the type Bert Schneider began to shoehorn into Hollywood films. The one sign of the changing social mores consists in the gay killers Mr. Wint and Mr. Kidd sauntering through *Diamonds Are Forever*, only to be dispatched with homophobic glee. The two are a rare acknowledgment that during the time that elapsed between the book (1956) and the film (1971), two gay men could openly hold hands (in the book version, Wint and Kidd's sexuality is consigned to Felix Leiter's case files). As for the other social transformations engendered by the 1960s, they find no representation on screen in the James Bond films. There are no hippies, no feminists, no student protesters, no draft dodgers, no Black Panthers.

You Only Live Twice is no different in terms of what is on screen—it is just as square as all the other Connery outings. But it is different thanks to its song, specifically because of who sings it, and because of the sound of its music more generally. Cubby Broccoli had initially asked Frank Sinatra to provide a song for the movie. But the producers eventually settled on his daughter Nancy. A woman closer in age to Kissy Suzuki than to David Niven; had costarred in a Roger Corman movie with Peter Fonda; and was associated with the styles of Carnaby Street and Swinging London (go-go boots, miniskirts), fashions supposedly from Bond's own backyard, but seemingly light years removed from his world by 1967.

Choosing Nancy Sinatra was only one way that Broccoli, Barry, and Co. showed they were paying attention. They had little choice. Dusty Springfield's "The Look of Love," the bust-out hit from *Casino Royale*, stayed on the airwaves all through the production and opening months of *You Only Live Twice*. The parody outclassed the original: Burt Bacharach's catchy melody and rich harmony, the sensual bossa-nova groove, and Hal David's just barely sexualized lyrics projected an ideal representation of Bond's sexual economy—all the while maintaining its decorum as a post–Tin Pan Alley pop record. Beyond the blond, transatlantic twenty-somethings at their center, the two songs share languid tempos, fancy harmony, varied arrangements, delicately "exotic" rhythms, and a reassuringly old-fashioned structure that places the main hook at the beginning and end of each chorus. More subtly, the two songs possess a deliberateness that somehow amplifies their sexual charge. And perhaps their very *slow-ness* allows us to take in their forward- and backward-looking elements all at once.

But Sinatra's song intensifies the contrast between these elements. Where "The Look of Love" creates a harmonious blend of traditional and up-to-date features, "You Only Live Twice" rather sets them at odds: a cheesy faux-oriental marimba motif juts out against the smooth violins and quickly disappears; the elegant vocal melody contends with a fuzz guitar; a quaint bolero rhythm is dusted off and treated as if it still had a whiff of otherness; heavy electric bass tells your gut this isn't your moth-er's pop record. This uneasy mix puts past and future, dreams and real-ity, memory and real presence momentarily up for grabs. "You Only Live Twice" is addressed to a square, who tamely "drifts through the years" and lives only in his dreams, and who is seduced out of his security by love. It was with good reason that Matthew Weiner chose the song to close the fifth season of *Mad Men*: Nancy Sinatra's song is the siren call of the future, of youth and of the counterculture wafting over the picket fence.

> You only live twice or so it seems,
> One life for yourself and one for your dreams.
> You drift through the years and life seems tame
> Till one dream appears and love is its name.

Living twice in Sinatra's song refers to something quite different than in the book. However opaque the book is in spelling out for the reader what "living twice" actually means, it is clear that it is referencing a sequential process—you live once, then you get reborn and get a crack at a second life. The two lives Sinatra sings about are simultaneous, "one life for your-self and one for your dreams." Leslie Bricusse's lyrics are about those rare moments when the life you imagined for yourself and the one you're actu-ally living might come together as one—moments that are scary, danger-ous, and evanescent. In the first version of the song recorded by the singer Julie Rogers, with a set of completely different lyrics by Bricusse, the two lives were similarly lived one after the other. Somehow when the repre-sentative of 60s culture came aboard as the singer, the two lives "you" live moved next to one another. What you live and what you dream came face to face, and "tamely" keeping them apart was an act of cowardice.

As so often in Bond songs, Bricusse's lyric is not actually about James Bond. Bond's life has never "seemed tame," and his dreams, as far as we can tell, are far less outlandish than what actually happens to him. "Staring death in the face," as Bond does in the novel *You Only Live Twice*, is something most first-world denizens don't do on a habitual basis—lucky the life, then, that is lived only once. But the condition Sinatra describes in the song is universal—in fact, Bond may be one of the few men alive who is exempt from her sweeping statements. The pronoun "You" in James Bond songs often has a hard time attaching itself to Bond specifically; it has a tendency to drift, to speak of the villain, the singer, the listener. When Paul McCartney sings that "you used to say 'live and let live,'" surely he isn't referring to the man with the license to kill; when Shirley Bassey imputes to "you" a "dream of gold" in "Moonraker," it seems an ill fit for 007.

At the same time, even if it has a hard time speaking to his life, the song clearly is about Bond. As the iconic string theme introduces the song, we see Bond's lifeless body, with blood running from a gunshot wound. Yes, "living twice" means somehow surviving this fatal shooting. But the problems the song speaks about have little to do with Bond's double life in the movie. "Living twice" in the song is one thing; in the movie it's quite another; and in the song as it occurs in the movie, the phrase becomes ambiguous. It concerns Bond and us viewers, but withdraws from both of those referents at certain points. It seems to concern Bond as seen by us, or us in light of Bond. The lyrics point to the phantasmatic character of the Bond persona: He lives "twice" because he persists in two contradictory lives that can come together only in a fantasy—our fantasy.

LIVING TWICE FOR BEGINNERS

So what *was* our fantasy in 1967? The film's original American trailer thinks it knows. With the Bond franchise securely established, this three-minute preview doesn't need to provide any description of the lead character, draw connections to the Fleming novels, or indeed hint at the movie's plot. It gives us a brand rather than a character, a montage instead of a premise. In what was becoming the typical economy of blockbuster film trailers, it presents slices of the big set-pieces—explosions, elaborate sets, cast of thousands—intercut with a parade of sexually available women, plus enough shiny objects to fill a trade show. This trailer stands out, however: its emphasis on branding pushes things toward an odd sort of abstraction. The film's lead villain gets reduced to an acousmatic voice, a pudgy hand stroking a cat, and a foot operating the wah-wah pedal of death—no name, no face, no credited actor, just a "they" who "don't stand a chance." Even Bond himself is basically a name repeated again and again, a Scottish accent, a hairstyle, a custom shirt. He does "die" twice, in the trailer, but it hardly seems to matter.

This trailer makes the Bond *franchise* the brand; it's no longer the character himself. The film's Japan setting, too, simply serves the brand. Japan says "Welcome, Honorable 007" and discloses itself in a series of easy-to-read images. But audiences knew that Japan could've been anywhere—anywhere that might convey Bond's, and the viewer's, mobility. Discontinuous images of traditional/hi-tech Japanese culture broaden our range of motion while taking space away from the film's Cold War theme and North Atlantic cultural politics. The fantasy, then, is that this barrage of heterogeneous images and sounds will hang together and become our life. The trailer gambles that its audiences no longer want a secret life, or a chance to start over, or a "real me" to break out of its shell. This fantasy is purely capitalist-consumerist; the magic of the market will somehow make it add up.

But the grippier fantasy actually concerns the central figure who receives cursory treatment in the trailer, whom the trailer renders as a straightforward branding mechanism. Bond is a patchwork, hanging together only as a name, a voice, a fast-decaying look, a function in the plot, a set of actions, and the fragmentary discourse around him. The stability of his brand can't quite mask the impossible aggregation of elements he has become. He's young and old, modern and traditional, cosmopolitan but very British; a covert agent who gets celebrity treatment. This makes him available for fantasy. His fancy stuff, his mobility, his interactions with people and spaces, his "look": it's a lumpy mix in which anything can come to the fore.

You Only Live Twice pictures its "second life" as painless and continual self-reinvention—like merely changing the settings on one of Bond's gadgets. As far as cinematic economy is concerned, this approach starts to change what we care about as viewers. It changes *how* we care. We're not moved by the lead character, the progress of the plot, or the emotions we witness: we invest in the *process* that swirls them around. The novel still presented Bond's transformation as something we care about, our hero pushed to his limits and beyond, but emerging a stronger (though reinvented) man. That sweep is gone in the film, where Bond's transformations are just devices for moving along the plot, and the film never pretends differently. This swirl supplants the "pure" capitalist enterprise of a *Goldfinger*. *You Only Live Twice* invents a kind of fantasy capitalism, telling us that's all there is. It sells it as a kind of realism, while still expecting us to believe in magic. This precarious doubleness soon breaks down, as we'll see in the prosaic *Diamonds Are Forever*: there, capitalism is sex, period. But *You Only Live Twice* expends considerable energy trying to keep those two together yet separate, no matter how this tears at the fabric of its protagonist.

What does this fantasy economy ask of a theme song? Nancy Sinatra's record both reflects and manages the swirl. Of all the Bond songs thus far it lay closest to the advancing edge of its music-historical moment, and it tapped in right at the point when pop records were becoming more collage-like—when they were starting to heap up more material than they could safely contain. So if the film places Bond and the Bond world under threat of disintegration, the Sinatra record does the same with its lead vocalist and its musical arrangement. Sinatra's voice does help hold things together. It provides a throughline that reassures us we're hearing a pop song. But when the arrangement pits the voice against a fuzz guitar's quicker (and catchier) melody, having already softened us up with the fake-Asian marimba figure and the bolero beat, it compels the singer to *earn* her place in the spotlight. The vocal melody makes this harder. You might find it relaxed and dreamy until you try to sing along: its wide range and disjunct motion are tough to navigate. When the singer has to strain against her accompaniment and the very melody she's presenting, the whole record begins to sweat.

This song's surprising mix of elements contains nothing really novel or extreme. But every element is compromised, trying to do two things at once. The electric guitar's distorted timbre allows it to work as a signifier of rock culture, but its violinistic melody leans classical. Punchy marimba scoring may have been trendy, but here the instrument is drawn back into the orbit of loathsome orientalist stereotypes. The electric bass provides harmonic underpinning of the most traditional sort, but its big sound and low-frequency heft suggest it wants to do more. The crisp bolero groove comes out of midcentury exotica, but its up-to-date sonic presence reminds us that percussion instruments and rhythm guitars can power a song without having to lock into a single rhythmic motif. The brass section swells and falls, just filling out the harmony, but its jazzy voicings generate power for a riff that never comes. And so on. All the elements are working overtime but nothing tells us what they add up to—this is a central part of the pop record's aesthetic in the late sixties.

Sinatra's vocal track too is compromised. Many late-sixties pop records operate like this: they assert the sonic materiality of the voice, the conceptual primacy of melody and lyrics, and the clarity of traditional AABA form, but they allow "secondary" features to run wild. The lead voice becomes part of the swirl. The lyrics can fragment: a word pops out here, a whole verse gets lost there. This approach disarticulates melody, vocality, and communication. Affect gets distributed across the song in unpredictable ways. Here the text-setting of the title phrase—"you" and "twice" as long notes thudding on the downbeats; "only" as the registral highpoint—seems designed to drain it of whatever sense it has. The rest of the opening line ("or so it seems") unfolds so slowly that it flaunts its pointlessness. In a painful/pleasurable way, the voice makes us want more; to get this "more" we must reach out to the instruments. This centrifugal force turns the song into an assemblage, matching the film's impossible economy. Sinatra actually turns in an impressive performance. She does her job, which isn't just negotiating the tricky melody and the busy arrangement: she's both fully present and willing to give herself up to the swirl.

Connery's Bond doesn't quite achieve this flexibility—the novel's lumpy elements are smoothed over in the film, and Connery doesn't register contradiction as much as he just purrs over it, looking to convince us that the whole thing coheres. Sure, it's possible to "live twice," don't even worry about it. Only the song and the music register the tension between these two lives, and therefore they end up registering the friction that the movie elsewhere studiously downplays. Across the soundtrack, melody puts pressure on the exotic elements of the instrumentation, the force of the rhythm section, and the pop record's ever-increasing emphasis on sonic materiality. Uniquely for the Bond cycle, this soundtrack makes its film's tensions productive: it continually registers the odd constructedness of the Bond world. Film scores were mostly sounding like this in 1967, but here the music's lumpy mix of elements stands for everything that was threatening the Bond-world's stability and adequacy. And the movie doesn't acknowledge those threats in any other way.

Only in the music do we get a response to what's impinging on the film from outside. Partly this means showing us what the movie's hiding: rock culture, black culture, working-class culture, not to mention Japanese culture. Like the credit sequence's nude dancers, the soundtrack foregrounds what it doesn't quite reveal. The music's refusal (or inability) to really give us soul music, heavy rock, funky jazz, latin boogaloo, psychedelic, or any other truly contemporary style helps it hit a sweet spot. Soundtracks that go further become late-sixties period-pieces; more timid examples seem embarrassingly conservative. The soundtrack for *You Only Live Twice* perfectly fits the ill-fittingness of the film's project. Right in time with the film's untimeliness, the music *sounds* as though it is willing to believe what the film as a whole makes hard to swallow: that things will all add up somehow; that "living twice" is something the rest of us can pull off.

Alice Cooper

THE MAN WITH
THE GOLDEN GUN

Lulu

LIVE AND LET DIE

Paul McCartney and Wings

DIAMONDS
ARE FOREVER

Shirley Bassey

WE HAVE ALL THE TIME
IN THE WORLD

Louis Armstrong

"When You've Got a Job to Do"

The 70s

Starting with 1971's *Diamonds Are Forever*, the songs that open the Bond movies do double duty. They hearken back to their recognizable and iconic forebears, but they do not blindly chase their famous antecedents; instead they put them into dialogue with musical styles and genres that were new to the franchise. "Diamonds" both does and does not sound like a song from 1971, and this was to become typical for the Bond song of the 70s and beyond: they were almost laughably of their moment, grasping at fads they could never catch up to. But at the same time there was a part of them that wallowed nostalgically in the world of Las Vegas casinos and big-band dance clubs—the world Fleming's Bond had inhabited, but that since vanished, and quite deservedly so.

This was possible because new and old had, by the time *Diamonds Are Forever* hit screens, noticeably, and that means audibly, separated. *On Her Majesty's Secret Service* eschewed the title-driven pop song in favor of a more with-it instrumental number. When the vocal theme-song reappears, in *Diamonds Are Forever*, it's the first historicist Bond record, a deliberate throwback clearly legible even to the most casual listener. Tom Jones's "Thunderball" represented the last time a Bond song tried to use bluster to cover up its outdatedness. By the time "Diamonds Are Forever" came out, composer John Barry and lyricist Don Black (who had collaborated on *Thunderball* and returned for *Diamonds*) had given up on any such attempt. Their song in most respects sounds like a mid-50s pop production, and the new elements they introduce to the formula (culled from more up-to-date genres like soul and funk) draw attention to the disconnect rather than paper it over.

But if it was an anachronistic song even when it was released, "Diamonds Are Forever" is not just a relic, obsessed with another time and insensate to its own. Rather, "Diamonds" introduces a very peculiar dynamic into the Bond-song canon and its relationship to the past. The disconnect between the musical language owed to the genre's origin in the early 60s, and the new idioms brought in to rejuvenate it, tells a compelling and at least partially self-reflexive tale of a very 70s set of anxieties. Precisely by being outdated and by tacking absurdly closely to a musical formula established more than a decade prior, "Diamonds Are Forever" manages to talk about its historical moment with surprising eloquence.

It wasn't easy being a song in the late 60s and the 70s. Yes, the music industry was booming. A tremendously wide range of stuff could happen on a pop record: songs could take many shapes and sizes, incorporate a crazy mix of elements, change tone, switch addressees, collapse into giggles. And still sell. Most people didn't care whether a record was "too pop"; unless you really identified with rock critics you weren't bothered by the professionalization and corporatization of popular-music production. But even so: the sixties had left behind a set of tensions that pulled the pop song this way and that. Where was pop supposed to turn—toward its "sheet-music" roots or toward an emphasis on *sound*? Toward kids or grownups? Toward a race-neutral "popular" style or toward "black music"? Toward rock or away from it? Songs of the seventies often did all of the above. So much so that when a chart-topping seventies pop record actually sounds like nothing but a pop record—remember Debbie Boone's 1977 "You Light Up My Life"?—it stands out as such.

The Bond songs of this moment not only reveal these tensions, they seem particularly susceptible to succumbing to them. From "You Only Live Twice" through Lulu's grating contribution to *The Man with the Golden Gun*, these songs present themselves as lumpy mixtures of "timeless" pop and the sounds of "today"; they make a problem of the pop song's traditional blend of familiarity and novelty. Paul McCartney's "Live and Let Die" does so the most cannily. Filling out this group are the two puzzling offerings from 1969's *On Her Majesty's Secret Service*: besides the instrumental low-modernist pop-rock march that serves as its title song, the film includes Louis Armstrong's ballad "We Have All the Time in the World" and the more obscure "Do You Know How Christmas Trees Are Grown," sung by the Danish vocalist Nina Van Pallandt.

The early-70s Bond songs exhibit a characteristic set of anxieties, most of which revolve around the idea of work and having a job. These Bond songs were about the job of being a heartbreaker spy, but beneath the surface that job stood in for another one, one that was changing radically around the Bond songs: the job of being a pop musician. Unlike most 70s pop songs these Bond-song entries have a clear raison d'être: they're there to serve a movie that brings them into being. We don't have to ask why they exist. But because their job is simply to *be* professionally produced pop records, commissioned to fit an already-existing title, they tap into 70s anxieties about labor, and especially affective labor. This is a decade, after all, during which the notions of what it meant to do a job and be a professional were broadening, but the prospects of actually having a job were increasingly precarious. And any possibility of not *having* to work a job was feeling a lot less attainable, or even attractive, than in the late 60s. So a pay-for-play pop song raises questions about what's actually being paid for, and who's getting the gig.

Shirley Bassey's "Diamonds Are Forever" features the singer dutifully doing what she's done once before, but the world around her has shifted so much that she ends up doing more than she gets paid for: she puts her gender, sexuality, age, and ethnicity into the song's unstable musical mix.

McCartney's "Live and Let Die" works similarly while reminding us that the no-longer-young rock star was emerging as a particularly odd sort of cultural spectacle. The man singing that nothing really matters "when you've got a job to do" didn't need to work for a living anymore, and had to worry that anything he did after the Beatles would be considered "just" workmanlike. Lulu's "Man with the Golden Gun" makes clear that professionalism and purpose are no antidote to bad taste.

FEAR OF A BLACK PLANET

"Diamonds" represents a musical return to the Bond of the 60s, delivered by the quintessential Bond singer of the 60s. Still, Bassey's song ironically produced something quite different, setting the tone for the 70s Bond songs. The songs are asked to squeeze into increasingly tight confines: on one side they've got a Bond franchise digging in its heels against changing mores and geopolitics, and on the other they have Bond soundtracks pushing outward toward new sorts of music. The best of the 70s Bond songs seize the space between the chairs into which a changing zeitgeist had maneuvered the Bond franchise, and the new soundtrack of the 70s, to explore and explode the ideology of the Bond songs. It is amazing what fit into that space: anxieties about race and gender, about liberty and libertinage, about the "artistic" and "commercial" aspects of songs, and about the history of pop and its politics.

The most noticeable element of the traditional Bond song that both returns and becomes transfigured in "Diamonds" is none other than Shirley Bassey's voice itself. The song plays to her strengths, perhaps more than "Goldfinger" had. Thanks mostly to "Goldfinger," Bond songs had been stamped with the impress of strong female voices. But Bassey's "Diamonds" marks the first time since "Goldfinger" that a song tells its story from what is explicitly a woman's perspective. In "Goldfinger" Bassey had slipped into the skin of a grizzled femme fatale dispensing advice to more inexperienced "golden girls." Femininity, in that song's universe, existed as a mere supplement to male desire. Bassey's voice provides guidance on how to respond to Auric Goldfinger's appetites without entering his "web of sin." At the center of the song remained Goldfinger himself, and his primary libidinal attachment, his love of gold.

The lyrics of "Diamonds" tell a story of female desire. Men appear much like the "golden girls" did in "Goldfinger": as substitutes for the true object of desire, diamonds: "I don't need love, / for what good would love do me? / Diamonds never lied to me / for when love's gone / they luster on." Diamonds are not just better, more transparent, more permanent than men (and specifically more so than a certain famously inconstant British spy), their evocation has clear masturbatory undertones. Diamonds are "all I need to please me," they "stimulate and tease me." The first diamond we see "lustering on" in the main title sequence of *Diamonds* is draped around a cat, which may be an indelicate hat tip to just those undertones. Barry is supposed to have told Bassey to imagine that she was serenading a penis when recording the song, but "Diamonds Are Forever" is really all about pussy.

If "Diamonds" is a song about how unnecessary a thing the phallus is, it is also a song about how unnecessary a thing white people are. Bassey returns to the Bond franchise not as a colorblind chanteuse, or a latter-day Lotte Lenya, but rather explicitly as a singer of color. "Diamonds Are Forever" marks a formal departure in several respects, most of which pay deference to changes in soul and funk, rather than developments in mainstream rock. That is, the new sounds this song grapples with aren't just different for the franchise, they are differently pigmented—black sounds—in ways that would have been recognizable to film audiences. The song depends on these new sounds, but it seems scared of them as well.

Is Bassey a "black" singer? Does the song treat her like one? A lot rides on these questions, financially and aesthetically. Gordon Parks's *Shaft*, released a season earlier in the summer of 1971, gave MGM a rare box-office triumph. Its crossover success showed you could have a black protagonist—a black *professional*—and present blackness as a kind of multiplicity. Equally notable was the way the film outed Hollywood's racism by making whiteness look pathological. *Shaft* told Hollywood that the old notions of "black" and "white" audiences didn't make sense. Isaac Hayes's top-selling soundtrack demonstrated that black music, composed and performed by a popular African American artist in his prime, could be fully adequate to the needs of a mainstream film. Bassey's "Diamonds" too took advantage of a profound shift in mainstream pop: middle-of-the-road, easy listening, and adult contemporary had drifted inexorably toward black music, even if the faces on the album covers remained white. Soulful singing, grooving rhythm sections, and jazzy harmonies were now part of pop's lingua franca. This blackening of grown-up pop meant that Bassey, a showbizzy Anglo-Nigerian Welsh belter who was never associated with the soul-music tradition, fronting a bunch of British studio hacks, could count as a soulful—yes, "black"—singer asserting African American musical authority over what was a very white film.

Bassey's soulfulness gives *Diamonds* new ways of conveying the urban, the modern, the cosmopolitan, the "mature." Her implicit conflict with Connery's Bond suggests an alternative picture of having a gender and embodying an ethnicity, and of being not-so-young. Bassey has a commanding ease and presence where the rest of the movie has to huff and puff: Bond struggles to seem himself, the Americans mostly bumble around, the director has lost his touch, and the blockbuster film's cinematic economy simply provides a little bit of everything at a uniformly mediocre level. Unlike Connery, Bassey makes a virtue of reprising a role. As a singing voice and a political subject she has *arrived*.

"Diamonds" hardly gives itself over to soul. On paper there's nothing particularly "black" about it. It's a Tin Pan Alley construction that puts melody, harmony, and lyrics up front. It doesn't need a soul singer. Black music is certainly a factor in the song, though. Right from the beginning the arrangement and production signal contemporary soul. The slightly busy mix of electric organ, flute, harp, strings, delicate percussion, and electric-guitar swells operates along the grain of Philadelphia soul. The prominent, staggered entrances of electric bass and drums tell you the rhythm-section instruments matter. Later the drumbeat gets funkier, the rhythm arrangement becomes more active, and a telltale electric guitar enters the soundstage with a wah-wah pedal and phase-shifter. As soulful touches proliferate across the length of the song, Bassey pushes further in this direction—bending notes, varying her vibrato, playing with the beat, getting a bit breathy, even adding a little grit. But the stop-and-start rhythm arrangement never allows the groove to take over. The drums are placed too low in the mix, and performed with too little vigor. And the record ends too early, on a cold close, denying Bassey an opportunity for extended vocal ad-libs: we never reach the crucial moment when the soulful diva takes control.

"Diamonds" is ultimately a soulful pop record, lightly updating the 60s formula perfected by Dionne Warwick and Burt Bacharach, and the 5th Dimension and Jim Webb. As ever, the Bond songs fail to learn an important musical lesson: 60s pop-soul is blockbuster music, mixing powerful singing, an attention-grabbing rhythm section, active horn and string arrangements, a heaping-up of additional instruments, and aggressive production values that put it all up in your face. Nor did "Diamonds Are Forever" get 70s-soul's memo about how you could stretch things out, allowing time and space for individual musical elements to assert themselves, as long as you provided an insistent groove.

The record's pop-friendly emphasis on its composed vocal melody matches the images it's set to. Just as the musical mix doesn't really invite you to follow the rhythm section or seek out the other instruments, the image forces your attention toward the center of the frame. The beginning of the credit sequence leaves nothing to chance, zooming in on a naked lady's diamond-accessoried crotch in all its soft-focus glory. When Bassey enters with the title phrase, the film's title card appears simultaneously in yet another stodgy centripetal composition. The black action films and their soundtracks encouraged viewers to look and listen deeper into the mix of elements they presented. *Diamonds*, on the other hand, wants to keep the blinders on. None of the song's soulful features connects with anything we see in the credit sequence: even as the syncopated drumbeat enters and the wah-wah guitar funks things up a bit, the camera, the cutting, and the figures in the frame continue to move very deliberately—the single dancing nude gyrates in slow motion, as if to some other song. And the film and soundtrack as a whole give no space to African American music. Black culture never enters the picture. The film's only black character is the unflatteringly named and not tremendously competent Thumper, one of two female bodyguards keeping a kidnapped Howard Hughes–like tycoon on ice.

This discomfort with nonwhite visibility (and audibility) whenever it reared its nonwhite head was to be emblematic for the Bond songs of the early 70s. The plots of those movies found James Bond traversing the remnants of the British Empire in vague recreations of Ian Fleming plots set before the territories in question gained their independence (South Africa in *Diamonds*, Jamaica in *Live and Let Die*, Malaysia in *The Man with the Golden Gun*), and through them runs a cruel streak of racial panic vis-à-vis the erstwhile colonial subject. Many of them are stories of reverse colonialism, of formerly subjugated nations and peoples sinking their talons into the metropole. *Diamonds* stages a crackerjack sequence that details a smuggling operation connecting the mines of South Africa to Amsterdam; in *The Man with the Golden Gun*, Scaramanga sends a golden bullet with Bond's name on it to London from his South China Sea hideout; and the voodoo priests of *Live and Let Die* pump drugs from their Caribbean redoubt into the heart of urban North America. No longer does Bond set out into the periphery to pacify them for the Empire (which had been the template most of the novels and the first Bond film followed); instead he's desperately trying to keep the racial other out of Britain. Meanwhile, the songs for these films replay this dynamic of attraction and repulsion with respect to music coded as "ethnic," and specifically black.

The axis that bedevils and ensorcells the music of the Bond of the early 70s is the one enshrined in the plot of *Live and Let Die*, where the Caribbean voodoo priest Dr. Kananga turns out to be the same man as the Harlem heavy Mr. Big. The colonial and the metropolitan subaltern strike an uncanny alliance—and they do so primarily through music. The film *Live and Let Die* introduces the villainous Baron Samedi (another ally of Kananga's) to the frenetic beat of colonial-era "tribal" drums, which segue directly into Paul McCartney's opening song. The other end of that secret pipeline is Mr. Big's Harlem jazz club (called appropriately

"Fillet of Soul"), as well a New Orleans establishment where James Bond, bewitched by the voice of a black woman performer, is abducted into Big's world. As she sings the film's theme song onstage, his table drops into the club's basement, where Big's henchmen are waiting. Music has become a conduit through which a nonwhite element has snuck into Bond's version of the West. The songs themselves experience this element as a threat, and seek to marginalize it.

Not that the franchise's one earlier foray into the black music of the global South did it more credit in that regard. *On Her Majesty's Secret Service* includes "We Have All the Time in the World," a Barry composition sung by New Orleans jazz great Louis Armstrong just a few years before his death. More than almost anyone else Armstrong had defined the "black voice." But the film tucks the song away in a romantic montage, burying its blackness under a haze of nostalgia. In a gesture of supreme bad taste, a hack trumpet player mimics Armstrong's style on the instrument the older musician could no longer play. The song places black music on the opposite end of sonic modernity—it's the music you remember from your youth, it seems to insist, nothing new, nothing threatening to see here. And it's actually worse than that: though Barry concocted a bullshit story about needing the poignancy of an older singer, the song is a shameless rip-off of Armstrong's then-recent comeback hit, "What a Wonderful World." Hearing Armstrong reprise his drawn-out "world," with its characteristic kaleidoscope of changing vowel-sounds, is nothing short of sickening. This is the beginning and end of the story of African American musicians in Bond films until Gladys Knight's song for 1989's *License to Kill*. The Bond songs were as aggressive in courting a kind of "black" sound as they were in marginalizing it.

The 70s Bond films' "fear of a black planet" parallels their anxieties about women as figures of authority. *Diamonds* can handle a minor character like Thumper, whose incompetence is both gendered and raced, but it can't make space for Bassey's blackness, which means it squanders both her sexuality and her professionalism. Bassey does what she can. She creates a wry, self-ironizing sexual persona out of a ridiculous lyric, using the very distance between "Diamonds" and "Goldfinger"—biographical, historical, and stylistic—to increase the erotic charge. And she vocalizes her way into the soul tradition, drawing on whatever she can find in the musical arrangement around her. Bassey's mode of professionalism here is to sing as if the song, the film, and early 70s culture at large need her to be black. But somehow the film doesn't hear her.

In *Diamonds Are Forever* the fear of a black voice sets in at the exact moment when that voice begins to speak of feminine desire—not the desire to be desired, not a grim warning of men's desire, but a desire that finds its objects independent of men. If the films of the seventies grapple anxiously with the proposition that once-colonized peoples could become entirely self-sufficient, and might no longer require saving by a handsome white man, then *Diamonds* traffics in the equally nerve-racking idea that women may not require men to satisfy themselves and may become erotically self-sufficient. The fear here as there is that James Bond, the British Empire, and white men more generally might no longer be invited to the party.

Not surprisingly, though, the song that opens the original James Bond's triumphant return to the screen does not come out and deny Bond's relevance and sex appeal. The question gives it some anxiety, but song and film manage to work through those anxieties just fine, thank you very much, and by the end all is well again. Whether the self-contentment of the diamond-infatuated onanist persona Bassey projects ends up successful, or whether she is just kidding herself, becomes the crux of the song, and the question never gets fully resolved. At first blush the song seems to present the story of a successful diet, as the singer weans herself off destructive men in favor of trusty diamonds. There is no last-stanza conversion, no wavering in the singer's abjuration of men.

Except of course diamonds are never really extolled on their own virtues, but always only as substitutes for men. Everything we find out about them matters only because men, according to the singer, are the exact opposite. Diamonds seem to have no qualities of their own, that is to say, without reference to men. The song should really be called "Diamonds Are Forever (and Men Aren't)." The singer may have liberated herself from men, and may "linger" autoerotically with her new toys, but men remain a necessary frame of reference.

Only if we listen harder than the film does can we grasp the radical self-sufficiency of Bassey's voice. Heard as what it really is—a soulful pop record powered by a professional singer giving it better than it deserves—"Diamonds" can trick us into forgetting that maleness and whiteness could ever have been a frame of reference. We can almost imagine it doesn't need Bond, men, white people, Britain, action, sex, anything. Almost. Unlike the Bond songs at their best ("Goldfinger," "Live and Let Die"), "Diamonds" isn't fully detachable. But letting Bassey's voice bore into us we can hear this record as the 70s-soul-diva feature it kind of wants to be. By doing her job Bassey remains capable of seducing herself—and us.

"WHAT DOES IT MATTER TO YA?"

If "Diamonds Are Forever" was haunted by the space between the sound of "Goldfinger" and the sounds native to the 70s, and was largely unconscious of just how eloquent its contradictions were, the Bond song that followed it, 1973's "Live and Let Die" demonstrated that a canny artist could actually use the outdatedness of the Bond-song format to reflect on his or her own work and biography. When he was asked to record the song for the next James Bond film, Paul McCartney demanded complete creative control, and he got it. He used the song to stage his own story, or a version of it: McCartney casts himself as a man at risk of outdatedness, threatened by new sounds, a man having to cope with a tougher, less welcoming musical landscape.

The song's lyrics, written by Paul and Linda McCartney, talk explicitly about the tectonic shift away from the world of *Goldfinger*. It's a song about the passage of time, about lost innocence and lost illusions, about the need to adjust to changed circumstances. The McCartneys are supposed to have written the song in one afternoon, and its lyrics read a bit like a therapy session. McCartney, who commented that coming up with "a song around a title like that's not the easiest thing going," seems to have tapped into his own anxieties and preoccupations for the song's lyrics:

> When you were young
> And your heart was an open book
> You used to say "live and let live."
> But if this ever-changing world
> In which we're living
> Makes you give in and cry
> Say "live and let die."

What the song leaves open is who exactly the "you" is who's receiving this advice. It doesn't seem like a sound lesson to impart to James Bond, who in neither Fleming's novels nor the earlier films had ever flirted with a "live and let live" attitude. Nor is this advice implicitly gendered, applying to potential Bond girls, or those drawn in by either Bond or his nemeses.

Of course, there is one possible addressee who would have been at the forefront of audiences' minds in 1973. A man who may not have actually said "live and let live," but who had said things very much like it. A man who was now finding himself stranded in an "ever-changing" world, a world that required a new kind of mantra, a newer, meaner kind of sound. That man was of course McCartney himself. Three years after the end of the Beatles, with the acrimonious court battles over royalties and the Beatles' legacy still in full swing, McCartney had returned to the charts with *Red Rose Speedway*, the million-selling second album he recorded with Linda and his band Wings. *Red Rose Speedway* had a successful single in "My Love" and an *Abbey Road*–like concluding suite that demonstrated what rock culture still regarded as high ambition. Nevertheless McCartney clearly remained worried he might become a has-been from the 60s, coasting on his earlier successes to new ones—or a mere pop meister.

The Bond song was the perfect vehicle for McCartney's public skin-shedding. Sure, James Bond had never been a hippie or hung around with gurus, but James Bond was McCartney's kindred spirit, in that they were both artifacts iconically linked to the 60s, to the point that their raison d'être in the 70s was somewhat murky. And if there was any part of the Bond franchise that had aged more poorly than others, it was their songs, which had started to sound like relics long before McCartney decided to write one. Ironically, that made the genre a perfect fit for someone in his position, someone who was likewise wondering how much of his 60s output could be salvaged and remain relevant in this new decade with its tougher attitudes and new musical idioms.

The song's music once again reflects this shift: "Live and Let Die" is a self-admonition to toughen up, to go with the time, and to leave behind the spirit of the 60s, and "All You Need Is Love." Its lyrics tell the story of a man whose heart was once "an open book," who abandons his optimism in favor of a more jaundiced, perhaps more practical mindset. "What does it matter to you, / when you got a job to do, / you gotta do it well," the song intones, and the twangs of guitar and clavinet that accompany the line suggest that it's not the most respectable job in the world. Whatever job it is, whether it's killing for a living or writing a song about it, somebody's got to do it.

Most of the Bond songs of the 70s emphasized craft over art. Of course, Tom Jones and Matt Monro had been craftsmen in their own way. But the need to emphasize the fact that the craftsman puts his skills at the disposal of the highest bidder rather than some vaunted ideal was an innovation of the 70s. The songs talk about spycraft, and they talk about music-making in a similar way—the Bond singers are guns for hire, and they don't mind letting the audience know.

The songs share this emphasis on professionalism with the films they accompany: *Diamonds Are Forever* opens with a famous montage detailing the highly developed diamond-smuggling ring Bond spends most of the film tangling with. The whole thing has a feel of uncharacteristic realism, and it takes almost until halfway into the film for this well-run machine to turn into another laser-based world-domination scheme. *The Man with the Golden Gun* opens with the hit man Scaramanga honing his craft, and *Live and Let Die* shows off the extreme efficiency of Big/Kananga's criminal outfit. In Bassey's "Goldfinger" villainy was mythic, in Tom Jones's "Thunderball" heroism was too—killing, like music, was a path to superstardom. In the 70s Bonds, making music and killing are jobs like any other. That too made the genre hospitable to someone in McCartney's situation, an erstwhile superstar determined to win accolades on the strength of his new efforts, not on the back of his iconic status.

At the same time, "Live and Let Die" is a record of struggle. The song is perhaps the most genuinely menacing since "Goldfinger." It is no accident that Guns 'n Roses, a band that specialized in creating a sense of menace without having anything actually menacing about it, decided to cover the song. But the song isn't just unsettling to listen to. It is itself unsettled. The elements that sound scary, roughly half the song, the other half seems genuinely scared by. The song constitutes a sneering taunt of a man who may not have gone with the times and gotten tough, and that taunt is cast in the musical idioms of the new decade—musical idioms that sound black, colonial, subaltern.

"Live and Let Die" is the first bona fide rock-and-roll Bond song, but its sound also constitutes a deliberate nod to the film's Blaxploitation elements. Unlike in *Diamonds*, these sonic elements are indigenous to the film's plot—to the point that the producers initially wanted the song written by McCartney to be sung by someone other than McCartney, preferably a black singer. As a compromise, the song is actually performed in the film itself (by the British soul singer B. J. Arnau) in Mr. Big's New Orleans nightclub. While the song's addressee is left tantalizingly ambiguous in the McCartney version, the "you" in this performance is clearly Bond himself. Arnau increasingly zeroes in on Roger Moore sitting in the front row. In her hands, the song becomes a sneering attack on his manhood: Bond is too soft to keep up with Big and his operation.

In McCartney's version, the song is pervaded by a different sort of angst. McCartney insisted that he and Wings be allowed to perform the song over the opening credits, and he wound up essentially tacking a sly bit of autobiography onto a commercial picture. It helped that the composer for the film (and the song's producer) was George Martin, who had worked with McCartney during the Beatles years. *Live and Let Die* was a reunion, albeit one under completely changed premises. Their kinship meant that song and musical score meshed much better in *Live and Let Die* than in the Bond outings to follow. The song's melodic line recurs frequently in the score, but conversely the song gathers up the multitude of often competing sounds that reverberate through the film—for instance the frenetic bongos of the voodoo cultists, or the jazzy timbres of the film's nightclub scenes.

But these orchestral touches are really limited to the song's famous chorus. *Live and Let Die* has an unusual structure. There is a marked stylistic break between the piano-driven poppy verse and the menacing hard-rock chorus, and there's a bridge that fits with neither: a reggae pastiche with goofy clavinet playing and—is that a kazoo? The verse is pretty flimsy, two sentences repeated without much variation. Accompanied by solo instruments—acoustic piano in the first iteration, piano plus cello in the second—McCartney sings the line, "When you were young, and your heart was an open book, you used to say 'live and let live.'" At this point backing singers chime in with a high-register "you know you did." If Guns 'n Roses' otherwise abysmal cover of the song got any element of *Live and Let Die* right, it is the sneering nastiness of this line. It's a schoolyard taunt, high-pitched and deliberately off-key.

It's with the title phrase that both the style and the instrumentation change dramatically: the chorus (which is even terser than the verse, consisting simply of the phrase "live and let die") introduces the hard-rock-guitar power-chords but also unleashes a cacophony of strings, booming brass, swirling flutes, clattering xylophone, and frenetic percussion. The song changes abruptly from solo singer and instrument to the clamor of the collective, from the anodyne comforts of piano and cello (an instrument prominent in "Yesterday," lest we forget) to the apocalyptic fury of 70s "world-music" excess.

McCartney and Martin deliberately play two worlds off each other. The schizophrenia between the two, between "live and let live" and "live and let die," becomes a self-portrait of McCartney. The small-scale world of the verse, talking about a bygone time of optimism and generosity, is dominated by pre-rock songwriting, by solo instruments, and, perhaps just as importantly, Western classical instruments. It sounds, in other words, not unlike the music-hall pastiches McCartney wrote during his Beatles period. The chorus, by contrast, is an orgy of sound without much in the way of text, and instruments that point beyond pop and rock. In particular the transition from one world to the other seemingly involves sounds redolent of jazz arranging: woodwind and brass trills, for instance, muted trumpets, or bongos.

In other words, it's noticeable that what besets the Beatles-like sound-scape of the verse is generally marked as ethnic, and usually black. At the same time, while the song seems apprehensive about this new sonic landscape, the whole point of the lyrics is that going with the times requires accepting it. And the modernist brass arrangements remind us that the origin of the James Bond theme itself was big-band jazz. In the book and in the film, the racial Other threatens white folks (above all Bond) as though it were a force of nature—an extension of practices and beliefs as old as time into the modern era. The soundtrack to *Live and Let Die*, and above all the title song, grant this Other a history: the black music we hear in the film embodies a historical trajectory, from the jazz of the New Orleans funeral, to the soul of Mr. Big's club, to the Blaxploitation-style grooves we hear on the film's own soundtrack.

The title song picks up elements of all of them, and hands large parts of the song over to them. Like "Diamonds are Forever," it's anxious, but it isn't phobic. Somehow musically James Bond had an easier time with superannuation than as a film. The film seems terrified that the erstwhile colonial subjects might take over and make white men obsolete. The song seems to accept that as a given, and tries to be okay with it. Whether or not this is McCartney's doing, or owed to Martin's influence, the resulting song recapitulates the basic gesture of "Diamonds": admitting new elements into the carefully redlined ghetto of the Bond song means opening it up to those that weren't allowed to speak or sing or narrate in the Bond novels or the earlier movies. In *The Man with the Golden Gun*, the film that followed *Live and Let Die*, we get a first sense that the series would extend that understanding to questions of gender as well.

"WHO WILL HE BANG?"

It's safe to say that Lulu's "The Man with the Golden Gun," written for the 1974 movie of the same title, is no one's pick for best James Bond song. When serious-minded critics write off the Bond songs for being retrograde and sophomoric, "Man with the Golden Gun" may well be the one they have in mind. The song's gender politics are icky, its puns juvenile, and the music is content to rehearse all the tired flourishes of the Bond songs of old, without adding anything truly its own. Barry dusts off his stabbing, low-modernist orchestral fanfares yet again, this time in the service of an uninspired combination of boogie-rock chorus and funk-rock bridge. Lulu's brassy vocal anchors things with all the awkwardness of a Broadway singer trying to pretend she understands rock and roll; her Sancho Panza is a barely competent session-musician spewing distorted-guitar leads. It'd count as a glam-rock record if Lulu sounded a little less polished and Barry had asked two-thirds of his studio orchestra to take the day off. What is more, in what seems like a fatal mishearing of 60s blues-rock groups like Blood, Sweat and Tears, already highly unfashionable when Lulu recorded her song, the fuzz guitar and too-large horn section sprawl across the entirety of the song. The record heaves and groans across its section-breaks, further emphasizing its Frankenstein-monster construction. Musically it's one of those whose-idea-was-this-and-why kind of records.

The lyrics have been understood as straightforwardly retrograde, certainly by critics at the time, on the mere technicality that they are. Even so, just as *Diamonds Are Forever* and *Live and Let Die* live off the fact that tectonic shifts in the zeitgeist had made the 70s a foreign, and in many respects hostile, shore to the world of Ian Fleming's Bond, *The Man with the Golden Gun* registers similar shifts with respect to the series' sexual politics. In other words: yes, its song is nastily retro, but this song can't be as retro as it would want to be—because once again the ground has shifted. So it may be just as crass as critics thought it was back then. But it may be more interesting than they gave it credit for. The film was released two years after *Deep Throat* burst into the American multiplex, and perhaps it is a nod to 70s "porn chic" that Lulu's song discards the series' habitual double entendre for what is now pretty much just a single entendre. Not that Fleming's novel had been squeamish about the meaning of the titular golden gun: Early in the novel Fleming has Bond peruse a dossier that opines that the "golden gun" is likely a substitute for the "masculine organ." And the film's villain Scaramanga, who harbors a professional man-crush on James Bond, makes no bones about the quasi-erotic nature of his obsession.

But the song's lyrics are unusual in that they abandon all coyness and feel almost jarring in their crassness. "His eye may be on you or me," Lulu coos, describing a situation well rehearsed in the Bond murder ballads since *Goldfinger*, only to add, as the rhythm section drops out and the tempo slows: "Who will he bang? / We shall see. Oh yeah!" Unless English usage has shifted enormously since 1974, when we're told that someone is "banging" someone else, gun violence is not the first thing we think of. If anything, then, the listener's mind is likely to have to leap *back* to the golden gun, after first making the perfectly straightforward connection that the Man with the Golden Gun's "million dollar skill" involves sex. Sex is not the subtext—the golden gun is.

The song's title as subtext—it's a strange situation, to be sure. And the rest of the song seems to forget for stretches that it's supposed to be about a golden gun, and just prattles on about sex. When we're told that "Love is required / whenever he's hired," the next line is, "it comes just before the kill." Lulu swallows just enough of the word "it," however, and the lyrics are just nonsensical enough, that many a listener will probably hear that "he comes," and is thus left with the even less appetizing idea of Scaramanga ejaculating as he shoots Bond.

These examples suggest two things. For one, the song's sexuality works on a different level than that of previous entries. There is a level of explicitness, in both senses of the word, that's unprecedented in the Bond canon, and that seems to point to a qualitative difference. Sex is impossible to talk about in the nudge nudge wink wink, ha-ha idiom employed by earlier Bond songs and films ("My name is Pussy Galore." "I must be dreaming."). In those earlier entries, another (usually a woman) offered up some piece of discourse, and all Bond had to do to make it tawdry was to raise an eyebrow—now the raised eyebrow is no longer up to the task.

For another, note that both the examples cited require the listener to suspend not just logic, but really all sense of grammar and usage. We can credit "who will he bang" as double entendre if we pretend that "banging" is a commonly used English word for shooting someone. "It comes just before the kill" either makes no sense whatsoever, or we have to mishear it. That may point to shoddy songwriting (and both Barry and lyricist Don Black have expressed their regrets over the song), but it probably points to something else too: the song no longer feels it can use double entendre the same way.

Double entendre was an operation of language that suffused the earlier Bond entries, and it made sense in a fairly circumscribed historical context. Puns were an important part of the Bond song. Moons, diamonds, thunderballs, gold—there was nothing that the Bond songs touched that didn't sound faintly louche, like a dirty joke you only barely understand. By pushing these puns to their groan-inducing extreme, to the point where we actually have to remind ourselves that there exists a surface on which the song is *not* talking about sex, "The Man with the Golden Gun" reflects on the disappearance of certain linguistic operations that were central to Bond's gender politics.

After all, the pun is a masculine domain in the Bond movies, a way for James Bond to assert control over very young and usually not very bright women. He sees meaning that the girl who makes the joke without realizing it doesn't see. In *The Man with the Golden Gun*, Bond encounters a young woman named Chew Mee. She announces her name with the characteristic innocence of the Bond girl, who doesn't understand she is a walking, talking joke. Roger Moore's brow goes up immediately, of course, and we get to laugh with him, and at her expense. He sees more meaning than she can, and it puts him in charge; it also makes him our surrogate.

In fact, we may see even more meaning than Bond, as we try to puzzle out which puns we're to follow: seasoned Bond-watchers learn that Denise Richard's nuclear scientist is named Christmas Jones with a sinking feeling. From then on we're waiting for the other shoe to drop, that is, to hear the line "Christmas came early." The double entendre, such as it is, gives us a sense of security that even Bond does not have: we suddenly know, in a dirty, perverted epiphany, the linguistic operation that will end the film.

In "Man with the Golden Gun," these operations no longer work with the effortless felicity with which they operated before. The song works itself into a real lather trying to recreate an operation of language that is no longer available to it. It's a panic that seeps into Lulu's voice, a panic that comes to infect the song's musical language. Lyricist, singer, and producer return to a well that has stood the Bond franchise in good stead for more than a decade—and they find that well poisoned.

Of course, "Man with the Golden Gun" finds the most Bond-appropriate way of dealing with this stress—victimizing a woman, in this case poor Lulu, who after all has a job to do. A parade of dumb sexual puns, cast in the form of a glam-rock showstopper, would embarrass a grown-assed woman even if the song's melodic/harmonic materials weren't so loathsome. What was she to do? Try to bring knowingness to abject stupidity? Or just be a pro—block out the sex-gags, focus on surface meanings, step into the batter's box and swing for the fences? These are rather unappealing choices—become a hyper-Brechtian Alice Cooper, or do Chew Mee with feeling. Lulu's performance suggests the latter. She gamely powers her way through the song. The stupider the lyrics get the greater her intensity. A listener comes away with a sense of her professionalism, despite the song's dopey affect. What did it matter to her? When she had a job to do, she had to do it well.

Doing her job and doing it well: this means more than that she hits the notes, conveys the lyrics more or less intelligibly, and makes the thing somehow hang together. She's behaving as if the pointless musical activity swirling around her actually added up to something. By the end her vocal timbre has almost merged with the sound of the fuzz guitar. With enough amplification the final chorus can trick our guts into thinking they've just been hit by a rock song. Sonic materiality can almost overwhelm the lyrics. The power of female vocality nearly shuts down the punning. That is not to say "The Man with the Golden Gun" is somehow a misunderstood feminist intervention into its sexist linguistic operations. Or that the song represents the female vocalist's triumph over the verbal and instrumental idiocy men have forced her to sing. It is, if anything, the macho subject's freak-out over the fact that these linguistic operations aren't as readily available anymore. And that different musical languages and different voices have emerged, and that not yielding to them can make you sound utterly square.

The Man with the Golden Gun could have had its properly masculinist theme song. Alice Cooper wrote and recorded the ideal mid-70s heavy-rock Bond song for the film, apparently on spec. (Unused in the film, the song soon appeared on Cooper's next LP, the appropriately titled *Muscle of Love*.) Its neo-garage-rock distorted-guitar sludge is perfectly pitched for 1974 album-oriented-rock radio. This is a Barry pastiche that exceeds its originals while achieving an up-to-dateness Barry and Co. never even sought. And this song has everything (allowing for the perhaps excessive runtime of four minutes): the pompous vocal melody placed a bit too high in the mix; the too-frequent repetitions of the title phrase; the major-minor inflections that derive from Monty Norman's original theme; bridges with turgid harmony; abrupt changes of gear; blaring brass; oddly juiced-up arrangements; orchestrated chromatic asides; a slow build to the climax; plus of course the double entendre about the "the man with the golden gun in his pocket."

It even does outdatedness right: Cooper's song sports Liza Minnelli on backing vocals, reminding us that the Bond song is ever-ready to employ old-fashioned singers with zero relation to the contemporary rock, soul, and pop charts. And again—Cooper's "Man with the Golden Gun" truly sounds like a mid-70s rock song. Unlike the Barry record it has an echt rock rhythm section, arranged, played, and produced in an idiomatic manner. The drummer adds tasteful fills. The lead guitarist doesn't overplay. It rightly concludes with a drawn-out, 70s-masterpiece ending: we hear the musicians basking in the sound they've created and we maybe believe we've experienced something special. But the producers went with Barry and Lulu. John Burlingame's eminently useful book on the music of the James Bond films doesn't uncover a real story behind this decision; he offers only conjecture, something about boa constrictors and a chicken. Burlingame surely gets it, though. Never mind the farm-animal-based onstage shenanigans: Barry, Broccoli, and Saltzman simply didn't like rock music. Alice *who*? What's an alice?

Here's the irony: everyone connected with the film would've considered Barry the musical authority and Cooper the village idiot. Barry was composing at his desk and hanging around in executive suites while Cooper was acting crazy onstage, pretending to kill people, messing with poultry, spreading mascara to the bridge of his nose. But it turns out Cooper was the pro's pro and Barry the amateur in over his head. Even presented with the perfect model in Cooper's song, Barry was unable to learn from it. His song for Lulu tries to say "*I don't need 'Alice Cooper,' I can do *that*"; but he couldn't. It was Barry who behaved unprofessionally: he didn't do what he was paid to do.

Barry's failure here is a failure of nerve in the face of a changing audience and a changing marketplace. But more immediately it's a failure of taste and discernment. This is another amusing irony, as the stentorian film composer was outclassed and out-discerned by the auteur behind *Muscle of Love*. And this failure runs deeper, into the whole of the Barry Bond-song canon. Barry's "Diamonds," like the film as a whole, falls short precisely because it cheapens African American culture, the erotic, and the orbit of professionalism. Mistake number-one lay in failing to see how these depended on each other. Highly professionalized soul was creating new modes of eroticism in the 70s, for example; as this connected with images of labor, it contributed to a peculiarly 70s erotics of disenchantment. Soul musicians realized what Barry did not: that professionalism was both a practical necessity and a crucial aesthetic category. Professionalism was also a moving target, which is why Barry and his bosses couldn't recognize it when they encountered it in Bassey and Cooper, nor note its absence when their British session-musicians fell down on the job.

Not only did Barry, Broccoli, and Saltzman shy away from the sonic modernity of black music and rock culture, they failed to grasp how primitive their concept of the song was. Music had changed around them since the early 60s as much as the rest of the world had. You weren't going to make good records if you didn't understand that post–rock and roll popular music had fully entered the sphere of professionalism: every facet of the production process had its specialists, every sort of sound had its new piece of gear, every decent studio musician wanted (and mostly received) greater microlevel aesthetic control. You couldn't just draft a song on sheet-music, phone up one of your pop-singer cronies, and hope for the best.

Listening again to Barry's "Diamonds Are Forever," "The Man with the Golden Gun," "We Have All the Time in the World," and the others, we can see that they set themselves and their singers an impossible task. These records attempt to transcend the contingencies of their production, and to make us forget the distance between the then and the now. They encourage their singers to find a song's—and a film's—hidden powers and possibilities, only to shut it all down once the song is over and the film starts up again. By contrast McCartney's "Live and Let Die," for all its flamboyance and eclecticism, is an exercise in the art of the possible: he and Wings and George Martin know what they're doing, and it shows. Barry's quixotic attempts at pop records tried to make the impossible possible; they succeeded in making the possible impossible. Along the way Barry forgot they had a job to do. . . .

NEVER SAY NEVER AGAIN
Lani Hall

ALL TIME HIGH
Rita Coolidge

FOR YOUR EYES ONLY
Sheena Easton

NOBODY DOES IT BETTER
Carly Simon

MOONRAKER
Shirley Bassey

LICENSE TO KILL
Gladys Knight

IF YOU ASKED ME TO
Patti LaBelle

"We're an All Time High"

James Bond, Pop, and the Endless 1970s

You might imagine, remembering how little they seem to change over the years, that the Bond songs feed only on themselves—cannibalizing "Goldfinger" or "Live and Let Die" until only the bones are left. Or conversely you might think about the parade of artists and styles that have left a mark on the Bond-song canon and decide these songs behave like most film songs, trying to draw on current musical trends; it's just that they're always a little late and a bit clumsy. But the reality is more complicated.

A lot of stuff impinges on Bond songs, whether they want it to or not. Musical sounds and cultural practices bombard them from all sides. Bond records, like all pop records, are the products of many hands; many voices speak through them. The Bond song artist has his or her canon. The song's lyricists, composers, producers, and session musicians have their own styles and histories. Past Bond songs have a weight that exerts its pull on the new composition. A particular recording studio has its sound. The mix of elements in the film makes its own demands, as do recent musical trends. And meanwhile the film's producers butt in with bizarre ultimatums. All these elements have to fight it out on a Bond record's musical surface. At different points in the history of the franchise, different elements win out.

Two things happened to the Bond songs of the late 70s and early 80s. Three of the five songs composed for Bond films between 1977 and 1983 weren't written and produced by the usual suspects. Starting with 1977's *The Spy Who Loved Me*, the music of Bond was briefly loosed from John Barry's stranglehold, which meant that a new set of voices could cut through the mix. Partly as a result of this shift, the Bond songs moved in a strange, and strangely consistent, direction. They locked into a particular late-70s musical approach, perpetuating it well into the Reagan era, as if the 70s would never end. They take the late-70s well-crafted, studio-savvy, good-sounding, trend-aware, black-music-friendly pop record—drawing on the elements that make 1977 pop's last golden moment—and try to do it for the Bond films. The results were mixed, of course, but these Bond songs are all notable for the way they pursue this particular vision of the pop song—at the expense of Bond song conventions.

If we want to get a sense for how atypical the Bond songs of the late 70s and early 80s were, we needn't look much further than the titles. For decades Bond songs had worn their idiotic titles with pride, constructing reasonably competent songs around words and phrases that sounded as though they'd been uttered during a bad mescaline trip in a Barstow motel room. It was a simple rule: the song had to repeat the movie's title, and even though some of the performers and writers must have cursed Ian Fleming for his titles, they obliged. Most Bond songs of the late 70s and early 80s broke that pattern; somehow asking someone to construct a song around a nonword like "Moonraker" or "Goldfinger" was okay, but "Octopussy" was over the line.

Even a song of this era that *did* evoke its film's title, "For Your Eyes Only" (1981), uses its title phrase in such a slapdash way that it's not even grammatically integrated into the lyrics—it's there because it has to be. "Nobody Does It Better" likewise actually does contain the title phrase ("the spy who loved me"), but you'd be forgiven if you missed it. It's a telling departure: part of the job of a Bond song, hell, part of the *fun* of a Bond song, was watching a competent lyricist and a competent singer struggle in the face of the utter, demented vapidity of these title phrases. It's not an accident that Paul McCartney's meditation on the phrase "live and let die" eventually stumbles upon the line, "when you've got a job to do, you gotta do it well."

This was the deal: a Bond song was a job, and taking it on meant accepting certain rules. Before the late 70s, the best Bond singers had had the courage of their convictions. Shirley Bassey is completely straight-faced in belting out the name "Goldfinger," and the charm of the song comes at least in part from the tension between her conviction and the utter ludicrousness of what she's saying. The performers of the late 70s were no longer willing to scream out their titles like that. They were professionals and they knew what sounded good, and what was sayable and sellable, and a song called "Octopussy" just wasn't any of those things. Their professionalism exceeded the limits of the Bond song, and they rethought the Bond song to fit their own sense of the job.

Their vision of the Bond song was the Bond song as love ballad. These are monogamous songs—they are sung from one partner in a couple to another, and the nature of the relationship has none of the ambiguities of earlier songs. Gone are the triangular relationships between villain, Bond girl, and superspy. The speaker has secrets that "the spy who loved me" is keeping safe, another has a side of her personality that exists "for your eyes only," while the third rhapsodizes that "we're two of a kind, we move as one." The songs rejected the ballad forms of earlier Bond songs, which in some way filled in the story, and instead emphasized the power-ballad form as a kind of snapshot of feeling. As the song progresses, we're not given more information (oh, yikes, Goldfinger is even *worse* than we thought), we're given a fuller and fuller picture of the kind of feeling described. Think of the statement that "nobody does it better": the sentiment is right there in the first line. The song doesn't nuance that statement, or ironize it, or reach for even more superlatives.

It's probably not wrong to think of these songs as more conservative and more timid than their forebears, but it's not as though the Bond songs had ever been positively daring or experimental. No, what sets this group of songs apart is their sense of stability: the central relationship doesn't conflate sex and killing, or hatred and voyeurism. When Shirley Bassey warned of Goldfinger, there was more than a soupçon of admiration in her voice. When the divas of the late 70s and early 80s serenade James Bond, admiration is admiration, love is love. The Bond songs of the 70s had largely been about work (the work of being a spy, of killing, of making music), and we'll see later that the songs of the mid-80s return to this pre-occupation, albeit under very different premises. The songs of the late 70s and early 80s drop the topic entirely. They are ostentatiously straightfor-ward love songs: they frame their movies as love stories that just happen to have exploding submarines and underwater fortresses in them.

The composers and lyricists that gave the songs this new direction were brought on board for mostly silly reasons: John Barry ran afoul of the UK's policy of taxing people who made boatloads of cash, which also drove the Stones to record *Exile on Main St.* in Keith Richards's basement on the Côte d'Azur. When Barry decamped for Los Angeles, he had to be replaced. The producers of the off-franchise *Never Say Never Again* had no intention of hiring him in the first place—although their upstart Bond turned to Michel Legrand, whose achievements, like Barry's, had peaked by the mid-60s. Hiring Legrand may have contained the hope of return-ing the music to Bond's halcyon years of 1964-67.

Carly Simon's "Nobody Does it Better" was written by *The Spy Who Loved Me*'s composer Marvin Hamlisch, with lyrics by Carole Bayer Sager, his then-lover (who'd go on to marry and make music with Burt Bacharach). Barry briefly reemerged for 1979's "Moonraker," a throwback-song if ever there was one (reuniting him with Bassey), but Sheena Easton's "For Your Eyes Only" was written by Bill Conti, with lyrics by Michael Leeson. "All Time High" saw the return of Barry as composer (with half-baked lyrics by *Jesus Christ Superstar*'s Tim Rice), but the song sounds more like its immediate predecessors than the clas-sic Barry songs. Michel Legrand's "Never Say Never Again," sung by Lani Hall (formerly with Sérgio Mendes & Brasil '66), which isn't really a canonic Bond song, nevertheless clearly belongs to this group. These people weren't cutting-edge by any means, but they were tastemakers and hitmakers closer to the zeitgeist than the Bond songs had gotten, Paul McCartney excepted.

The success of Simon's "Nobody Does It Better," which went to number two on the pop charts and was nominated for an Academy Award, helped drive this brief Bond song cycle. The Bond producers certainly weren't above trying to engineer a direct borrowing: in 1987, for example, they and Barry would hire Duran Duran fans a-ha to more or less reproduce the success that Duran Duran's Bond song had had in 1985. Barry's fake-rock "The Man with the Golden Gun," sung by Lulu in 1974, was surely beholden to the commercial triumph of the rock-oriented "Live and Let Die" in 1973. Bond songs always repond to their immediate predecessors.

But "Nobody Does It Better" represents a special case. It was that strangest of Bond songs, in that it doesn't sound out of joint with its historical moment. Its sound and audience-appeal make it a perfect representative of the late 70s—the last golden age of the pop record. It did well on the easy-listening, album-oriented-rock, and AM-pop radio formats. It successfully appealed to kids, adolescents, 60s people and oldsters. It engaged both pop and rock sensibilities. It managed that magic combination of being trendy and universal all at once, in both music and lyrics. The record's sound stands out too. "Nobody Does It Better" may start unpromisingly, with its rinky-dink piano intro, but by the time it ends (especially in the longer version that was released on record), it has come to sound as good—in terms of sheer sonic impact—as "Live and Let Die." The Bond songs of the late 70s and early 80s stand in its shadow, edging aside for a moment the 60s and early-70s examples that normally serve as the inevitable point of reference.

In general these five records don't sound like Bond songs or "read" like Bond songs. Their form (instrumentation, rhythm, melody, voice) and content (lyrics and address) make them something of a mini-cycle within the larger group of Bond songs: certain tics and concerns dominated in Bond songs before and after, but for some reason they took some time off in the late 70s and early 80s. The four Bond-franchise songs are straight-up love ballads. ("Never Say Never Again," the non-franchise outlier, is in the tradition of the Bond girl's address to the hero.) One can certainly argue that whenever the Bond song talks about violence, or about spycraft, it really talks about sex. But "All Time High," "Moonraker," "For Your Eyes Only" and "Nobody Does it Better" barely pretend to talk about spying or shooting anymore—when Carly Simon invokes the title phrase of the "Spy Who Loved Me" who is "keeping all my secrets safe tonight," it's completely beside the point whether she's addressing Bond. She's just a girl, serenading a boy, and using espionage vocabulary because it makes the song more interesting.

Sonic materiality is key to the success or failure of these five songs. The sound mostly trumps the lyrics. Rita Coolidge's 1983 "All Time High" became a top Adult Contemporary (and middling Pop) hit despite, not because of Tim Rice's hastily-written lyrics. (Coolidge called the song "unfinished" and for many years declined to sing it onstage.) What it had, besides Coolidge's sure-handed vocal performance, was a producer like Phil Ramone (who spent a lot of time on the charts in 1983), and crisp drumming and bass-playing. The other big commercial success in this group, "For Your Eyes Only" by Sheena Easton, also got a raw deal in the lyrics department, but sounded okay because the recording-session was led by Easton's regular producer, Christopher Neil. "Never Say Never Again" had more Bond song-friendly lyrics and a fine mix of personnel; it's probably better than you remember it. But the record's production values seem notably thin: somehow the instruments lack punch. The record did nothing on the charts, despite the film's success.

If one fact tells you how unusual a period in Bond music the late 70s were, it is this: The biggest failure of this group was Shirley Bassey's reunion with Barry on 1979's "Moonraker." This was hardly Bassey's fault. Nor do its words hit bottom quite as hard as those of "For Your Eyes Only" or "All Time High." True, the song demonstrated Barry's peculiarly labored lyricism in a most unflattering way. But the melody wasn't the problem. It was the record's *sound*. We tend to think of Barry's style as lavish, as an "expensive" approach: we know the big brass and string sections cost money. But in a way Barry was actually quite stingy.

Recording in England, using ordinary studio-musicians, he failed to take advantage of the sounds and possibilities that L.A.'s or New York's top session-musicians could have provided. (Sidney Margo, who contracted the musicians for the English Bond sessions, is partly to blame.) If we compare a song like Barry's "Moonraker" to an exemplary love ballad of the later 1970s, like, say, "Love Ballad" by L.T.D., we can hear the difference instantly. The guitar, bass and drums more or less jump off the grooves of the L.T.D. record, even at its much slower tempo, while the rhythm section of "Moonraker" just sits there as if they're still waiting for the red light to come on. "Moonraker" was lacking in the one department at which the rest of the late-70s crop excelled—competence and professionalism.

Whether they succeeded or failed, all five of these songs converged on a late-70s aesthetic of smoothness and polish that encompassed a lot of pop, soul and rock. Taking advantage of the recording studio, this approach borrowed from the genres that swirled around pop (like soul, disco, rock, country) in such a way as to make the borrowed materials available to be noticed: you could notice them and enjoy the song because of them, or not notice them and enjoy it anyway. The blend of elements in this late-70s aesthetic may have been smooth, but the overall *sound* typically had a bright, crisp, sparkly high end, a well-defined, warm midrange, and full, rounded lows: in its own ways this sound was quite assertive. This was a style and approach that pushed Barry's "Goldfinger" aside, for a time, along with formerly indispensable motifs from the James Bond theme and "007." None of those sonic tics and well-worn motifs make an appearance in any of the songs of the era.

However atypical these songs were for the Bond-song format, in their own way they still partook of the Bond sound. What we've been calling the "Bond sound" has identifiable sonic features: the big-band brass arrangements, the melodic motifs, the slightly soggy sound of the English rhythm sections. This is the part of the Bond sound that went missing when the Bond songs briefly flirted with competence in the late 70s. But the Bond sound is also a musical aesthetic and a set of cultural practices. It's a way of musically experiencing the world. It operates even when the songs don't include the familiar Bond motifs. The Bond sound conditions the *way* a song borrows from current styles as well as *what* it borrows and which styles it borrows from. This "sound" is a way of *filtering* whatever elements the Bond songs borrow. This approach worked partly because most of the people who were asked to contribute to the Bond sound were respectful of the Bond song canon and willing to play along. And it was especially well suited to the kind of commercially successful late-70s pop that "Nobody Does It Better" represents.

1977 may have been pop's last golden age. It seemed like everything was selling—and everything was. The record industry was on a growth spurt. To be sure, some of the songs that populated the Top 40 that year have since been forgotten, and a lot of the songs we remember from that year were underground or otherwise outside of the music industry's mainstream. But an opposition like underground vs. pop doesn't really do justice to how enormously capacious pop music was in the late 70s. We may find it hard to imagine that 1977's "Strawberry Letter 23" by the Brothers Johnson, Parliament's "Tear the Roof Off the Sucker (Give Up the Funk)," Foreigner's "Long, Long Way from Home," and Ram Jam's version of "Black Betty" became top-20 pop-chart hits; or that the Ramones' "Sheena is a Punk Rocker" and "Rockaway Beach" made the 1977 pop charts. Surprising too, in retrospect, are the catchy pop-songwriting hooks you can hear on albums like *Talking Heads: 1977* and Wire's *Pink Flag*. Pop's values were everywhere, guiding even the efforts of those who operated far, far from top-40 or adult contemporary. Even oppositional styles "did" pop and did it well—pop's musical values could be heard all over post-punk, heavy metal, funk. In return pop was the generous, inclusive center of the music world, eager to encompass hard rock, soul, new wave, disco, and even the occasional progressive rock song.

Meanwhile the blockbuster films of the era interacted with the pop charts in striking and not-so-striking ways: the themes to *Star Wars* and *Jaws* charted, were turned into disco tunes, and film songs like "You Light up My Life" could outperform the films they were written for. For decades the Bond songs had been the interesting, perplexing, aggravating artifacts they were thanks to the tension between styles, between modes of listening, between competing audiences. All that tension could be smoothed over in 1977, and the Bond songs of the era are weird precisely by virtue of how un-weird they are. As a result, though, they momentarily stopped sounding like the freakish chimeras of old—they stopped sounding like Bond songs.

DOING IT BETTER (AND WORSE)

Carly Simon's "Nobody Does It Better" lacks the reputation of iconic Bond songs like "Goldfinger and "Live and Let Die." But more than any Bond song before or since, Simon's record is fully representative of its moment. It is, shockingly, an up-to-date Bond record. This hardly means it's free of old-fashioned elements: at a cultural moment when disco, soul, new wave, country and even mainstream rock sought pre-rock glamour, competence, smoothness, simplicity or innocence, looking backward was basically a structural requirement. But the earlier Bond songs weren't in its field of vision: it drew from past styles on its own terms, and not through a Bond-song lens.

Its dopey opening piano part is one of these backward-looking features. You hear clunky plain triads, a clumsy rising baseline, a tipsy bit of cocktail-piano, all performed without the feel or touch that you'd expect from a high-quality piano player. It sounds like what's sometimes called "arranger's piano": something a songwriter might bang out as she demonstrates a song, rather than something actually performed by a professional keyboardist. It's as though the singer were pitching an idea of the song rather than actually presenting it. But why on earth would a Bond song begin this way? No one ever accused Bond songs of feeling off-the-cuff. Why start with a gesture that not only looks back toward Tin Pan Alley, but that can make one faintly queasy, in the same manner as the nauseating saxophone line that begins Rita Coolidge's "All Time High" several years later?

One reason is late-70s nostalgia: Tin Pan Alley sentiment, sophistication and indeed competence were then quite in fashion. Movies like

Martin Scorcese's *New York, New York* looked back at the Great American Songbook through the lens of classic 40s noir and romanticized the hell out of it. New recordings of classic ballads were coming in waves. By beginning their song this way Hamlisch, Simon and producer Richard Perry leapfrog the Bond franchise, sail past John Barry's late–rock and roll synthesis, and claim a direct connection to the Golden Age of popular music. And by doing so they manage to place themselves within a vital part of the musical present circa 1977. But what about what *fails* in this piano introduction—the bad playing, the tipsy affect, the exposed ugliness of the stupid note-choices? It all works in context as both a "realistic" depiction of the songwriter's art (putting the old-school Hamlisch in front of the camera, as it were) and a sign that, as Simon put it, they were thinking about this whole project in a way that was firmly "tongue in cheek."

This old-fashioned, sparse and vaguely gin-drunk opening also provides a perfect foil for what follows. For one thing it gives Carly Simon the opportunity to start slow. She begins by singing with a bit of a breathy timbre. She uses no vibrato in her presentation of the first stanza, and in general she seems to be holding back. This opening gives the song something to build from, but it also points to the trick embedded in its basic structure: the song refuses to offer a clear sense of what's the verse and what's the chorus. Simply put, if you consider only the lyrics—which section has the title phrase, which focuses on specifics and which deals in generalities, which varies more from iteration to iteration—the song's form appears to be chorus-verse-chorus-verse. But if you take the music independently, the song says verse-chorus-verse-chorus. Simon delivers the title phrase clearly, but sings as if she's delivering a verse, not a chorus; this preserves the ambiguity, an ambiguity that's dispelled only in the song's intense final minute.

Just how up-to-date Bond's sound was, for once, is noticeable immediately after Simon concludes her first stanza. A perfectly placed drum-fill happens in the gap between the first and second stanzas. Listeners might notice that the toms' timbre has a bit of an edge. Normally rack-toms go *dup dup dup* but in this fill and throughout the song they go

DOOM DOOM DOOM, with a pronounced downward trail. They are in fact Syndrums, a kind of electronic percussion instrument that had only just come on the market. "Nobody Does It Better" is one of the first recordings on which Syndrums appear. Of course they were advertised as producing "realistic" drum sounds, but they hardly did. Their aesthetic and practical point, especially in disco, where they gained wide usage, lay precisely in making artificial-sounding sweeps and swoops. In "Nobody Does It Better" their sound falls somewhere between a well-produced big rack-tom sound and a deliberately attention-getting synthetic swoop. Syndrums work as a hook both here, because they jump into an otherwise fairly sparse and conventional texture, and throughout the song, as the drum fills become more frequent and more intense.

These Syndrums represent a Bond record on the cusp of the new. But of course they can be written off as merely a novelty effect. What's truly up-to-date about them is the taste and precision with which they're played. Jeff Porcaro, a young but in-demand studio musician who later co-formed the supergroup Toto, was a marvelous drummer who had already played on many groove-oriented songs across the spectrum from soft rock to disco and soul. He performs these fills with the intensity and groovingess he would have been asked to bring to a dance track. His playing in general says black music, and not middle-of-the-road pop, even though the song begins at the exact geographic center of that road (and even though Porcaro himself is white).

In general this record gets better as it goes along, partly because it presents a textbook power-ballad buildup. The old Bond ballads put a lot of their arsenal out front—a short intro, a couple of bars of singing and then the entire ensemble quickly gets in on the action. "Nobody Does it Better" rolls its instruments out gradually: an electric piano quickly joins the original acoustic piano, adding sonic depth and nudging the acoustic-piano player toward a smoother, fuller, more nuanced feel and sound. The brass section hits the beginning of the second stanza, along with a discreet and well-played lead guitar; the texture starts to seem full. Simon's voice is doubled starting halfway through the song, adding a sense of weight and authority that allows the instruments to play harder. The song's harmonic rhythm, which hasn't drawn notice so far in the song, speeds up into an attractive turnaround figure right after Simon sings the film's title, adding momentum. At this point the song becomes notably more intense—the drums are more present, the string section becomes a factor, Simon sings with more oomph.

These are unusual features for a Bond song. The "Goldfinger" template had committed the songs to start out with their thesis—if they didn't blurt out their title first chance they got, they at least established their sonic universe right away. Just as the opening title sequences don't really have any plot (instead acceding to a musical logic: water, then magma, then water again, now some guns, more guns, magma again), these songs don't develop. Simon's song confidently jettisons this generic feature along with many of Barry's orchestrating tics. The string arrangement is active without turning into Barry's churning low modernism. Similarly the brass at the end has more to do with disco and soul than with Barry's big-band shtick: if it looks back in time, it's toward George Martin, not Barry; and in any event it's dominated by an echo-effect that puts it squarely in the late 70s.

"Nobody Does It Better" makes the ideal package, even before we get to thinking about its lyrics. This record was heard as such, by all accounts. The film's producers appeared to recognize its commercial potential right away. Beyond its Academy Award nomination, it sold briskly as a 7" single, meaning that little kids and AM-radio-listening grownups were buying it, and drove sales of the soundtrack album. It became Simon's second-biggest-selling single and has remained in her canon, prominent on all her greatest hits compilations.

Hamlisch made some good decisions that added to the strength of this record. For one thing he engaged Simon's regular producer, Richard Perry. Equally important, he and Perry decided to do the main tracking in Los Angeles but record the string sessions at Abbey Road Studios in London. This shows a keen sense of priorities. Hamlisch and Perry knew they'd need a top rhythm section to create a big pop-chart hit in 1977. And they were thinking about questions of tradition as well as sound and feel, and wanted to achieve a proper balance between professionalism and, yes, sentiment and a sense of fun. Recording a string section at Abbey Road is, precisely, a *fun thing* for an American producer and a youngish New York songwriter who had had his head turned by the Beatles and George Martin. And hey, maybe the British string players were charmed that a jaded L.A. producer had schlepped all the way over for a simple string session, and gave it something extra.

The outchorus is where the song really shines, partly because it's only there that the song disambiguates the question of what's the chorus and what's the verse. During the recording session Simon improvised a melody over this final section. Once she had arrived at the definitive version of this attractive new melody—which was not implied by the original composition—she sang it over and over again, maybe to make sure she'd really gotten it. The producer realized that Simon had hit on something special, so he built up a rich vocal texture by overdubbing multiple iterations of Simon's presentation of this line; the richness derives partly from the slight differences between iterations. This is how back-loaded the song is: it has a major hook arriving about forty seconds from the end. And the same might be said of other features that come forward in this increasingly intense outchorus: there's a new chord progression with a rising bass line (which redeems the clunky left-hand piano figure of the song's opening); the horns introduce a catchy unison melody that stands out partly because of some extra high-end and a slapback-echo effect; the string section becomes more active and more sharply articulated, and thus hookier, especially as it interacts with the horn line. And Porcaro continues to play his crack Syndrum-fills. This minute-long outchorus may be the sublimest moment in the Bond-song canon, particularly given where the song begins. It certainly shows the Bond songs at their most anthemic.

TOO MUCH OF A GOOD THING

But guess what: this beautifully constructed flag-waver ending, the song's best feature, doesn't actually appear in the film. Every recorded version includes it, but in the title-sequence to *The Spy Who Loved Me*, the song

fades out before this special minute of music commences. Just at the
moment when a Bond song—as song—could put pressure on its film, the
film instead applies its own pressure to truncate the song. The song comes
between another indifferent ski-chase sequence filmed by stunt camera-
man Willi Bogner (his second Bond film out of four), and another bit of
dreary exposition by Bond three-timer Lewis Gilbert.

Between those two sequences, something unprecedented happened
and the films had to make sure to shut it down. The kind of pop song that
builds in a sense of collective, participatory aesthetic experience—the
anthem, the flag-waver, the tearjerker, the headbanger, the power ballad,
the singalong—all of this exists in tension with Bond-song aesthetics. The
Bond film actually has a problem when it gets a really good record on its
hands. Once we start to care about a Bond record as such, and about each
other as sharers of a common experience listening to it, Bond starts to feel
ignored—he pulls the plug and goes home.

Sheena Easton's "For Your Eyes Only," composed by Bill Conti, seems
like it was engineered to avoid this problem. It plays by Bond song rules
while still seeking the charts; it was indeed ensconced on the U.S. pop
charts for nearly six months, where it reached number four. In a canny
way the song accomodates itself to the needs of a demanding pop subgenre: records designed to succeed both as title songs in blockbuster films
and as pop singles. This was an old subgenre—and a more or less constant
presence on the pop charts since about 1960—but it was especially lucrative in the late 70s and early 80s. The Bond song would seem well posi-
tioned to participate in this boom. But most of the film songs in question
were instrumental, if not conventionally cinematic. (Think of the themes
from *Star Wars, Close Encounters of the Third Kind, Chariots of Fire*, and
remember Conti's extraordinarily popular theme for *Rocky*.) Records like
this bore a trace of their origins as title themes; unlike the Bond songs
they didn't even pretend to offer themselves up as typical pop singles.

To write a Bond song you can't just write the best song possible and
stick it in a Bond film. There are rules to follow that may make you cringe
as a professional; but part of your job is to balance the demands of the
sound against your sense of how a pop song should work. "For Your Eyes

Only" manages to work as both a pop record and a movie theme-song. Following "Nobody Does It Better" it does what it must to be an up-to-date pop record without disqualifying itself as a Bond song. But it does much more to accomodate itself to its role in the film, and not only because it repeats the title phrase eight times: framed by song-sections without the rhythm section, it builds in the segues into and out of the film proper.

The song's portentous opening recalls Vangelis's *Chariots of Fire* theme, which was released right as Conti was starting work on the song. It begins in the Vangelis manner, with a tonic-chord wash dominated by artificial-sounding synthesizers; a repeated horn-call figure jumps from synth to synth. There's no guitar, no bass, no drum-set, little sense of a pulse. The verse continues in this vein; Easton delivers the title phrase, set to the horn-call melody. The full rhythm section doesn't enter until the verse's final line (about fifty seconds in, an eternity in a pop song); when it does the record becomes a more conventional love ballad. From then on the record oscillates between late-70s ballad and Vangelis pastiche. Easton sings fine, the bass player is legit, the drummer's not bad at all, but it's once again a few steps behind U.S. production standards—which means the song belongs again safely to Bond's sonic universe.

But even with these concessions to its function in the film, the song's lyrics, form and musical arrangement bespeak an uneasy synthesis of elements that suggests you can't just drop a little bit of spycraft into a love ballad and call it a Bond song. This was something that would become even clearer in the lyrics to Rita Coolidge's "All Time High," the song that opened *Octopussy*. That song is maddeningly straightforward. The remarkable thing about it isn't some hidden layer that would require two cunning academics to draw it out—there really isn't such a layer. What is remarkable is that the song insists, against all evidence, that there *is* such a layer.

When Coolidge darkly intones that she "had no intention to do the things we've done," we believe her for a moment—her voice briefly dips into a Shirley Bassey register, and the lyrics she's singing dip with it, into the wellspring of ambiguity and sleaze that made Bassey's Bond songs so potent. The next line is "Funny how it always goes in love, when you don't look you find"—if there is a Platonic idea of cliché it's that sentence—and any ambiguity and darkness just floats away. You realize the brief note of regret that made that earlier line so tantalizing was a pure accident, like a chimp banging on a typewriter and writing a line of Hamlet only to follow it with a page of gibberish. Coolidge's song doesn't have any depth, but it sort of knows it's supposed to.

So it simulates depth. She claims that she and Bond are "doing so much more than falling in love." There runs through the song a constant insistence that there's *more* going on than "just" a love song, but the listener pretty much has to take the song's word for it. (This same problem raised its head in the lyrics for "Nobody Does it Better": the song wants to have its cake and eat it too, writing a bouncy ballad about "doing it" and wanting us to hear sex *and* something else.) But what on earth would that "so much more" even be? It is as though the song knows it's supposed to have two levels of meaning, but it just can't get itself to actually activate them. It's like the pope's daughter trying to tell a dirty joke.

"For Your Eyes Only" operates similarly. It combines disparate elements in an awkward stop-and-go synthesis; it's professionally done, and holds up as a pop record, but it doesn't really work when we encounter it in the context of a Bond film. There we think the song will say something about the world of the movie, about the world of the main character, about danger and seduction. Mixing "Chariots of Fire" with a spy theme is tough enough, but how do you put that together with a love ballad about a man who has "brought out the best in me." It's as though someone tried to write a theme song that could feature in both *Terminator 2* and *Ghost*. "For Your Eyes Only" is the early-80s version of late-70s pop: it's more content with schematic, cut-and-dried elements, and it's okay with you seeing how they've been assembled. But it's still very much an example of the kind of 70s pop song that does and has everything. It even has an awareness of how it can and should function in a film. Just maybe not a Bond film.

If Easton's song runs into problems because it isn't willing to leave behind the pop charts in favor of the paltrier pastures of a totally outdated mid-60s aesthetic, the opposite is true for Barry's sole effort during those years: 1979's "Moonraker." Shirley Bassey and Barry reuniting for a Bond song may seem like a time-capsule for 1979, something doomed to come off as a rehash of glory days. But that's not really true: 1979 was perfectly primed for a Bassey Bond. Disco had brought many older divas back onto the charts. The resulting songs ranged from the sublime to the you-can't-be-serious—from Jackie Moore's "This Time Baby" to Ethel Merman does disco—but altogether this trend helped recast the look and feel of who could sing as a sex object. You could be older, blacker, fleshier, brassier and still sing as a desirable vixen. This is the sort of thing that Bassey could have succeeded mightily at.

But Barry just wasn't the man to make it happen. Disco for him, as for Hamlisch, meant the Bee Gees's disco-inflected pop. Listening past Barry's typical arching melodies and the song's draggy feel, we hear a pastiche of the Bee Gees' "How Deep Is Your Love": bass and drums provide a slightly-heavier-than-pop grounding for an electric piano that makes the chord progression seem more soulful than it is. A touch of extra percussion beyond the drum set—a samba-derived triangle—represents the only other element that signals disco and late-70s dance music. All in all this was a missed opportunity: pop-disco's mix of "mature" sexuality and urban nostalgia could've been ideal for a Bond ballad. As it was Barry assembled the ingredients of a disco-era song—and created the perfect pop-disco song for the year 1964. "Moonraker" was a record addressed to no one.

"YOU WON'T NEED TO READ BETWEEN THE LINES"

Carly Simon, by contrast, is the poet laureate of interpellation, the queen of second-person pronouns. It seems she's always talking to you, yes you, unless you think the song is about you, in which case no dice, you self-important dirt-bag. Her two biggest chart-toppers are basically letters written in the second person singular—the more famous one by far is "You're So Vain" (her only song to chart at number one), but there's also "Nobody Does It Better," which charted at number two. The former song inspired decades of speculation about who the "you" in the song was, but a similar mechanism is at work in "Nobody Does It Better" as well.

Not that either of these songs needs much speculation. Take "Nobody Does It Better": the addressee can only be Bond, and "doing it" can only be sex. As for "You're So Vain," we have Warren Beatty, who actually said in public that he thought the song was about him. While plenty of other names have been floated as possibilities, only Beatty really clicks. Like the fictional James Bond the real-life Warren Beatty was known for his frequent having of sex. For the actor as for the superspy, sex became part of the job. Especially when a film like 1975's *Shampoo*, starring Beatty as an oversexed hairdresser, brought it all together—sex like a pro, on and off screen, and a prescient tagline: "Your hairdresser does it better." If the "You" in "You're So Vain" turns out to have been some random L.A. guitar player in tight pants, well, why would we even care?

Wondering who exactly was vain enough to think "You're So Vain" was about him of course missed the point of the lyrics' cute language game. Because the moment you think the song is about you, the song *is* about you thinking that very thing. And because the song implies that, if you think the song is about you, it is no longer *really* about you, except in your own stuck-up little head. Which means that the song really *has* no referent: it's very clear about who it's *not* about, namely *you*, but it never gets around to actually being about the person it's actually about. "Nobody Does It Better" similarly floats above a sea of possible references, and like "You're So Vain" it seems designed to make us think that maybe, just maybe, the song is about us. This time it's an ode to "you," and "you" seem to be pretty much perfect. It's almost impossible to hear a song address someone as "you" and to not apply that pronoun to yourself.

More specifically, the use of the second person singular signifies the end of the kind of specific scenes imagined by previous Bond songs: this song could literally be sung by anyone to anyone. You could imagine people belting it out at 50th birthdays, or at a silver wedding. Not exactly something you could say about "Goldfinger" or "Live and Let Die." The highly specific metafictional settings imagined by "Goldfinger" and its immediate successors were long gone by the time "Nobody Does It

Better" came out, but "Nobody" is certainly the furthest away from that of any Bond song.

It's another strategy to make pop music as broadly appealing as possible. Any specific situation you imagine in a pop song implicitly excludes some listeners—gender and sexual preference being the most obvious ways, but that's just the beginning. Even "You're So Vain" is actually about a fairly specific, albeit universal, story. Its metafiction is pretty detailed: from an apricot scarf, via horse-racing in Saratoga, to a sexual encounter a few years back. "Nobody Does It Better" doesn't take any such chances. It basically doesn't explain anything. Who is "I"? Who is "you"? What gender are they? What's the nature of their relationship? What is "it" that they're apparently so good at? The song levitates in a kind of studied meaninglessness.

As in most globalized pop, its intensity is unencumbered by anything that would bound and restrict that intensity. Specificity would serve to curtail appeal and would force us to reflect more precisely on the feeling described. This is how the song functions when we look at it as a pop song. But it looks quite different when we encounter it in a theater, or as the opener to a soundtrack album. Then the roving, universal reference is replaced with the one, the only possible one. "You" could only refer to James Bond, who, no less than John Shaft, is supposed to be "a sex machine to all the chicks." We think the song is about him—does that make us vain?

This doubleness—this song addresses literally everyone, or just one single fictional person—points to another tension between the adult-contemporary pop ballads and the Bond canon into which they sought to wedge themselves. A love ballad wants to provide unthinking affirmation—it has one thing to say to its love-object and it's gonna spend three minutes saying it. Bond songs can do affirmation, of course, but they do it through specificity: Bond is the most lethal, the most demanding, the most relentless. That's not the "you" of Easton's, Coolidge's and Simon's Bond songs. Their affirmation is as global as the songs' appeal: everything about "you" is just awesome, why'd you have to be so good? Perhaps affirmation is harder than we think.

Just how hard it can be we can glean from the text Mick Leeson wrote for "For Your Eyes Only." These lyrics are, to use a technical term, a huge fucking mess. Not by some vaunted professorial standard, but simply by the standard of putting words together in sentences that might possibly convey some meaning.

> For your eyes only can see me through the night
> For your eyes only I never need to hide
> You can see so much in me so much in me that's new
> I never felt until I looked at you

What makes these lyrics such a mess? Well, the affirmation of the pop song serenading "you" requires one vocabulary, and the Bond song requires another. And in these lines the two pass each other like ships in the night. The Bond-movie honchos made certain demands—"start with the title phrase," for instance—but those demands set the record on the road to nonsense. The song starts with a sentence that requires us to re-interpret the title phrase hallway through. Because what do Conti and Leeson do to turn that phrase into a song that might yet sound universal and find success in the charts? They use the title phrase a million times but never in an appropriate way either grammatically or syntactically: they repeat it almost like a mantra, and they pretend to embed it in a context, but the phrase never actually gels with that context. For instance, they decide that the first use of "for" is a conjunction ("*because* only your eyes can see me"), but the second "for" is a preposition ("*in* your eyes"). They make the title phrase mean something entirely different in its first iteration than in the second.

At some point Easton intones "But you won't need to read between the lines." Indeed not. This should be a song about secrets that are for your eyes only. But whatever confusion there is derives from a muddled surface, not some incredibly deep subterranean meaning. Just like "You're So Vain," "For Your Eyes Only" creates no depth, but just surface agitation, endless circulations of phrases. Wouldn't a title like "For Your Eyes Only" suggest that the *speaker* is the mysterious one, rather than the addressee? You'd think so, but instead it seems to be the one being looked at who is invisible. As in Carly Simon's "Nobody Does It Better," the song is all about "you;" the person who exists "for your eyes only" doesn't seem at all interesting. This wouldn't be a big problem coming from a singer-songwriter, who can invest the song's persona with what the late 70s would've recognized as personality. But Easton is very much a singer-who's-not-songwriter, and what could have come off as idiosyncrasy instead just comes off as almost pathologically bland. "All Time High" pushes this problem even further, because while the song avoids making "Octopussy" its title phrase, it replaces that title phrase with one that doesn't make any sense. What does it mean to "be" an "all time high?" Are we *experiencing* an all time high? Are we demonstrating what two people on an all-time love-high would look like? Are we just saying we're awesome together?

It's tempting to think of Bond songs as just an assemblage of pieces that happened to open a franchise of movie, and to say not much connects them beyond that. But here's why we have been insisting that there is a tradition, an idiom, and indeed a "sound" that connects these songs. The 70s songs were among the most successful in Bond's history: chart success, fantastic production teams—why not live in 1977 forever? But the Bond songs didn't do that. There were a few more Bond songs that seemed to take the smooth adult-contemporary hyper-competence of "Nobody Does it Better" as their lodestar, most successfully Gladys Knight for 1989's "License to Kill." But by 1989 her song was an outlier. After a brief interregnum the Bond songs had decided to renew their vows to 1964. "Goldfinger," a song that had confined the Bond songs to a straitjacket of turgid chord progressions and semi-competent rhythm sections for twenty years, was once again the model, and "Nobody Does It Better" was suddenly forgotten. The Bond songs had finally captured the zeitgeist, and then they retreated into the kind of anachronism that had haunted them for decades.

The reasons had little to do with charts, with radio play, with promotion—in all of those departments "All Time High," although probably the least successful entry of the trilogy of Bond love ballads, did perfectly fine. They had to do with aesthetics. With the lyrics. With an incompatibility between Bond and the love ballad, between Bond and hyper-competent adult contemporary, maybe between Bond and competence tout court.

The next time the Bond songs collided with competence it was on 70s ground: 1989's *License to Kill* included songs by two crucial 70s soul singers. Gladys Knight provided the title song and Patti LaBelle sung "If You Asked Me To" over the closing credits. Both records were high-quality, up-to-date R & B ballads that tried to connect with adult-contemporary listeners and 70s-soul fans—a.k.a. grownups. This they did, which wasn't easy in 1989. It had taken the Bond franchise twenty–seven years to hand the microphone to legitimate soul artists; by that time the grooving rhythm sections had been replaced by drum machines and digital synthesizers, African American ballad-singers could hardly make the pop charts, and soul music was something you sampled. Knight and veteran producer Narada Michael Walden knew how to create drum-machine-driven soul: you include both the drum machine *and* the live rhythm section, with top studio-musicians, programmers and engineers doing their jobs; and most importantly you sing like a soul singer, with so much groove that it sounds like your voice, and not the drum machine, is generating the beat. LaBelle received a fine song from Diane Warrren, a key architect of the power ballad, and turned in a memorable performance.

But again, these two songs were too smooth, too canny, too competent for the Bond franchise—even though aesthetically and stylistically they stayed within the orbit of the late-70s Bond ballads. LaBelle's song makes zero concessions to the Bond sound. Knight, who expressed some anxiety about singing lyrics with violent imagery, studiously avoids articulating the word "kill," despite its prominence in the song's main hook. And Walden actually got punished for the one Bond-sound touch he included. "License to Kill" alludes to the opening of "Goldfinger," borrowing the I-♭VI chord-oscillation and a bit of the rhythm; Knight ad-libs magnificently over Walden's new arrangement. John Barry's people came after him with papers, demanding co-songwriting credit. We know how Walden *should've* responded: "Seriously, guys—hearing Gladys Knight ad-lib over your bullshit chords should be payment enough, you cheap tax-dodging fucks." But alas, he signed. How very late-capitalism . . . paying a professional to perform affective labor and then threatening to sue him for performing it too well; refusing to hear the difference between homage and plagiarism; treating everything under the sun as fungible IP; the franchise's left hand reaching an out-of-court settlement with its right hand. In late-capitalist Bond world, doing your job at a high level could land you in trouble.

If there was one truth the songs of the long, long 1970s learned the hard way it was that you could be too professional for the Bond song. When Carly Simon sings "Nobody does it better," the very idea of *doing things at a high level* ends up taking precedence over the sex and the addressee. We've moved past the late-60s "doing your thing," past "doing it" as the quintessential mid-70s sex-euphemism, and we're on the road to Nike's insufferable late-80s "Just Do It." Somehow "doing it" got purified of the "it"—and the *why*. This is the story of affective labor, of the "service economy," and it didn't turn out well for the Bond songs. At the end of these transformations we may find ourselves asking how we became so concerned with the service that we forgot about making songs that actually sound like we know what we're doing. The problem was not Carly Simon's song, or the nature of its goodness; it's just that the Bond franchise wasn't ready to be so good. A little bit of amateurishness went a long way in negotiating the demands built up over decades of films and songs.

This was certainly the lesson new wave bands took away from their immediate forebears, when they got a crack at the franchise in the mid 80s. "I swear my nerves are showing," intones Morten Harket of a-ha in "The Living Daylights"—and a lumpy, nervy, uneasy amalgam seemed to sit better with the Bond franchise than the professionalism offered by the Eastons, Coolidges, Simons of the world. There was a kind of amnesia to the efforts of the late 70s, and if the world was ready to reward the Bond songs for trying something new after twenty years of retreads, producers maybe weren't convinced that James Bond was still capable, or even deserving of a new beginning. So the songs beat on, boats against the current, borne ceaselessly into 1964.

A VIEW TO A KILL
Duran Duran

THE LIVING DAYLIGHTS
A-Ha

WHERE HAS EVERYBODY GONE
The Pretenders
IF THERE WAS A MAN

Looking the Part

James Bond's New Wave Years

Singing a Bond song would make anyone nervous. Who could feel comfortable delivering a speedwritten song with half-baked lyrics about a moonraker, a thunderball, or (god help you) an "all-time high"? Who would want to deal with fussy studio bosses, a severely image-conscious brand, an imposing canon of Bond songs, and a bunch of contemporary musical styles you have to both gesture toward and swerve away from—only to find your song sharing a credit sequence with wiggling nudes? But it's one of the peculiar features of Bond songs that the singers do a good job hiding their discomfort. Except, that is, for the 80s new wave singers whose job it was to actually sound nervous.

The Bond films went against the grain when they dabbled in 80s new wave. Yes, Duran Duran had fully embraced mainstream dance-pop by 1985, and the Norwegian synth-pop group a-ha had fully embraced Duran Duran. But still: it's hard to imagine the typical new-wave voice—tense, anxious, amateurish—as the right fit for a Bond song. So what happened when Duran Duran and a-ha brought their jittery comportment into the hallowed space of the Bond-film title sequence? What were the stakes when Simon Le Bon's voice cracked in the middle of a high-profile performance of Duran Duran's Bond song? What did it mean for a-ha's Morten Harket to "swear" his "nerves are showing"?

Think about how a movie song usually works, and how the Bond song departs from this type. Theme songs want to grab us, get us jazzed up and ready for the film ahead. Set to an opening montage or aerial shot, they often enough seem intended to get us through some rather dreary exposition. Watching Michael J. Fox skateboard for three minutes, or airplanes getting refueled, certainly goes down much more easily when accompanied by Huey Lewis or Kenny Loggins. And that seems to be the point: theme songs are accompaniment. At least in the context of the film, we're never really left alone with its song until the credits roll and we file out into the lobby to an end-credit reprise.

The Bond songs are different. Of course they too are accompanied by visuals, but those visuals almost invariably fail to contribute anything to the film's plot. Sometimes they contain rudimentary bits of foreshadowing (the opening to *Moonraker* has a moon, *Diamonds Are Forever* has diamonds, and so on), but a good many of the title sequences don't even have that. In the majority of James Bond films the exciting opening sequence deposits us in a darkened theater with nothing but meaningless shapes gyrating like a late-90s screensaver—and with a voice. A voice that is, as a rule, kept out of the film itself (a rule the Bond films broke only once in over a half-century); a voice that exists only here, and that in this brief interlude has absolute control over us.

This isn't how film songs are usually consumed. If anything, our silent vigil before the Bond song resembles the way we listen to our favorite singer in our dorm room with the shades drawn, our pillow clutched, and our eyes closed. For very few of us, those singers would have been Carly Simon, Rita Coolidge, Duran Duran's Simon Le Bon, or even Shirley Bassey. Those three minutes in the dark in a movie theater or living room are strangely intimate encounters with voices that in another situation would have us reaching for the radio dial or the remote control. They are part of the Bond films' odd alchemy, these three minutes we spend alone (or almost alone) with the voices of second-tier stars warbling largely meaningless variations on the film's convoluted title.

The voices of Bond are of an unusual kind, even if they are voices we have heard before outside of the movie theater. Even those voices—iconic voices like Louis Armstrong's, Paul McCartney's, and Madonna's—sound different when doing a Bond song. We register a disconnect between the singer and the work of performing a Bond song. This may not have been true in the earliest Bond films, but as the decades wore on the spectacle of the Bond song was a familiar voice doing somewhat unfamiliar things. As we suggested in our introductory chapter, these artists are not really doing "their" thing.

The lyrics these Bond singers belt out and the visuals they accompany give few clues to a movie that seems to have gone on a three-minute hiatus for no apparent reason; it's the voice itself that becomes responsible for anticipating what is to come. More than the instrumentation or the song's lyrics, it's the materiality—the very substance—of the Bond singer's voice that sets the tone for the movie. One need only compare the Shirley Bassey of "Goldfinger" and "Moonraker" to see how differently the same person can introduce two very different motion pictures. It's the same person, and the producers clearly want the later song to sound like its more celebrated forebear. But still, Bassey's voice is altogether different. The Bassey of "Goldfinger" sounds squeezed, clenched like a fist, choked with either fear or regret over Auric Goldfinger's devious machinations. It is a voice redolent with the deliberately disembodied and affectless quiver of Lotte Lenya—the voice as a scene of the crime, or a scar borne as a sort of trophy.

A very different Shirley Bassey sings the opening to "Moonraker"— "Goldfinger" was disembodied, "Moonraker" is all body. The opening visuals depict deep space, but for once they feel redundant rather than scant: all of space is already in Bassey's alto. So deep, so engulfing, so maternal is Bassey's voice that the menace it registers has none of the sneer and swagger of "Goldfinger." It is the siren song of oblivion, the temptation of cutting the line and drifting into outer space—a temptation all too familiar to 70s music with its profusion of astronaut songs. Ground control to Commander Bond. The harsh shimmer of Bassey's voice in her first Bond song was the glare of a switchblade; the deep languor of her last one trembles with the fear of a black hole.

If Bassey's voice grew more languid with each of her Bond songs, the twenty-first-century Bond songs got great mileage out of putting pressure on their singer's voices. Where earlier songs had granted them space, after the millennium the singers' voices began sounding boxed-in, cornered. As the Bond films grew more conflicted, and the Bond persona veered from Roger Moore's bemused, even avuncular ironist to the constantly traumatized and retraumatized incarnations portrayed by Pierce Brosnan and Daniel Craig, the voices of the Bond songs became seismic detectors for the fault lines within the character. When Madonna, in the first auto-tuned Bond song, 2002's "Die Another Day," sings of "closing my body" in the clenched metallic shimmer characteristic of digital sound-processing, the seductive vixen of "Moonraker" has turned into a victim of trauma.

Or consider the post-traumatic wail with which Jack White and Alicia Keys ricochet through "Another Way to Die" (for 2008's *Quantum of Solace*). The voices strain to reach notes that seem deliberately pitched to distress them; Keys and White, two very different singers, end up sounding interchangeable at certain points, each as hoarse and battered as the other. It's a fitting song, and a fitting set of voices for a film in which both Bond and his girl are considering what can be done to repair damage done by violence.

Independent of styles, independent of whether they were drifting with their time or hopelessly chasing after the zeitgeist, the Bond songs manage to communicate a lot with their voices. We spend more time with them than with your average film song (no one talks over them, they never phase in or out), and we certainly spend more *quality* time with them. The voices of the Bond song speak *of* different things, and *for* different things, than the instrumentation or the lyrics. The instruments are owed to current fashion and Bond-song tradition, the lyrics are owed to the whims of Ian Fleming and whatever poor writer has had to turn Fleming's title into a pop song. But the voices are the song's own.

No one forced Bassey to give her voice the shallow luster she imbues it with in "Goldfinger"—she could have sung it the way she sang "Moonraker," and it still would have sounded pretty fantastic. But it wouldn't have been "Goldfinger." It wouldn't have had that wonderful shimmer, it wouldn't have sounded like Lotte Lenya, it wouldn't have gone so well with Jill Masterson's gold-covered body. Bond voices are not just another admixture to the alloy—they well up from some deeper place, speak of anxieties, fears, hopes and promises that the songs can't talk about in their lyrics.

"I SWEAR MY NERVES ARE SHOWING"—PLAYING BOND

The distressed and post-traumatic voices that have come to dominate the Bond songs in recent years owe their existence to a shift in the way the Bond songs relate to their singers, a shift that occurred in the mid-80s. For much of the 70s, the voices of the Bond song had pulled their own little world into the Bond universe. Sometimes they did so to great clashing effect, sometimes it was more subtle. But in each case the power of the voice, or rather the type of voice it was, created a gravitational pull that put the entire song under its spell and bent it ever so slightly out of shape. Why is there a solo cello in the middle of "Live and Let Die"? It's not there because of the dictates of the Bond-song form, nor in an effort to tweak those dictates. It's a bit of the Beatles universe called forth into the Bond song by Paul McCartney's instantly recognizable voice. The Bond song was never a capacious genre, but its rigidity made it easy to distend, and for those distensions to be noticeable.

Consider Rita Coolidge's "All Time High," the opener for the 1983 Roger Moore outing *Octopussy*. Why does the song's arrangement add strange touches of country music—in particular the sound of a pedal steel guitar, which in 50s pop might have passed as a Hawaiian signifier, but by the 1970s was a trademark of country? There's nothing country about the lyrics of "All Time High," nor about the film, which is a high-seas adventure and Egyptian travelogue. It is the singer's identity, her voice, that pulls the music in the direction it wants. And that direction is back to the late 70s, when Coolidge had her greatest successes, and countrified pop could coexist on the charts with disco, hard rock, and everything else.

This changed with the song that followed "All Time High." Starting with Duran Duran's "A View to a Kill" (1985), the music of the Bond song no longer accommodates itself to the voices. It's the other way around. The voices begin to cower before the up-to-date, percussion-heavy arrangement; they're at its mercy. Together with the song that followed it, a-ha's "The Living Daylights" (1987), "A View to a Kill" constitutes the Bond series' most open hat-tip to the eighties zeitgeist. But while Bond's brief foray into new-wave territory may amount to little more than an opportunistic—and characteristically belated—flash in the pan, it reconfigured the genetic makeup of the Bond songs in ways that were to endure: they changed how voices functioned and how they related to the massive production that is a Bond song. They mirrored something about how the solitary singer related to the world of capitalism he or she was supposed to celebrate.

The mid-80s found the Bond franchise buffeted by market forces its runaway success had thus far shielded it from. The Bond movies were pulled into the wake of MGM's financial travails, with MGM's extensive library (including the Bond films) becoming a football to be wrestled over by various alliteratively named sharks, including Ted Turner and Kirk Kerkorian. Meanwhile court battles over the Bond property led to the bizarre spectacle of two Bonds, an upstart starring an aging Sean Connery and an official one with an equally bedraggled-looking Roger Moore, in direct competition at the box office in 1983. Bond had been a brand for a long time, but by 1985 it was no longer altogether clear whether he was anything more than that.

It took a little while, but eventually the worry that Bond had become a mere simulation seeped into the Bond songs as well. In the 60s these songs had talked about the making and unmaking of the self (think of Nancy Sinatra's "You Only Live Twice," for instance), while in the 70s both the singers themselves and the lyrics emphasized the craft, labor, and professionalism involved in both the job of being a musician and the job of killing for a living—the line "what does it matter to you / when you've got a job to do / you have to do it right" may well function as the poetics for the Bond songs of the 70s.

Both the job of being a superspy and the job of being a musician seem to have become matters of make-believe by the mid-80s. Duran Duran and a-ha provide a Bond sound for the age of union busting: what you are matters little, what you can do is beside the point; look the part and people will pay you money to do the job. Generally speaking, the traumatized, overwhelmed, outgunned voices of the later decades of the Bond franchise are traumatized not so much by world-historical events, or by Bond's tawdry past, but rather by their distance from the origin—by the sense that they can never reach whatever standards were established by the earlier songs. They suffer from impostor syndrome.

With Duran Duran's entry into the series, the New Romantics briefly took the reins of the franchise—and it was an awkward, though revealing, fit from the first. The bands of New Romanticism were post-punk poseurs embracing glamor and indeed an aesthetic of late capitalism. They looked the part, not so much of tortured or starving artists, but of entrepreneurs of pop. Sometimes they embraced an explicitly corporate look: Heaven 17 wore pinstripe suits and worked the phones on the cover of their debut album (see Fig. 6.1). Depeche Mode sang about shaking hands and sealing contracts. These bands were playing at working in the new way in which the 80s thought of work: carrying briefcases and owning mobile phones. Drum machines and synthesizers replaced guitars, although they of course also amplified punk's DIY aesthetic. Now literally anyone could be in a band—even a drum machine.

The synths and the drum machine led post-punk down the road to pop. Not only did it make their records danceable and thus open up new markets, it also encouraged the musicians to acquire the kind of skill sets that the guitar-strumming punks and rockers either didn't need or hid if they had. They became not just good instrumentalists, but songwriters, producers, and programmers as well. At the same time New Romanticism was a return to sentiment and sentimentality; these songs were many things, but they were never spare. Lushness and grandeur, full

Figure 6.1 The cover of Heaven 17's debut album (1981): New Romantic style as (ironic?) DIY corporate chic.

textures, big feelings—in these areas the New Romantics could give the most baroque progressive rock a run for its money.

New Romantic style was thus in some respects self-contradictory. It retained post-punk's ironic and oppositional DIY aesthetic, but in doing so started producing bestselling records that became parts of the same system of commodified top-40s pop records it claimed to be mocking. On the one hand these songs trade on their imperfections, on sounding DIY, but at the same time they're always at risk of being hypocritical sell-outs. One way or the other, these songs are posing. They have to work so hard looking and sounding the part that they risk being unmasked at any point—a topic that frequently trickles into their lyrics and their sensibility.

The Duran Duran and a-ha entries into the Bond-song canon seem incredibly 80s to us today, but it bears remembering that they actually combine a number of distinct 80s strands, and navigate rather fraught terrain in doing so. Musically these songs tend to play it safe: they gesture toward the defining sounds of the 80s without going too far. These records don't come off as too "programmed" or "synthesized"; the instrumental parts don't have the metronomic regularity of automatically sequenced keyboards. There is something almost grudging in their introduction of drum machines and synthesized percussion rather than "natural-sounding" drums—which would have been hopelessly outmoded by 1985. Most of all, they reassure mainstream pop and rock listeners with a group-oriented sound and a lot of frisky live playing. It helped that Chic's Bernard Edwards coproduced "A View to a Kill": he was a 70s disco-master who successfully took dance music into the digital age without rejecting the idea of the live rhythm section. This is not the mid-80s world of one guy in his bedroom with a MIDI keyboard and a drum machine.

And—shockingly for the franchise—these two Bond songs are danceable, in an eighties-white-people sort of way. Both records derive their momentum from synthesized drum-sounds and heavy bass lines rather than melodies; in this they reflect the dance-music turn that happened once new wave and post-punk groups got their hands on prosumer drum machines in the early 80s. But these records are still far more melodious than groups like New Order had been earlier in the decade. The two songs present new wave as dance pop. They rely on conventional harmonies and melodies, and on vocals more compatible with mainstream masculinity than new wave at its most deliberately spare, androgynous, and post-human.

Sprinkled throughout, we find reassuringly retro gestures. In "The Living Daylights" the synthesizer even gestures toward a surf-guitar riff in the mode of "You Only Live Twice." The Duran Duran record surprises us not only with its danceability. What really makes it unusual is how well it could pass for a non-Bond song. The group was at its prime in 1985, and for all their post-post-punk amateurishness they had actually developed a fashion-forward sound that sold briskly, fit nicely into a number of radio formats, and didn't embarrass itself on the dance floor. "A View to a Kill" was one of the band's top-selling singles, perfectly representative of what the group did best. It combines a groove-oriented approach with the pop-song credo that you never go more than three seconds without presenting a hook. A simple drum-machine pattern is striped across the whole song. It's crude, but its persistence, big sound, and basic catchiness allow for a lot of flexibility around it.

This is a lesson the first drum-machine-driven dance-music outfits learned from disco: you create a musical texture in layers, starting with a prominent drum-pattern, and you can do more or less whatever you want over it. But Duran Duran also had a credible bass player and a versatile guitarist who knew how not to overplay, plus a live drummer who added things in and around the drum machine. Though the band had frequent recourse to trendy synthesizer-sounds and special effects, they typically grounded their songs in a solid bass-and-drums groove beneath a shifting palette of guitar and keyboards.

"A View to a Kill" begins very un-Bond-like, with a distorted-guitar screech followed by the entrance of the drum machine. The groove quickly fills out with a busily funky bass line and a crisp rhythm-guitar part. The song's first gesture toward the Bond sound happens when a few hits of sampled (or highly processed) brass create a gappy ascending melody while we wait for the voice to enter the texture; as the song continues, the sampled-brass hits provide a stuttering commentary between vocal phrases.

Whether intentionally or not, the ad-hoc brass arrangement creates a brilliant musical pun: it's both a punchy brass-band assault in the Barry manner *and* a well-judged use of still-trendy digital samplers. It succeeds as a hook because it's old, and it succeeds as a hook because it's new; the Bond-song archive contains nothing else that works so cannily. The Barry-supervised recording session included a full orchestra along with the band. But Barry uses the orchestra quite discreetly—to fill in the harmony (thus bringing out the pop-friendliness of the verse and prechorus) and enhance the brass-stabs. In this respect, but also more broadly, the record actually sounds like Duran Duran—just on a good day, a touch heftier than usual.

a-ha's "The Living Daylights" too allows its artists to sound like themselves, just a little better. The collaboration between Barry and the huffy Norwegians did not go swimmingly, and the band apparently preferred its self-produced later version. But the original soundtrack recording is as good as anything the band ever released, partly because imitating Duran Duran—which was clearly part of what they were hired for—may have been their strongest suit. Duran Duran's hybrid sound reportedly helped get a-ha past its initial synth-pop phase. "The Living Daylights" reveals this connection clearly: the light-voiced singer fitting the verse's melody around a built-up, partly electronic groove already recalls "A View to a Kill," and the keening prechorus deepens the likeness. "The Living Daylights" also follows its immediate predecessor in its use of sampled horns to signal the Bond sound.

Altogether the Bond-film version of "The Living Daylights" has a pleasantly lumpy mix of elements: the cold keyboard textures of synth-pop, real and synthetic horns, distorted guitar leads and nylon-guitar strums, breathy vocal-sounds washing in and out, and an eclectic group of sampled percussion instruments along with a live drummer playing tons of fills. All this may have been too much for the band: their "authorized" version of a year later sticks much closer to their synth-pop roots. Whether or not the original version's varied palette was influenced by that old-school soundtrack Svengali Barry, it comes off as decidedly new wave. Something a bit hipstery governs the way the song melds the traditional and the newfangled; the mixy-matchy collection of musical elements sounds a little excessive; and the lead singer's nervous energy seems hard-pressed to keep it all together.

Duran Duran's contribution may have achieved greater commercial (and aesthetic) success. But its seams show even more clearly. This is how new wave and its progeny operate. Everything pretty much works, but the heterogeneity of this record's elements—human versus mechanical, acoustic versus electronic, distorted versus clean, futuristic versus retro, and so on—can make us wonder whether the song will fall apart, starting with a malfunction of Simon Le Bon's less-than-ideal singing. Which sort of happened: performing "A View to a Kill" on the big stage of Live Aid in the year of the song's release, Le Bon had a horrible voice-crack. Except that it didn't matter—yes, he was terribly embarrassed, the rest of the band was pissed, and the moment survives in (YouTube) memory, but the show really did go on. Perhaps it was enough that Le Bon looked the part. Or, more likely, the audience already knew that Le Bon's imperfect voice would never be able to hold its own.

And this is what's most remarkable about the years when the Bond songs took on the new wave sound: those voices. Under Barry's aegis, the Bond franchise was actually pretty shrewd in melding new-wave and Bond-sound elements—but when it came to the voices, no such luck. Neither Simon Le Bon nor Morten Harket (of a-ha not-really fame) are the seasoned professionals that belted their routine way through the Bond songs of the 60s and 70s. And it shows. Their voices sound pinched, driven by the instrumentals and the backup vocals, at times even overwhelmed by them. Forlorn in their own arrangements, set upon by the musical world they themselves have conjured, these are bewildered voices, pan-icked. They are voices that say nothing less than that you no longer have to be able to sing to be a pop star.

Not for nothing do they appear at the transition from Connery and Moore to Dalton and Brosnan. Connery and Moore are profoundly vocal Bonds. Connery's velvety purr was deep and seductive and threatening in the same way Bassey's "Moonraker" voice was; by 1983 Moore certainly didn't really *look* the part anymore, but he still quite *sounded* it. You looked at him, his eyes wide open as though in constant fright (lest the viewer notice the wrinkles), and you thought that that couldn't pos-sibly be Bond. Then he opened his mouth and you were, at least for the time being, reassured.

Dalton and Brosnan by contrast look the part, but their voices lack the rollicking timbre and the expressiveness of the earlier Bond voices. Bond was well on his way to being a look rather than a sound—Omega watches, Parker pens and Yves Saint Laurent suits. Likewise Duran Duran and a-ha had the right stuff only in the looks department. This was to some extent new wave's point—against the anachronistic hypermasculine strutters of rock and roll and punk they deployed singers who recapitulated for the concert stage the buffeted and panicked vagaries of middle-management masculinity. Let Mick Jagger or Sid Vicious sound like ancient deities rebirthed into the late twentieth century; Le Bon's and Harket's voices were those of the wunderkind money-manager caught by his boss at Le Cirque with the company credit card.

The films if anything foregrounded that fact. The visuals that accompany the songs of this era are stolid and posey, leaving us more alone with songs that don't do so well under close scrutiny. They had a cruel way of stranding the lonely voices that anchored them, of highlighting their weaknesses rather than hiding them with visual panache. *The Living Daylights* opens with one of the most dynamic sequences of the entire Bond series—a chase around the Rock of Gibraltar set to a Bond theme with a pulse-pounding drum-machine beat. Then Timothy Dalton introduces himself as "Bond, James Bond," the screen goes black—and all the energy generated by exploding jeeps and Union Jack parachutes seems to dissipate.

The title sequence that accompanies a-ha's song is as static as the opening chase has been dynamic. The overall pace of the editing feels glacial. The sequence relies on rippling water rather than the usual undulating bodies (see Fig. 6.2). The customary feminine silhouettes seem to have been set adrift in a fishpond, a far cry from the roiling water and magma eruptions of, say, *You Only Live Twice*. The colors seem straight out of Jean-Jacques Beineix's *cinema du look*, in films like *Diva* (1981). The frame is often dominated by negative space, with guns sticking inertly into the middle of the frame, and even more often just lingering at the edge (see Fig. 6.3). The title sequence for *A View to a Kill* is similarly static, with an Asian woman in static poses. The girls look like models waiting for a shutter to click. The opener for *License to Kill* is literally presented through the shutter of an Olympus camera. The look has become product placement (see Fig. 6.4).

In terms of their lyrics the two new-wave songs follow the pattern set by the late-70s/early-80s entries. They very deliberately marry a James

Figure 6.2 Stagey, inert, posey: from the title sequence of *The Living Daylights* (1987).

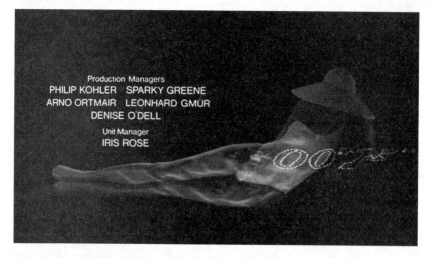

Figure 6.3 Stranding the audience with the singer's voice: model posing in the title sequence of *The Living Daylights*.

Bond sensibility—a vague nimbus of danger, eroticism, and betrayal—to preexisting genres of pop songs. "The Living Daylights" interprets its title phrase as a kind of carpe diem: don't let the morning come, because it will force us to separate. It's a theme as old as love poetry, with John Donne as perhaps the most famous example in a long tradition.

Figure 6.4 Product placement has become the gaze: the title sequence of *License to Kill* (1989) is apparently brought to you by Olympus.

"A View to a Kill" meanwhile is one of those Bond-song texts that mostly say things that sound like two people might be either killing each other or fucking. If anything, what exactly is happening seems less clear than in earlier songs, and not because of ambiguity or double entendre, but rather because of zero-entendre, that is to say, the lyrics don't make a lick of sense. "Dance into the fire" is a case in point: it's a nice phrase, but ultimately little more than that. It sounds like an imperative at first (go on, dance into the fire!), but it turns out to be about two people dancing into the fire. What exactly transpires when they dance into the fire is murky too: lots of stuff happening is described as "fatal" (nice songwriting, boys), but it's not even clear if dancing into the fire is a good thing or a bad thing (we, for one, would like to know before we attempted it). There's a lot of sound and fury here, but it depends on our mishearing (when we think the lyrics are exhorting us), on our taking a part and neglecting the whole that surrounds it.

The lyrics are at once remarkably detailed and maddeningly elusive in the kind of story they're telling. The second stanza of "A View to a Kill" starts with "Choice for you is the view to a kill / between the shades, assassination's standing still." We analyze texts for a living, and we have no clue what the hell that's about. But what we can say: it's deliberately opaque, but also quite specific. Two people are meeting after many years, there may be tears, killing, dancing, or some combination thereof. The lyrics are also incredibly hard to say out loud—the lines just quoted are a veritable tongue-twister, and "assassination's standing still" is almost impossible to make out without relying on a lyric sheet. The songs sound as though they were written by nonnative speakers of English, or maybe written with those kinds of speakers in mind. They make up in things they *might* be saying for the things they really aren't saying.

Although good old series stalwart John Barry cowrote the song with the group, the song is pure new wave. The lyrics have a killer hook in a cool title phrase, and then barely bother to invent lyrics *around* that cool phrase. (Pop quiz: Why should you "keep feeling fascination"? What's the point of "burning down the house," and will a raincoat be employed? Does Gary Numan enjoy receiving visitors "in cars"?) New wave songs often had the kind of lyrics that you sing along with until you realize you've got no clue what the hell you're even saying. That again was probably a reaction to the self-seriousness of 70s rock. New wave lyrics aren't cryptic so much as they are cheerfully unencumbered by meaning: oh, I'm sorry, you were expecting us to give a shit about our lyrics? Sorry to disappoint, mate.

But this free-floating intensity that seems to come out of nowhere and that dissolves into a puddle of incoherence the moment you look at it too closely of course also has something of a slogan in search of an argument. The title phrase looks the part of a Bond-song title, the song looks the part of a thrilling spy-ballad, but there's little beyond that general look to convince us they really are that. It's the "there you go again" of lyrics—a snappy line with nothing to back it up, hymns for a decade whose defining conflicts were with the Falklands and Grenada. Dancy and bouncy, intense and full of gestures of sex and violence, with very catchy group-sung melodies, they feel like anthems, but they're no such thing. Can you really picture yourself singing along to "A View to a Kill" or "The Living Daylights" at a crowded bar? One fakes one's way through those lyrics like a schoolboy who hasn't practiced his prayers—"dance

umm umm umm fire umm umm kiss umm umm kill"? This is not
exactly "We Are the Champions."

At least when it comes to the lyrics, "The Living Daylights" gives us
more of the same. There's a driver, but who the hell is he or she? What's
the point of mentioning "hopes" that were dashed, the "blame" that "a
hundred thousand people" seem to cast? The song doesn't clarify any of
this, and it doesn't seem to know. But it manages to create a generalized
atmosphere of anxiety—whoever "I" is in this song, he is worried he's not
good enough, worried people may be disappointed in him, worried hopes
may have been stoked that he can never satisfy:

> Hey driver, where're we going
> I swear my nerves are showing
> Set your hopes up way too high
> The living's in the way we die.
>
> Comes the morning and the headlights fade away
> Hundred thousand people . . . I'm the one they blame
> I've been waiting long for one of us to say
> Save the darkness, let it never fade away
> In the living daylights.

The song looks the part, but its nerves are showing—one wrong move and
the song's Bond is revealed as a fake, and the Bond song is revealed as a
fake alongside him. "The Living Daylights" is, in its own way, the perfect
song for the Bond films of the 80s. There's the creeping sense it's going
through the motions, the worry that it just doesn't stack up, the fear that it
can't meet expectations. Its Bond is an anxious Bond: what used to come
naturally now requires effort or feels strange, what people loved about
you now incites anxiety. In a song that replicates all the parts of the Bond
song—percussion, blaring brass—but does so synthetically, there is a fear
of being a substitute, an empty shirt.

There's something almost sadistic about the way the opening sequence
abandons Morten Harket's voice. The synths overpower him, the lyrics seem to out him as a fake, the visuals strand him with meaningless
static poseyness. The sequence reaches a pinnacle of banality when the

Figure 6.5 The headlight . . . fading away! Get it? From *The Living Daylights*.

line "and the headlights fade away" is actually accompanied by a head-light on screen: it flashes up, when called on by the vocals, then indeed dutifully fades away (see Fig. 6.5). It is this brief moment that betrays the sequence's anguished dialogue with a genre that the title sequences of the Bond songs helped create over the decades, but that by now had provided a visual vocabulary that actually competed with that of the Bond-song sequences. That genre is the music video.

The first Bond song to be accompanied by two separate sets of visuals was "All Time High" in 1983. From then on all songs had essentially *two* videos—one of which was in heavy rotation in movie theaters, while the second was (ideally) in heavy rotation on MTV. The static posers in the title sequence of "A View to a Kill," to cite the most extreme example, thus squared off against a very 80s concoction directed by Godley & Creme, in which the band members saunter around the Eiffel Tower in Roger Moore's footsteps. That sequence was way more fun than what accompanied the song in the film: dynamic, cheeky, visually inventive, everything that the Bond-opener was not.

The music-video aesthetic had made its way into the Bond films' opening sequences before. For decades, the Bond singers had been visually absent from the opening sequences, but the opening credits of *For Your*

Figure 6.6 From the music video for Duran Duran's "A View to a Kill."

Eyes Only, released in 1981, the year MTV went on the air, actually feature very little beside the singer Sheena Easton. The way her face is framed and overlaid with other visuals recalls the promotional videos ABBA made in the late 70s. But in *For Your Eyes Only*, the song's opening credit essentially doubled for the music video. The film simply ingested the visual aesthetic of ABBA and pre-MTV music video, and made it conform to the Bond formula—they could still coexist in the same visual frame. *A View to a Kill* has the first opening sequence that seems to understand that those two aesthetics were either intrinsically different, or in the process of diverging.

The cheeky music video for "A View to a Kill" points to the fact that here the new audiovisual medium of the music video stands in an uneasy relation to an earlier audiovisual form. Throughout, the band members are shown viewing action from the film through binoculars and on screens. But because the video itself has the VHS shimmer characteristic of early music videos, what they "see" through their lenses and screens looks quite different—they are, the editing seems to imply, not so much *in* the film as watching the film (see Fig. 6.6).

It's a sequence that plays Moore and the musicians off each other: they are both in the same space (on the same set, in fact), but at different times, and made to coexist only through editing. By bringing together Moore and Duran Duran, but bringing them together in a way that they remain

Figure 6.7 "Bon, Simon Le Bon": from Duran Duran's "A View to a Kill."

noticeably separate, the music video seems to ask us to compare the group and Bond. But in terms of what? Is one the real deal, the other one a fake? Are they both just acting a part? Is it real man versus little pipsqueak, or withered sex symbol versus new, legitimate sex symbol? At the end of the video Simon Le Bon says the line "The name's Le Bon, Simon Le Bon" (see Fig. 6.7). What's the implication? Is he a successor, or a poser? Is it more absurd when he says the line than when certified old person Roger Moore claims to be "Bond, James Bond"? The visuals produced by men Moore's age for the actual film appear far less willing to give Duran Duran the upper hand, but the music video seems a lot less decided.

Still, we're watching Duran Duran watching Roger Moore perform. They are audience surrogates, playing dress-up and singing over a movie that singers like them are barred from by generic contract. Shirley Bassey sang three Bond songs, and she never appeared in a single frame of any of them. Other than Sheena Easton's turn, none of the Bond singers ever appeared on screen until Madonna's cameo as fencing-instructor Verity in *Die Another Day*. Even when their song was sung within the movie, it was sung by someone else. By appearing in the video, the members of Duran Duran thus make clear that that video is *not* like the opening sequence—when they appear, they appear again as fake Bonds, as would-be Bonds, as substitutes. In the music video for "The Living Daylights," the

Figure 6.8 Stepping into Bond's shoes: From the music video for a-ha's "The Living Daylights."

three members of a-ha open the song by reenacting the iconic gun-barrel sequence that opens almost every Bond film—but rather than shoot, they reach for the microphone, the keyboard, and the guitar (see Fig. 6.8).

This is the Bond sound of the 80s: in over its head, keenly aware that it's incapable of the kind of craft and professionalism that had characterized the songs of the late 70s. This was no longer the music of union guys, this was the music of union busters, of fake-it-till-you-make-it Wall Street hustlers. They've replaced their drummers with a machine, they've put the orchestra out to pasture, they've streamlined their work-process and promoted synergy. Now they feel a little guilty about it, stranded on the stage all by themselves. The shame these songs felt, the shame they were made to feel by the films that incorporated them, was that of Charlie Sheen vis-à-vis Martin Sheen in Oliver Stone's *Wall Street* (1987)—the Wall Street whiz kid versus the union man who works for the company that to his son is just an item on a spreadsheet.

Through some kind of strange institutional memory, these songs and the films they appear in retained the viewpoint of 70s professionalism. They hand the mic to Morten Harket and Simon Le Bon, but the gaze they cast upon them singing is that of the Martin Sheen character in *Wall Street*. While these songs tread new ground in the Bond song's relationship to synthesizers, to labor, but also to masculinity and authenticity, the films seem intent on disavowing any innovation—they'll let the kids play dress-up, but they won't confer any kind of legitimacy upon their play. They mark them as—to use the band name of the group that provided two of the in-film songs for *The Living Daylights*—Pretenders.

PRETENDERS

The Pretenders, another new wave act well-established enough for the Bond series' producers to feel they were safe to hire, wrote two songs for *The Living Daylights*—"Where Has Everybody Gone" and "If There Was a Man." They certainly sound like Bond songs. They were co-written by John Barry and incorporate instrumentation and themes from Barry's score. They're brassier, they avoid the familiar musical motifs of the Bond theme, but in typical Bond-song fashion they foreground an arch chromatic melodic gesture that often characterizes Barry's approach. But they enter the film in a new and exceedingly 80s way. One of the film's secondary villains is a trained killer named Necros, whose preferred method for dispatching his victims is to strangle them with the cord of his Walkman headphones—and the only cassette he seems to own plays the Pretenders.

In one truly neat scene, Necros strangles his way through an MI6 safe house. He first infiltrates it concealed as a jogger, then moves on to impersonating a milkman, each time wearing his signature Walkman. Before each kill we can hear the Pretenders blaring for a brief moment as he takes off his headphones and strangles another hapless victim. When he's finally discovered and the shooting and explosions start, an instrumental version of "Where Has Everybody Gone" appears on the soundtrack. The violence hidden under those plushy headphone pads has finally come out into the open, leaving the musical idiom of the 80s and turning into Bond music we can recognize.

There is a profound horror at 80s excess throughout the film, as Bond's traditional ways struggle against a new world dominated by finance rather than ideology. The villains turn out to be neither the Soviets nor the Americans, but rather a group of Soviets and Americans moving guns, money, and opium in a way that doesn't exactly downplay the allusion to Iran-Contra. In a final confrontation with the ultimate baddie Brad Whitaker (played with an exquisite Texas twang by Joe Don Baker), Bond characteristically shows up with his traditional Walther PPK, and is forced to square off against Whitaker's almost outlandishly disproportionate arsenal of newfangled weaponry. Normally Bond is the master of gadgets, but here he does his job in a deliberately old-school manner, against a recognizably 80s kind of excess. Whitaker's weaponry seems utterly excessive for a simple melée. When Bond has emptied the Walther's clip, Whitaker growls: "You've had your eight. Now I get my eighty."

The movie's villains aren't any younger than Bond—but they are clearly going with the times in ways Bond is not. Bond is pushed into the role of the traditionalist—not just by the opening songs and their twenty-something singers, but by the bad guys. Just compare Necros and Dalton's Bond. With his love of jogging, his sweatbands, his Pretenders tapes, Necros is basically a time-capsule of mid-80s preoccupations. Bond's concessions to the zeitgeist are minimal by comparison. He's a man out of the early 60s, and the villains, with their eighty-round magazines, their fancy Walkman thingamajigs, and their embrace of pop culture, make him look his age.

The song that blares so threateningly wherever Necros goes is another one of those abandonment songs. Just like "The Living Daylights" and "A View to a Kill," it's a song about being stranded and left alone, as a lone voice laments inevitable betrayal:

> Where has everybody gone?
> I've got this feelin,
> Goin' to end up here on my own.
> Where's my support now?
> Where's the ranks of the strong?
> In this faceless crowd, where can I belong?

Such is the idiom of the mid-80s Bond song: a single figure, anxious he or she might have been abandoned, looking for support or surety he or she can't seem to find anywhere. Notice that many of the phrases, above all "support," could be 70s psychobabble (Where's my support group?) or just as well 80s militarism (Where's my backup?). Is the speaker a soldier left behind enemy lines, or just some little shit missing mommy and daddy? It's hard to say.

Generational factors never seem to be far away when a-ha, Duran Duran, or the Pretenders worry about being all alone, about not fulfilling expectations, about being blamed. What has come naturally, almost automatically to Bond singers so far has suddenly become fraught—the vast instrumental armature that previous generations of Bond-singers deployed as backup has become something menacing, something potentially overwhelming. The traditional trappings of the Bond song, invented by members of another generation but imposed on their children here, have become malignant.

The Bond songs had a strange way of dealing with the new genres and sounds they were forced to incorporate during the 1970s. They treated these new elements with trepidation, they fetishized and feared them. By the late 70s they managed them by seeking out the least threatening exemplars, and that was largely the producers' approach to new wave as well. With Duran Duran and a-ha they turned (for the first time really) to relatively up-to-date artists in their prime. But still the Bond songs took a different attitude to the new sounds and voices they grudgingly incorporated. They strand them and make them come up short.

The members of a-ha and Duran Duran were children of the late 50s and early 60s, a new generation of Bond singers who clearly played up their (relative) youth. The insouciance with which the members of a-ha step into Bond's shoes in the video for "The Living Daylights," the naivety with which the members of Duran Duran interact with Roger Moore in the one for "A View to a Kill," all cast these young men with their jean jackets and their very eighties 'dos as the whippersnappers against old man Bond. Composer John Barry and director John Glen never saw eye-to-eye with either group, and Barry credited his miserable experience working with a-ha for making him exit the franchise after twenty-five years.

Bond had lost what in an earlier chapter we called his "double-agedness." For a long time the Bond character had existed at an impossible intersection of two generations: the young stud and the middle-aged grumbler. By the mid-80s, when this generational tension resurfaced, youth culture had become too young for James Bond's doubleness to remain plausible. Duran Duran and a-ha were bands for the MTV generation, and Roger Moore was a matinee idol for the generation of their parents. In his book about the music of James Bond, Jon Burlingame tells a funny story: in an attempt to audition the band for their new Bond film, Glen and Barry went to an a-ha concert, and found that "the oldest person in the audience was about 15." Just picture Glen (born 1932) and Barry (born 1933) in a raging mass of screaming teenyboppers, and you get a pretty good idea of how precarious an undertaking it was to sign a-ha to the Bond franchise.

Just as Thatcher and Reagan took a hammer to the postwar liberal consensus in the United States and the United Kingdom, the Bond consensus finally crumbled in the 80s. If James Bond had been the kind of hero both dads and sons could get behind on a rainy Saturday afternoon, a hero that they could read very different things into, that unanimity came apart in the mid-80s. For one side, the sight of Simon Le Bon climbing around on an Eiffel Tower set alongside Roger Moore made your skin crawl, like when the new owners were shown around the factory and they turned out to be your son's age. For the other side, Le Bon's presence on that set was long overdue—and the fact that he coexisted with Moore only due to the magic of editing seemed as insane as casting noted methuselah Roger Moore as a sexually attractive spy, or a sexually attractive *anything* for that matter.

For one side having to encounter someone like Le Bon in a movie theater was anathema; the other side didn't encounter his voice in the movie theater at all, but rather was introduced to the Bond song via MTV. Or they, like Necros, had the song on their Walkman by the time they walked into the movie theater to catch a Sunday matinee at the dollar theater.

SHAKEN AND STIRRED
David Arnold

GOLDENEYE
Tina Turner

**TOMORROW
NEVER DIES**
Sheryl Crow

**THE WORLD
IS NOT ENOUGH**
Garbage

SURRENDER
k.d. lang

"Your Life is a Story I've Already Written"

The Gay Panic Years

If the Reagan-era Bonds had suffered something of an identity crisis, which was transmitted directly into their theme songs, the songs of the 90s knew no such doubts. And why would they have? After a few years off between *License to Kill* and *GoldenEye*, the new films were immensely successful and their songs did well on the charts. Oddly enough, by staying still for a few decades, Bond had somehow become cool again. The 80s Bond songs would have been horrified by this turn of events, wondering what they'd done to find such good fortune and if they really deserved it. By contrast the 90s Bond songs plowed ahead—surely they must have done *something* to deserve their renewed profitability and restored cachet.

This made these Bond songs the perfect anthems for the Third Way 90s, the era of Clinton and Blair. The films were pragmatic and utterly unencumbered by history. If it had worked before, why reinvent the wheel? If something had become difficult to maintain, why not just jettison it? If money was coming in, why question what you'd done to earn it? There were no more communists to fight. Instead one just competed with other capitalists, may the best salesman win. And by the 90s James Bond was the best salesman of all: he sold wristwatches, cars, expensive liqueurs, and designer suits. Above all he sold capitalism itself, not any one object but the "system of objects," as Jean Baudrillard once put it.

But if all of James Bond became a single, slickly produced surface, the songs remained the place where the franchise's black heart kept pumping. Not that the songs weren't smoothed over too. They sounded much like the films looked—manifestly competent, exceedingly polished, and largely free of personality. But the memory of the franchise's long, difficult life was encoded in these songs, and they couldn't hide from the past as readily as the movies could. They told stories of dark desire, violence disguised as sex, voyeurism, and obsession, and they related these tales from unusual perspectives. The songs spoke of desires that veered into areas Bond songs had never ventured into—BDSM, homoeroticism, threesomes. And they took little joy in talking about those things; there was no dirty tittering like in "The Man with the Golden Gun," or gleeful double entendres like in "Diamonds Are Forever." If anything the songs seemed freaked out by the scenarios they described. These were James Bond's gay panic years.

After "Goldfinger," the Bond songs pretty quickly abandoned the ballad form, but they showed respect for one of its most salient features: sometimes it's easy to tell who is speaking in the song, who's being addressed, and why. Almost always the situation described in the song corresponds to an actual situation in the film, or one that we could easily imagine taking place somewhere around the film's plot—a Bond girl finds herself falling in love with Bond, a Bond girl is abandoned by Bond, a Bond girl is torn between her allegiance to both villain and hero.

Most of the early songs are indeed focalized through the Bond girl: they see the film's world, its problems, through her eyes. There are a few that don't narrate from an implicitly female perspective; "You Only Live Twice" is the clearest case. There are a few that *could* be narrated from a man's perspective, but where the focus on Bond still puts the singer in the position of desiring, taunting, obsessing over Bond—think "Live and Let Die."

This chapter is about a group of Bond songs that diverged from this convention. We've already discussed Bond songs that play with their conventions. Sometimes these conventions are pretty obvious to the audience (the convoluted melodies, the big-band brass arrangements), others are more hidden (the rarity of backup singers, to name just one). The focalization of the song lyrics is one of those hidden conventions. The Bond songs took forever to shed this particular convention, and when they did, they did so quite decisively. It was a very important move, with implications as to how the Bond songs related to their own pop tradition. Indeed, what's interesting about these Bond songs is that they're otherwise so boring: we have to listen past their smooth surfaces and complacent rehashings of Bond-song clichés to grasp how troubling their perspectives really are.

As we'll see, when the Bond girls fell silent, it wasn't Bond who piped up. Bimbos and vixens had held sway for thirty years by the 1990s, and now it was the villains' turn. In Tina Turner's "GoldenEye," the person who "watched you from the shadows as a child" is almost certainly Sean Bean's traitorous Agent 006. In k.d. lang's "Surrender" (the original song for *Tomorrow Never Dies*), we hear how "the news is that I am in control"—a clear allusion to the Ted Turner–like villain in the movie. The Garbage song "The World Is Not Enough" speaks from the perspective of Sophie Marceau's Bond girl/villain hybrid (the first time the series had combined these two archetypes), either addressing Bond or her co-villain Renard. Only with "Die Another Day," which Madonna recorded for the 2002 film of the same name, does the mode of address switch yet again: now for the first time Bond speaks for himself.

Even though there's one outlier in the bunch (after deciding that k.d. lang wasn't high-profile enough to open *Tomorrow Never Dies*, the producers replaced her song with one by Sheryl Crow, which speaks from the Bond girl's perspective), the villain's point of view is a remarkably consistent feature of the Brosnan Bonds. Never before "GoldenEye" did the villains wrest the bullhorn away from more ambiguously affiliated characters, content to be sung about or ignored. And never after "The World Is Not Enough" did they pipe up again: Bond was busy with his own demons and the villains were, at best, a tiny strand in his Gordian knot of complexes and dysfunctions.

What accounts for this strange interlude? It probably stems from the Bond franchise's relation to its own history. Not so much individual adventures or events—these are made to disappear with baffling efficiency at the start of each new outing—but just the weight of decades of Bond films. One of *GoldenEye*'s Bond girls (villainous Xenia Onatopp) was played by an actress who was born the year *Thunderball* came out; the other (sweetly forgettable Natalya Simonova) was played by an actress born while *Diamonds Are Forever* was in production. Maybe that's why the Bond girls fell silent around then—when Shirley Bassey had sung out her warnings about Goldfinger she was drawing on a long memory. By now, there was too much history for a Bond girl to recall.

Instead, the villains got to talking—*they* had become the series' memory. The actors playing them were older than the franchise, older than the man currently playing the superspy. They were often familiar with the name James Bond in much the same way that Shirley Bassey had been conversant with the name Goldfinger. The gaze they cast upon him is a weary one, freighted with history, often enough personal history. "You'll never know / how I watched you from the shadows as a child," Tina Turner intones in "GoldenEye"—the villain's memory is longer than Bond's. She knows, he doesn't.

The gaze of the Bond girl is of course entirely different: to steal Matthew McConaughey's line from *Dazed and Confused*, Bond keeps getting older, they keep staying the same age. Their memory cannot extend very far back because they're always young, always new, and, until recently, never allowed to display much intelligence. The villains by contrast are usually quite good at remembering—better even than Bond himself. SPECTRE, Blofeld, Jaws: villains, unlike Bond girls, linger and resurface. They become, if not the conscience of the Bond series, at least its black, toxic memory. More than the hero, who in the movies has a weird amnesiac streak, these villains are the source of continuity, the bearers of tradition. And in the 1990s when Bond stared into their abyss, they stared back. But what did they see?

THE MEMORIOUS GAZE

By the 1990s, the style of the Bond villains changed, although in an unexpected direction. They suddenly began resembling the kinds of opponents Ian Fleming had invented for James Bond. The books contain richly imagined villains, and their villainy usually springs from sources other than the greed for power and riches that motivates the Bond films' baddies. Many of them are products of British colonialism or British triumphs in war: former Nazis, bastard children of British officers, or (like the "Chigroes" Fleming seems nastily obsessed with in *Dr. No*) simply products of ethnic intermixing within the Commonwealth. They are by-products of historical processes—like Le Chiffre in *Casino Royale*, who gives himself that name because he is, at the end of World War II, "only a number in a passport."

A file on the villain offers the information that "racially, subject is probably a mixture of Mediterranean with Prussian or Polish strains." The operative word, as ever with Bond villains, is "mixture": where Bond stands in for purity, the villains come from a more complicated, muddled, and therefore debased world. As these examples make clear, one reason why the films gave these backstories a wide berth was that they were often unbelievably racist. Fleming very clearly feared any miscegenation between whites and nonwhites, between Brits and other peoples, or even other peoples passing as British when they were really not. It was a trope so noxious that it took until 2002 for the films to finally trot it out—*Die Another Day* presented a villain who *seemed* English, but was in fact a North Korean infiltrator after lots of plastic surgery (a plotline taken from the novelization version of *Moonraker*). Surely that's a measure of how troubling this particular plot-point was even in the not-very-enlightened atmosphere of the mid-60s.

The villains of the movies by contrast had been less troubling creatures. Even though many of them were played by Germans, at times with rather thick Teutonic accents, the movies never make their villains ex-Nazis—the two that come closest are *Goldfinger*, which features a sequence where Bond and the villain play golf over a bar of Nazi gold, and *A View to a Kill*, which has a bleached-blond Christopher Walken as a Nazi genetic experiment. Hugo Drax, who in the book *Moonraker* is a half-English ex-Nazi trying to get even with England, in the movies has some vague plans of starting over human civilization in space. And other than Dr. No (half-Chinese, half-German in both novel and film) and Mr. Big/Dr. Kananga (the Fear of a Black Planet personified), the films' villains aren't racially ambiguous.

All that changed when Bond returned to the screen in 1995 after a six-year hiatus: *GoldenEye*'s villain had a backstory steeped in British history—a member of MI6, he is the orphan son of Cossack Nazi collaborators who were returned to Stalin by England after World War II. *The World Is Not Enough* has Elektra King, daughter of a British oil and gas mogul and an Azerbaijani oil heiress. *Die Another Day* features the aforementioned Korean psychopath posing as a Richard Branson–type playboy billionaire. These villains have become repositories of historical memory. Whereas the villains Roger Moore battled had essentially ahistorical aims—raise money, make room for a master race, start World War III, and profit—the Brosnan films' villains are out for revenge for very specific and historically accurate actions by the British Empire. This is how they had functioned in the books all along, but only with Brosnan did the films follow suit.

It's tempting to tether this noticeable shift to some world-historic development or other by saying, "this is a post-1989 Bond," or some such. But that seems to presume an awful lot: Why would the end of the Cold War have occasioned this shift? Why would it be the villains who remember? Well, that last question may get us to a partial answer as to why the villains became so memorious from *GoldenEye* on. The world had changed around Bond, but the world had changed around Bond all along. What was new was that Bond was now determined to change with it.

Bond movies were supposed to look more like other movies of their time, and James Bond himself was supposed to be more recognizably modern, rather than a relic.

When James Bond reappeared in 1995, there was a nervier tone to the character and to the movies in which he appeared. *GoldenEye* opens with M calling Bond "a misogynist dinosaur, a relic of the Cold War," and the Bond films of the Brosnan and Craig eras became obsessed with figuring out a new home for a half-century-old character in a rapidly changing world. As such almost every Bond film since *GoldenEye* has been a course correction or a reboot. Earlier Bond films had tried to paper over the fact that the franchise was constantly starting over and trying to reinvent itself ("living twice," in the title phrase of the iconic 1967 film)—their Bond could be old *and* young, with it *and* anachronistic. That possibility, that consensus had evaporated by the 80s. From 1995 on, Bond was a driven man, always needing to reestablish himself.

The songs that accompanied these reconceptions, however, were deliberate throwbacks. Tina Turner, k.d. lang, Sheryl Crow, and Garbage's Shirley Manson all did their best Bassey-impressions. These songs are slick pastiches, capably made, often by pretty serious producers. U2's Bono and The Edge wrote "GoldenEye" for Tina Turner, and the song was produced by Nellee Hooper, who'd worked with Madonna and Bjork. Crow's "Tomorrow Never Dies" was produced and cowritten by veteran producer Mitchell Froom (Los Lobos, Suzanne Vega, Crowded House). And Butch Vig, producer of landmark albums by Nirvana and Sonic Youth, was the drummer/leader/producer of Garbage, who performed "The World Is Not Enough." Starting with late 1997's *Tomorrow Never Dies*, composer David Arnold took the reins of the soundtracks for the next five movies. His of-the-moment sampling techniques and percussive loops brought the Bond sound out of the 70s. Arnold had scored a handful of big-budget films before taking over the Bond franchise, but that's not what got him the gig: in 1996 John Barry heard some early tracks from Arnold's *Shaken and Stirred*, an album of Bond-song covers and remixes that eventually made the British album charts, and decided Arnold should be the next Bond-film composer.

All these players helped maintain the smooth professionalism that had returned to the Bond songs before the franchise's six-year hiatus. Like Narada Michael Walden and Stewart Levine, who produced Gladys Knight's and Patti LaBelle's Bond songs, Arnold, Hooper, and Froom knew what they were doing. One thing they knew was that you need to hire the right musicians and engineers if you want a record to sound a certain way—something Barry and his contractor Sidney Margo could never grasp. The right people meant the songs sounded good, were never embarrassing, and charted reliably (at least in the U.K.).

But, at least aesthetically speaking, they were remarkably conservative entries. Never mind that these songs drew on songwriters and producers with indie-rock résumés. Never mind that they used synths and samplers and up-to-date post-rock ambient effects. These songs were perfectly content to throw a few of Barry's low-modernist gestures at you—an angular muted-brass melody here, a timpani tattoo there—before quickly switching over to middle-of-the-road pop. Crow's "Tomorrow Never Dies" is typical in this regard: Arnold orchestrates his ass off for the song's first twelve seconds (very Barry, very "cinematic"), until the texture hollows out into bare octaves and finally gives way to pseudo-singer/songwriter posturing.

As a result, the acknowledgment of Bond's precarious status slipped into the cracks and crevices underneath the smooth, produced surfaces—into the lyrics. And perspective became the most potent way by which they acknowledged it. The women who sang these songs no longer sang from the perspective of grizzled observers or hapless Bond girls; they usually slipped into the role of the villain. And the gaze they cast upon Bond was tinged with a slightly sadistic erotic longing—a fact that seems to freak these songs out quite a bit.

Appropriately, Tina Turner's "GoldenEye" is all about voyeurism—at times the detached voyeurism of the gumshoe following a person through a crowd, at other times a voyeurism that borders on the fetishistic. Its voyeurism seems interested not so much in the innocence of its object, but rather in some sort of vague corruption. Lines like "See him move through smoke and mirrors / feel his presence in the crowd" suggest that whoever Tina Turner is sneaking after isn't exactly a standup citizen himself, and she seems to get off on it. It's of the "Every Breath You Take" school of stalker songs.

As so often in Bond songs there is an erotic tinge to the gaze, even if the speaker's main intention seems aggressive rather than amorous. This erotic tinge is probably what you notice first. The 90s Bond songs allow their erotic content to shape their basic affect; they're written, sung, and produced in a way that tends to hide the danger they describe. They do this partly by encouraging an initial mishearing—creating a fundamental confusion over what's being sung about—that can only be corrected if you attend closely to the lyrics. At first all you notice is a litany of erotic clichés caressed by a strong female voice: "On the wind I feel his breath," "I know when to talk / And I know when to touch," "I'll tease and tantalize with every line / Til you are all mine," "How you tease / How you leave me to burn," and so on. Only later do you realize the speaker is describing eroticized violence, not kinky eroticism.

Which makes the question of just who is talking all the more central. "GoldenEye" marks probably the first time in the Bond-song canon that even a casual listener has to pose that question. Because if Tina Turner slips into the Shirley Bassey role, the grizzled demimondaine who's got bets out on both Bond and the villain, she gives that role an odd new dimension: What sort of Bond girl, what sort of ex-plaything for the villain, would have followed Bond around for years, hidden in the shadows but following his dastardly exploits? What sort of *woman* in the world of Bond has that sort of persistence, that sort of permanence, that sort of past? Persistence, permanence, and past—those were by 1995 the domain of the Bond villains.

Sure, the song tries to cover its bases. At one point Tina Turner worries about "other girls gather[ing] around" Bond, but this simply isn't a girl's perspective, at least within the logic of the Bond universe. It does seem to line up quite nicely with the film's main villain—a sort of dark alter ego for Bond: Alec Trevelyan, Agent 006, an orphan like Bond. But unlike Bond it's not some sort of family tragedy that has made him so, it's the actions of the British Crown. He embodies, in other words, exactly the fear of encroachment by things un-English that so threatened Ian Fleming. Bond's tragedy is ahistorical—mountaineering accidents like the one that claimed the lives of Andrew Bond and Monique Delacroix are deaths of splendid isolation. Alec's tragedy is tethered to the turmoil of global history; it's not for nothing that he bears the surname of a great English historian. And unlike Bond, who uses his lack of family ties to serve Queen and Country, Trevelyan harbors an undying grudge against the Empire.

It is Trevelyan's gaze that Tina Turner makes her own in "GoldenEye"—the first time a female performer has taken on an identifiably male perspective in one of the Bond songs. He's the one "who's left behind," he's the one who "gets so close" just "to be denied":

> Goldeneye I found his weakness
> Goldeneye he'll do what I please
> Goldeneye no time for sweetness
> but a bitter kiss will bring him to his knees.

Just what sort of an object is this Goldeneye envisioning? An object of "bitter kisses," an object of tears, an object of a prying gaze—but a gaze that scans for weaknesses to exploit, for ways to "bring him to his knees." At one point it may have been a look of desire that Trevelyan cast upon Bond, but by now it's animated by desperation, by wounded pride, by jealousy that has turned murderous.

> You'll never know how I watched you
> from the shadows as a child
> you'll never know how it feels to be the one
> who's left behind.
> You'll never know the days, the nights,
> the tears, the tears I've cried
> but now my time has come
> and time, time is not on your side.

There is an erotic fascination here, but it isn't straightforwardly erotic. It's about control as much as it is about desire; it's about wanting to be the other as much as wanting the other. It is, in other words, a far more interesting erotic arrangement than most Bond songs had hitherto managed. And the song tries to walk back from it time and again; the song can't be about what it is fairly obviously about. A secret agent wanting another secret agent? A villain's schemes are not just a metaphorical dick-measuring contest with Bond, but actually aimed at Bond's dick? It had been there on screen at least since Auric Goldfinger pointed that laser at Bond's crotch, but there had always been enough window dressing to make for plausible deniability. The weird lasciviousness with which the villain went after the hero was at best a subtext. Now that it's in the text, the films have to deal with it, and it sends them into a panic.

The sadomasochistic dimension that enters the picture with "GoldenEye" becomes a mainstay of the Bond songs of the Brosnan era. Consider the first line of k.d. lang's "Surrender," which was the original choice for the opening song of *Tomorrow Never Dies*:

> Your life is a story I've already written.
> The news is that I am in control.
> And I have the power to make you surrender,
> Not only your body but your soul.

"Control" is the operative word in all of the songs of the Brosnan years—control, as "Surrender" puts it, over body and soul. The songs all cast this control as a violation, and in the case of "Die Another Day" it's even explicitly framed as a rape. To have another man so intensely interested in controlling your body fills these songs with profound dread. Being ogled and objectified by women was okay. Gladys Knight could "aim straight for your heart," and you were okay with the ambiguity because maybe she was trying to kiss you rather than kill you; gun metaphors in love songs are kind of a nonissue. But songs like "Surrender" no longer speak from the surety of a heterosexual woman's perspective—openly gay k.d. lang deliberately keeps the song androgynous, and keeps in play the possibility that a man might be wanting to control Bond and do things to his body.

The song's funny bit of indirect discourse—"*The news is* that I am in control"—points to the film's villain, a media tycoon. But it can also make us ask what kind of person would need to frame a statement like "I am in control" in such an overtly self-inflating way. Who *are* you, if you begin a first-person utterance with the phrase, "The news is"? A complete dick, that's who. And what if such masculinist self-regard becomes a song's only way to signal the oddness of its perspective—a polished female singer presenting a torturer's point of view? What if this dickishness is the song's only mode of self-reflexiveness?

That's what "Surrender" leaves us with—just the barest acknowledgment that there might be something weird about the relation between its words and its music. Its tunefulness and polish make us dig for the lyrics' dark message. And when we grasp what the words are saying, we listen in vain for some sense that the music has responded to their surprisingly dark perspective. Putting some gurgling synths behind the voice and the Barry-style brass arrangements, as Arnold does here, doesn't count as an attempt to engage with the lyrics' sinister point of view.

This disconnect between words and music governs all the Bond songs of the 90s. The lyrics of Sheryl Crow's "Tomorrow Never Dies" coalesce around a Bond girl's point of view. They dish out rudimentary Bond-film tropes ("Martinis, girls, and guns") and a more-or-less gothic longing for death, all in the second person, addressing Bond as the lover/murderer. Despite their familiar Bond-girl perspective, these lyrics share more with the other 90s Bond songs than with earlier Bond-song texts: here too the torture and privations seem more than just playful or metaphorical.

And like the other 90s Bond songs, "Tomorrow Never Dies" hides its dark character under a musical surface that keeps insisting we hear the song as conventional failed-romance pop. Sheryl Crow's performance is greatly responsible for this effect. Her delivery gives no hint of the song's deadly stakes. She swallows her consonants when she hits the chorus's soaring melody, and she leaves the occasional phrase unintelligible; this helps foreground the clearly presented title phrase, but deprives it of meaning and context. Not that the lyrics themselves are much help, with phrases like "the power of loving you near" and "Vacillations good Lord." Simply listening to the song, we may know who is speaking; but we don't know *why* she is, or whether it matters.

Garbage's "The World Is Not Enough" too raises questions about the identity of its speaker. And it too dissimulates about the kind of song it is. Like its three 90s predecessors, the Garbage record presents itself initially as a romantic song from a Bond girl's perspective. Its chorus addresses "my love," apparently confirming an intimate relation asserted in the first verse. Shirley Manson's close-miked voice brings out the intimacy and vulnerability that the words and melody can convey. Unless you've got your nose in a lyric sheet, you'll tend to hear the chorus and first verse as covering familiar territory: the present-tense experience of a romantic affair's uncertain future. This is *not* not a love song. Maybe somewhere, in the back of someone's mind, is the opening line of "To His Coy Mistress," Andrew Marvell's poetry-anthology chestnut: "Had we but world enough and time."

This song does want you to probe beneath its surface. Garbage's sound featured multilayered guitars and percussion, subtle noise effects, and a complex ambience; this was mostly the province of drummer Butch Vig, better known as the record producer who crafted Nirvana's *Nevermind* as a digital collage of multiple takes, outtakes, and recording-studio detritus. With the Barry-style orchestrations Arnold placed on top of Vig's basic tracks, "The World Is Not Enough" presents a highly differentiated sonic space. Manson's knowingness provides an access point for listeners seeking the song's depths. Burlingame's *The Music of James Bond* uncovers a 1999 quote from Manson that connects the Bond films and Garbage's music on precisely this register: both have "something you can enjoy on the surface but underneath there are lots of conflicting themes."

But in truth "The World Is Not Enough" doesn't quite make its tensions and complexities available to the casual listener. It may take too much effort to hear it as something other than a sonically updated but still backward-looking Bond song. Partly this has to do with Vig's sonic alchemy, which wasn't meant to demand notice. *Nevermind* sounded pretty raw, aggressive, and "live" to most of the millions who bought it; only a thin stratum of geeks heard it as the ProTools masterpiece it doubtless was. Things were different in the 70s, when the best sonic effects were the most obvious and you could hear subtlety a mile away. Vig's approach didn't foreground its sonic exploration. So unless you know it's worth listening deeply into the textures of "The World Is Not Enough," you may not hear its subtleties. And even if you do notice the sophisticated sonic effects, you may not connect them to the lyrics; you may not have reason to ask how these subtleties shape the speaker's perspective and the song's scene of address.

The song's most interesting feature is equally geeky, but it goes right to the heart of the question: Who exactly is the "I" of this song? Bond-song fans know that "The World Is Not Enough" is the only song to take a crucial line of dialogue from the movie and incorporate it into the lyrics. Strangely enough, though, that doesn't settle the matter of who the speaker is. Not only is the line, "There's no point in living if you can't feel alive," taken directly from the script—a gambit several earlier Bond songs had tried—it becomes an all-important clue in the film. It's a line that Elektra King (played by Sophie Marceau) utters to Bond, and that the terrorist Renard repeats later, making Bond realize that the two are in cahoots. But who then is speaking it in the opening song, Renard or Elektra? And who is it spoken to? For the film makes it abundantly clear that Renard and Elektra extend their sadomasochistic folie à deux to include Bond—Elektra sleeps with Bond at Renard's behest, and Renard taunts Bond with the fact that they are now connected through Elektra: "She's beautiful isn't she?" he sneers at Bond. "You should have had her before, when she was innocent. How does it feel to know that I broke her in for you?"

This is pretty much a classic case of what the late theorist Eve Kosofsky Sedgwick called the homosocial triangle. Two men who can't/won't get it on directly go through the intermediary of a woman they both fight over and sleep with. Is Elektra King speaking to Renard? Renard to Elektra? Elektra to Bond? Renard to Bond? The only one either spoken about or spoken to is Bond—he's the silent object of their attentions, or an ignored third party.

> People like us
> Know how to survive.
> There's no point in living
> If you can't feel alive.

We know when to kiss
And we know when to kill
If we can't have it all
Then nobody will.

"People like us"—the suggestion that the women who sing in the Bond stories are not unlike the man about whose adventures they sing isn't entirely novel. The grizzled personae adopted by Shirley Bassey were just as hard-bitten as 007. But during the period when the songs tended to ventriloquize the Bond girls any assertion of kinship sounded either shallow or slightly delusional: even when "All Time High" claims that Bond and Octopussy are "two of a kind" and "move as one," it rings a bit hollow—Octopussy is as feisty as Bond girls come, but the film doesn't position her as Bond's equal. But now the Bond girl, if it is indeed her speaking, is herself one of the villains, and may in fact be speaking to another villain. Who still occupies a safely masculine position here? Where is good old Mr. Kiss Kiss Bang Bang?

Could this sense of kinship between villain and hero stem from the villains' newfound relationship to history? They have become the repositories of history, in particular of painful and traumatic history—of *Bond's* history, no less. And by invoking a queasy, erotically tinged sense of camaraderie, they remind him that they embody what he represses—that time leaves scars, that replacing your love interest with every adventure is not the same as forgetting that the last one existed, that replacing your leading man every half-dozen movies or so isn't the same as withstanding the ravages of time. If Bond, always clean and fresh-faced and new, represents the logic of lather-rinse-repeat, the villains pick up on what time can't wash away.

These songs turn the villain's unremitting gaze into the Tell-Tale Heart of the Bond series, into the painting in the attic. The unwelcome eroticization of Bond by a clearly male gaze was really the only way these songs could talk about the wear and tear in the Bond persona. Their lyrics fasten voyeuristically on Bond's imperfections, on the repression and forgetting that is involved in starting over again and again. They turned the unavoidable bumpiness of a forty-year-old franchise that had gone through four actors in the same role, into the very essence of Bond: a man whose burden of forgetting grows with the wreckage of each adventure.

"IT WORKS"

Although it was Daniel Craig who eventually parachuted into the London Olympics with a fake Queen Elizabeth in tow, it was during the Brosnan years that James Bond became an important ideological buttress for Cool Britannia. After the Conservatives were swept out of office by New Labor, after another wave of Brit pop briefly made Yanks care about the antics of the Gallagher brothers, after soot-stained old London was reborn as a modern financial superpower, there was a sense of a British renaissance. In 1998 London was proclaimed "the world's coolest city" on the cover of *Newsweek* (long recognized as the coolest magazine at your dentist's office).

Though always more of a roving buzzword than an identifiable set of cultural products, Cool Britannia was understood by boosters and practitioners as a revival of 60s fashion and culture: Oasis sounded pretty much like pre-psychedelic Beatles, the Spice Girls drew on 60s culture for their outfits, Damien Hirst did Warhol but with a bigger budget, and James Bond, well, James Bond was still around, but somehow was suddenly cool again.

The Bond phenomenon reemerged as vital in this period that mixed nostalgia with new national pride. *Austin Powers* didn't do anything that the original *Casino Royale* hadn't done, but it brought back some of the sights, sounds, and lingo of Swinging London. When the Spice Girls got to making *Spice World*, their M-like record-label boss was played by none other than Roger Moore. Iggy Pop and Jarvis Cocker were covering Bond songs for David Arnold—it was an age of historicism and citation, and Bond became a conduit. After all, how much easier to cite a tradition that had never ended in the first place?

But Bond didn't just find his fortunes buoyed by a tide that lifted all boats—he became an active participant in the Blair government's promotional effort. Starting with *GoldenEye*, the films stopped showing generic palaces with beefeaters parading before them whenever Bond went to see M; instead they showcased the actual SIS headquarters at Vauxhall Cross, a postmodern ziggurat that the Thatcher government had deposited on top of a bunch of abandoned riverside factories. When *The World Is Not Enough* opens by blowing up that very building (it would get blown up once more in *Skyfall*) and following that explosion with a chase scene along the Thames, it's sure to take a detour through the docklands to showcase the gleaming towers, fine eateries, and expensive cars in the revitalized area around Canary Wharf. Even as the Bond films breathlessly imagined fantastical threats to British power, they celebrated the new, modern London and helped brand it abroad.

The Bond series entered the 90s with a sexy new leading man; with a country one could actually show on screen without people assuming it was a Monty Python skit about birth control; and with lucrative tie-ins with Swiss watch manufacturers, continental fashion designers, and German car manufacturers. And Bond was successful again—in 1989 *License to Kill* had failed to hold its own against Hollywood product, whereas *GoldenEye* was the most profitable Bond film since *Moonraker*.

Throughout it all Bond soldiered on under the motto that has become associated with Tony Blair and New Labor: "The challenge of modern democracy," Tony Blair once wrote, "is efficacy. Not accountability, transparency or whether it is honest or not, but whether it works." That was the ethos for the Brosnan Bonds: they aimed to please, not to dig too deep, to save the world efficiently and look fantastic doing it—they did what worked. It was a post-ideological Bond: in the title sequence for *GoldenEye* the female shapes take pickaxes to statues of Lenin—but they pointedly don't put anything in their place. That too was New Labor: ideology that refused to understand itself as such.

As in New Labor Britain, as in Cool Britannia, there was much unease to repress, but so many good reasons to repress it. Why rock the boat when things were going so swimmingly? Just as Russian oligarchs and Australian moguls were buying their way into British soccer and the British press, Bond was now for sale to the highest global bidder. But who cared, if Bond looked so damn stylish getting out of a BMW in his Boss suit? Arnold's soundtracks were basically pastiches, the old themes warmed over with only enough electronic elements mixed in to sound new without actually being new. But what did this matter at the box office? Your James Bond doesn't have a lot of charisma; he looks more comfortable modeling the tuxes than actually acting in them. But he looks right in magazine ads, so keep calm and carry on making money.

No wonder the Bond songs turned to the villains' point of view. In a period of state-sanctioned amnesia, in an era of irrational exuberance, of nauseatingly vacant ever-smiling pragmatism, their way of looking at the world—jaundiced, jealous, and old-fashioned—becomes a more interesting optic than that of the hero or his friends, who bounce from triumph to triumph without asking themselves why and whether they deserve to triumph in the first place. Because that's why Fleming turned to German, Chinese, Belgian, or Catalan bad guys in the first place: history's losers forced the English gentleman/spy to reestablish that the right side had won, had won for the right reasons, and had won decisively. "It works" is the opposite of that. It's the willful blindness of Wile E. Coyote refusing to look down in case the cliff has already ended.

During the Brosnan years it was an unbroken line of North American acts that did the looking down. Tina Turner, Sheryl Crow, k.d. lang, Garbage, and Madonna became the voice of what the glitzy, overproduced surface managed so successfully to hide, all the more successfully since it so obviously worked. But Bond's constant starting-over was taking a toll of its own, and by the early twenty-first century the enforced sunniness of the New Labor years was wearing thin. The series increasingly began to think of its constant need to start over as a problem. The preponderance of past that it carried along with itself had become traumatic. In the 70s it had shrugged off this repetition, because that was Bond's job, the director's job, the singer's job. In the 80s it had shrugged it off because, hey, as long as no one called him out on it James Bond would be just fine.

But the 90s Bond songs fell into a deadly trap, and almost took the franchise down with them: they saw themselves as *adequate*—both new enough and retro enough to "work." They had exchanged the pragmatism of the 70s, of having a job to do and wanting to do it well, for a more aggressive kind: the fake-it-till-you-make-it ethos of the new-wave outings without any of their anxiety. These songs forgot they were supposed to stick out, sound awkward, clutch at the past, find one of last year's trends and follow it badly, blink at the sight of the future. They were the perfect accompaniment to a Bond franchise that had become foolish enough to picture itself as of its time. By the end of the 90s, though, the series started to worry that the kind of sunny amnesia Bond displayed in those years might itself be a symptom of something far, far darker.

**YOU KNOW
MY NAME**
Chris Cornell

ANOTHER WAY TO DIE
Jack White   Alicia Keys

**DIE
ANOTHER
DAY**
Madonna

"Close My Body Now"

Bond's Traumas and the Compulsion to Repeat

Successful franchises ask two things of their audience: absolute memory and absolute amnesia. They expect us to recollect details and hoot with joy at callbacks. And they rely on certain things to recede in memory. Things feel new to a good sequel-watcher that should feel rote; past entries take on strange new dimensions once the latest film is out. *Star Wars* fans still upset over George Lucas's work on the prequel trilogy repress the fact that the original really wasn't a very good movie either. Indiana Jones fans who excoriate the second film for its racism conveniently forget that the first film was equally problematic in its treatment of Arabs.

The James Bond franchise requires less repression than most. Over the years it has become comfortable with repetition and pretty much discovered the pleasure of venturing up its own ass. But the critical fortunes of the franchise—which probably hit a nadir with the Moore outings of the early 80s, but went back on the ascent when Brosnan took over the role—have depended on a most peculiar bit of amnesia.

If you've read reviews of *Skyfall* you will remember many of them pointing out that this was a "new" Bond—vulnerable, traumatized, human, not the comic book hero of earlier installments. If you saw any reviews of *Casino Royale* when it came out in 2006, you would have heard about the new and tougher version of Bond, far removed from the fanciful heroics of earlier films. If you read what the critics said about *Die Another Day*, *The World Is Not Enough*, or even *GoldenEye*, you'd come across the same trope, and you'd find the "new" Bond hymned in much the same terms as he was in the reviews of *Skyfall*.

Film critics, in other words, have been fêting a "new" Bond every three or so years since 1995 (if not earlier), forgetting that they celebrated the last movie in pretty much identical terms. A lot of these reviews tie the new, tougher Bond to changes in the geopolitical landscape he inhabits—this is the Bond for the post-AIDS era or the post–Cold War era, this is the post-9/11 Bond, and so on. But that notion is contradicted by the very fact that the idea of a "new" Bond is older than the end of the Cold War—Rita Kempley opened her review of *The Living Daylights* in the *Washington Post* with the sentence "007's come a long way, baby," and that was in 1987! So it's not that the new, harder-edged Bond (or, in some tellings of the same story, the "return" to Ian Fleming's Bond) itself fulfills some deeper need. He's been around for a while now. It's instead the idea of starting over, the idea of a reborn Bond, that seems to hold reviewers in its spell—and, judging from box-office receipts, filmgoers as well.

By now, it seems, sitting through yet another globe-trotting adventure with our British superspy becomes more enjoyable (or perhaps becomes enjoyable in the first place only) when we delude ourselves into thinking that, surely, *this* one isn't just any old Bond, *this* one is different, *this* one "has come a long way, baby." There's something obsessive about it by now—about the need to reassure ourselves that, even though it may look like we're doing the same thing over and over, we're actually trying something new.

By the early twenty-first century, each new Bond song had become as much an act of recollection as of repression. A song like "Skyfall" acts as though there were a stable tradition called "the Bond song" and aims to recover it. And a song like "Die Another Day," which is far more hostile to that tradition, likewise assumes a kind of stability—a past canon, not just a catalogue, that it can dynamite. What both repress is that everything may have been tried already, that there may be no way convention can be tweaked in ways it hasn't been tweaked before. The Bond songs of the twenty-first century are haunted by the possibility that the past may be all there is, that there are no beginnings, that no newness may betide. The lyrics for Madonna's "Die Another Day" start with the high-flying hope of "shaking up the system," of "breaking the cycle," but that ambition quickly falters and devolves into the far more modest resolution to just carry on as before, and to postpone the inevitable until tomorrow:

> I think I'll find another way
> There's so much more to know
> I guess I'll die another day
> It's not my time to go.

The late Bond song draws on and is haunted by its past in much the same way that late capitalism relates to whatever came before it. Which isn't perhaps all that surprising. Within the Bond song as in the world at large, it feels like we've been doing the same thing over and over, but with diminishing returns. We've gone from making things to moving money around—or just parking it—by means of increasingly complex financial instruments. We've sped up and perfected the circulation of capital, people, and goods, but the newness this world brings us is just another iOS and even faster delivery for shit you don't need. We've stopped experimenting with new lifestyles, and instead have trained the herculean arsenal of our technologies on gilding our preexisting lifestyles.

And we've closed our eyes to the new world these endless circulations might yet bring about: we're climate denialists, peak-oil denialists, we sort our garbage but take fifty flights a year. Deep down we think: this is all there is, and it's so solid. Another world, good or bad, seems impossible. That sense steadies us, but it pains us too. We've been so good to the market, we've been so diligent in enabling job creation, we've been such good boys and girls and supported the "right to work." But it hasn't led to anything new and different, just more of the same. We live in a world without grand choices—capitalism or communism, religion or secularism. We inhabit the world we inhabit not because we think it's the right one, let alone because it's the good one—we inhabit it because there isn't another world, because we've come to distrust all those who'd seen such a world.

This is late capitalism, and this is the world to which the Bond songs offer their poison-pen hymns of praise. It takes something to gin up much enthusiasm for such a world, and the James Bond pictures are perhaps unique for the steadfastness of their enthusiasm. Any enduring romance requires repression—of slights, of mistakes, of the fact that it's all been said and done before. And toward the end of the Pierce Brosnan years the Bond songs had so much past to grapple with that they began to understand it as traumatic. As something they required counseling for. The high-70s songs—"Diamonds Are Forever," "Live and Let Die," "The Man with the Golden Gun," and "Nobody Does It Better"—had thought of carrying on the tradition as a job that you show up for and just do. From the end of the 70s through the early 80s the Bond songs keep going as if it were still 1977. The mid-80s songs had understood the job as acting a part and making tons of money while doing so. From "Die Another Day" onward, the songs worried that carrying on was a symptom, and they sought out a cure.

"SIGMUND FREUD, ANALYZE THIS"

It's amazing how quickly *Quantum of Solace* faded from memory. Sandwiched between the critically lauded *Casino Royale* and *Skyfall*, it shared their obsession with finding a *new*, more contemporary Bond. But unlike them it attempted to create this new Bond by simply stealing the visual styles of other movies popular at the time. *Quantum of Solace*, filmed in a shaky handheld style and edited within an inch of its life, was an obvious attempt to ape the Bourne movies that seemed capable of doing Bond better than Bond himself.

It may not at first be obvious why this would put pressure on the opening song. It does greatly impact the rest of the film's music: the Bourne movies had helped popularize a kind of noisy, electronic soundworld that effectively blended music and sound-design. In digital action cinema, it wasn't entirely possible any longer to distinguish between a percussion flourish and the sound of two cars banging into each other.

Traditionally, cinema had asked music to create mood and convey a character's emotion or experience. The music fulfilled this task by means of melody and harmony, mostly relying on familiar textures: string sections, brass choirs, solo wind instruments, and so on. The movies on which *Quantum of Solace* models itself no longer do this. Emotional beats are usually left unscored, the orchestra whips itself into a lather only when someone starts running or firing a gun. The "musicalized" sound effects do a terrific job reflecting a character's subjective experience; the music doesn't need to bother. This sort of film doesn't require a pop song. In fact it's inimical to the way pop songs integrate, or rather fail to integrate, into the soundscape of narrative film.

This is because Golden Age film soundtracks wedge themselves into the film's sonic world in a way that displaces all sense of realism. Peter O'Toole blows out a match, we cut to a sunrise in the desert, and the film's diegetic soundscape goes silent. And only in that silence is the orchestra able to do its work, that is to say play a piece that is marked as an interlude, a piece accompanied by sumptuous imagery but no important plot developments.

It's tempting to think this style of film scoring went out with David Lean, but that isn't true. That most quintessentially 80s of filmic devices, the montage over a preexisting pop song, relies on the same dynamic: diegetic sound and dialogue drop out (replaced by pumped fists and almost pantomimic facial expressions), letting the audience know that for the duration of the song the narrative will stick with this particular action (getting good at karate, delivering a pizza, having pottery-sex) as a kind of static vignette.

There is tremendous safety in these sorts of vignettes, which are full of sound and fury, but ultimately quite risk-free. No main character has ever gotten knocked off in one of these, no title-fight has been lost, no heartwrenching breakup has occurred. If these things happen, it's after the sequence is over. While the song plays, the world of the film coheres and we can feel reassured by its coherence.

This is the safety that modern action films seek to undercut. Many 70s thrillers did it by just not having a soundtrack at all, by pummeling their viewers with diegesis, and giving us no token as to whether a scene might harbor danger or not. Others opted for such minimalist scores that the signal effects of extradiegetic music were reduced. John Carpenter's scores work this way: by the time you realize you've been hearing a single note on the keyboard, the knife is already out and in some co-ed's neck. And of course action films in the Blaxploitation vein saturated their films with so much music that we expect every scene, intimate or spectacular, to take place against a grooving rhythm section.

By the late 90s there was a new approach, however, that flipped the old logic of the musical interlude on its head. Now everything was score, but the score was often little more than noise. Like the Blaxploitation soundtracks they relied on constant sonic saturation, but the effect on the viewer was closer to that of Carpenter's minimalist approach: the tension never let up. There were no safe spaces carved out by and carefully delimited by the sweep of melody and harmony. Instead a nervous background hum came to envelop everything.

It's difficult to imagine a sonic regime more inimical to the Bond song. The Bond song, after all, is the epitome of the musical idyll in which nothing of consequence happens. The Bond songs were the kind of artificially enclosed ecosystem in which extinct species could thrive decades past their time. Under pressure to reinvent itself, the franchise in the early 2000s destroyed that ecosystem. By that point, what magic the musical montage once held was gone, and the safety it afforded became a source of comedy or dread. It's no accident that the first opening sequence to allow the film's plot to infiltrate its Arcadian pastures stages that infiltration as a violent S&M scenario.

Whatever else these title sequences were, for nearly forty years they had been plot-free zones. Danger beset James Bond every minute of the plot, lurked in every shadow and in every far-flung locale—but during those three minutes of gyrating silhouettes, remarkably, nothing happened. When something did happen, after forty years of peace, it was a violation, an assault.

Madonna's "Die Another Day" took a hatchet to the conventions of the Bond song. And the sequence's visuals took a hatchet to the dreamy security of earlier title sequences: as Madonna's song plays, Bond is brutally tortured. Scorpions fill the screen, as does Pierce Brosnan's pain-contorted face. The traditional female silhouettes now flicker over fetishy leather boots. When a woman's face appears it is that of Bond's torturer, not his love interest.

The title sequences were the last idyll of plotless, protected privilege. In the films themselves women had learned how to reject Bond; the world had learned it could get on without him. In these sequences, it was once again all about Bond. He was safely at the center of the universe. Here women existed to be gawked at; beyond these three minutes of respite they weren't anymore. "Die Another Day" changed that.

The opening sequence and the events described in the song aren't plotless, just the opposite. They're as far as you can get from meaningless meditations on an already pretty meaningless title phrase. "Die Another Day" is all plot; the entire plot hinges on the title sequence. It's what Freud would call the film's "primal scene." The rest of the film simply works through the repercussions of what happens while the song plays. And what happens is that former colonial subjects, women, and communists finally get their hands on Bond.

The opening sequence finds Bond captured by North Koreans after a failed incursion into the hermit state. His captors drag him into a cell, and the film transitions into the title sequence almost imperceptibly (see Fig. 8.1). But the plot goes on as the song plays, as if fast-forwarding through months, maybe years of torture. Most of it is presented in the visual vocabulary we're familiar with from previous title sequences, but there are realistic shots interspersed—a grizzled-looking Brosnan getting pushed into a bucket of water, his torturer glaring at him through a doorway, scorpions being picked up by leather gloves. Those shots are

Figure 8.1 The plot invades the title sequence: the opening shot of the title sequence for *Die Another Day* (2002).

presented with perfect realism. The sequence doesn't stay in the world of silhouettes and symbols—it seems to want to stay there, but gets jolted from it time and again.

Similarly, the song Madonna provided for this sequence is pure dynamite. Few elements of the Bond-song aesthetic remain standing after she's done, and what elements remain have been subtly transformed. At first the song seems drawn to the safety of convention: it starts with some spooky strings, and seems to want to set up a catchy vocal melody. But there is something grudging about even that: the verse's melody is gappy and clipped, repetitious, confined to a four-note segment of the minor scale; the voice is digitally processed to the point that it sounds like an android Madonna. Pretty quickly, this seems like barely a melody at all, especially against the string arrangement that precedes and undergirds it.

As the song unfolds there are moments when the vocal melody seems like it's about to shake free, but then something barges in to obstruct it. All the while, a pervasive electronic-dance-music aesthetic keeps telling us that the voice can be heard as an unwelcome imposition on the synth-and-drum-machine-driven groove. It's a song that no longer has much use for a singer. For decades, Bond singers had gotten to play coy, had gotten to threaten, to menace, to entice—none of this is possible for

Madonna's voice in "Die Another Day." Just getting a word in, or perhaps a word out, in the sonic swirl around her, counts as a kind of victory.

The instrumentation, musical arrangement, and production, too, tell you this is not the typical James Bond song. Beyond the strings, whose presence signals the Bond sound, there are no traditional instruments. And even though the strings are real (not sampled), arranged by legendary film composer Michel Colombier, like Madonna's voice they're brought into the digital domain to be chopped up, distorted, and otherwise defamiliarized: "Die Another Day" preserves the string section and the emphasis on vocals of the typical Bond song, but it uses digital signal-processing to destabilize the sense of warmth and humanity strings and singing voices normally create. Most everything else is synths, and moreover synths that are programmed to *sound* "synthetic": like the scorpions that populate the title sequence the synths aren't pretending to be other instruments or voices, they are just pretending.

Madonna and her principal collaborator on the song, the French guitarist/producer Mirwais Ahmadzaï, were very resolute about bringing the Bond songs into the world of techno. This wasn't only a matter of using electronic sounds. It meant engaging with techno's history. To take one example: the synth-bass line that enters about thirty seconds in mimics the Roland TB-303 Bass Line, an artificial-sounding mini-synthesizer associated with techno, acid, and rave of the late eighties and early nineties. Madonna and Ahmadzaï likely understood that using the TB-303 in techno's accustomed manner, with overdriven-filter sweeps and the notes bending into each other, would create fissures not just in the surface of the Bond song, but in the Bond-song audience. The kind of middle-of-the-road hearing that united listeners of different generations and cultures around songs like "You Only Live Twice" was suddenly subdivided into those in the know and those that felt (and in fact were) left out. Some would hear such sounds and realize that they had a history, and specific cultural resonances, while others would just experience them as alienating and weird.

So the record presents a combustible mixture that both fulfills and subverts basic Bond-song conventions. Android or not, the voice is still recognizably Madonna's: you hear the Bond song's traditional celebrity-vocalist *and* a whole apparatus designed to make her sound strange. And despite the choppiness and the other characteristics of electronic dance music, the song still works as voice-driven pop. It's probably a virtue of this record that it was insufficiently "pop" for Bond fans and film critics (who heard it as flat, too electronic, repetitious, not hooky enough), and too vocalcentric for dance-music aficionados—while still reaching single digits on the pop and dance charts.

Whatever it was, "Die Another Day" was not neutral. It may have been the first Bond song that made you take a stand. Depending on whether you accept or reject techno as a plausible admixture with Bond-song pop, you experienced the song as either putting forward traditional pop elements only to squash them, or as a new (but still vocalcentric) Bond-song synthesis.

The lyrics meanwhile break down again and again, halting, revising. What meaning they do manage to convey between breakdowns is disturbing. The verses describe what is, in the best of cases, a person's panicked, disjointed thought process while being tortured. Given the pervasive aura of sex that enshrouds the Bond songs, it more likely describes the thoughts of a rape victim:

> I'm gonna wake up yes and no
> I'm gonna kiss some part of
> I'm gonna keep this secret
> I'm gonna close my body now

What sort of lyrics are these? Several lines aren't full sentences, some just break off midthought. The repetition ("I'm gonna") gives the whole thing an urgent note. But the urgency evaporates at the end of each line. The speaker will decide on one thing ("I'm gonna wake up"), only to then walk back that statement ("yes and no"). The speaker will decide on something ("I'm gonna kiss some part of") and then neglect to tell us what that something is. As much digital chopping as the song endures, it's not like it was ever coherent on the page. What it tries to say it cannot say; what it tries to say may not even be sayable.

And that's perhaps the most viscerally upsetting part of Madonna's concoction: given its location in the film, given what diegetic action it is used to underscore, it's pretty clear that its gappy, garbled, mechanized production is intended to reproduce the experience of a victim. Even the video for the song casts Madonna as a torture victim, so this isn't just the film appropriating a song that's talking about something entirely different. But at the same time the formal adventurousness has a sense of excitement about it: Madonna is trying to prove that new sounds can invigorate the Bond formula. The song can work both negatively, as a representation of torture or trauma, and positively, as a staging of what the lyrics call "break[ing] the cycle" and "shak[ing] up the system." Utter brutalization and a chance at a new beginning—the song declines to distinguish between them. While being ripped apart by torture, it thrills at the chance of a new beginning contained in the annihilation of the self. Not even victimhood is stable in "Die Another Day."

The reversals don't end there: because even while the destruction of the stable "I" is the dominant theme in "Die Another Day," that theme can obscure that it's the first time Bond says "I" in one of these songs. Because "Die Another Day" upends another storied Bond tradition, although one that fewer casual viewers or listeners will have picked up on: James Bond speaks in the song. When the previous Bond songs said "I," that "I" could be any number of people, but it was never Bond. The 60s songs (and some of the 70s songs) tended to situate the singers somewhere in the orbit of the villain—they seemed to know altogether too much about the lives of Auric Goldfinger, the Moonraker, the Man with the Golden Gun to be saints themselves. Some of them sneered at Bond in tones that suggested they were the bad guy's mistress or factotum, and some of them serenaded Bond in terms that made them sound like Bond girls.

This strain emerged as dominant in the late 70s, when a string of Bond ballads ("Nobody Does It Better," "For Your Eyes Only," "All Time High") clearly took the point of view of Bond girls smitten with Bond, but aware of the danger of getting into bed with him. It was this type of song, Gladys Knight's 1989 "License to Kill," that sang Bond into a six-year hiatus.

A completely different point of view greeted him when he reemerged in 1995's *GoldenEye*.

The Brosnan Bonds, as we saw, no longer speak from a Bond girl's point of view. When Tina Turner, k.d. lang, or Shirley Manson say "I," they are channeling the villain him- or herself. "Die Another Day" makes another change, and for the first time hands Bond the mic. This becomes possible only because the film's actual plot has invaded the title sequence: Madonna's lyrics make clear reference to the events on screen, providing a kind of thought-bubble for the man being brutalized as the titles roll. Of course, the song destroys even the possibility of anything as coherent and sustained as a thought—there are no questions posed, no metaphors reached for. What we hear are defense mechanisms, pure, simple, and instinctive. The lyrics themselves make this clear—there is no "ego" that says "I" here, only a quivering mass in pain that seeks nothing more than to avoid more pain:

> I'm gonna break the cycle
> I'm gonna shake up the system
> I'm gonna destroy my ego
> I'm gonna close my body now

Previous speakers in Bond songs had always gazed in repose: the bad guy watched "from the shadows," Shirley Bassey asked you "why do you hide," they remembered you from "when you were young." They took a long view of events, a view that itself implied a kind of continuity and safety. That too is gone: this speaker knows nothing but the present moment, and hopes to survive it for another day.

"Die Another Day" is almost surgical in the way it isolates the unspoken and unconscious conventions that have made these title sequences feel safe, and then turns those conventions on their head. We are given our first glimpse of the signature female silhouettes as Bond's head is being submerged in icewater. The next time we see them they play as shadows on a woman's leather boot. The song meanwhile has a string-section intro, but that intro is immediately disrupted—by flamenco-clacks and castañets. That may seem just like an unusual bit of sound design, but it's actually a sly commentary on the rules of the Bond credit sequence, and a tweak of those rules.

Those sequences had always depended on a thorough split: there's the unseen vocalist and instruments producing sound; and there are the feminine shapes doing their yoga moves on screen without making a sound. Sometimes you can hear a gun being fired in the sequence, but that's about as far as the events on the screen intrude upon the soundtrack. The eruptions, the water, the explosions, the running, the dancing—all of it happens as a kind of silent kabuki.

The flamenco-clacks and the castañets don't "come from" what's onscreen, but they acknowledge what we see in front of us: they refer to bodies colliding with objects and with other bodies. They acknowledge the song as a dance-song, but more importantly they acknowledge the physical bodies on screen. Flamenco-clacks are essentially a body as instrument; playing off against the very flamboyantly artificial synths and Madonna's heavily processed voice, they insist that underneath all this fakery, there *is* a body here doing things to another body. "Die Another Day" abandons the safe middle ground the opening songs had thus far occupied, and gets at once too close and too far away for comfort.

"Die Another Day" cites all the visual conventions of the credit sequence, but in citing transfigures them. The famous silhouettes? They appear as reflections on the boots worn by Bond's torturer (see Fig. 8.2). The characteristic lava motifs? They are far less metaphorical now, the fire that heats the implements of torture (see Fig. 8.3). The unmotivated shots of women's faces who don't show up again in the movie? Now that's Bond's torturer. The sequence has a strong BDSM-vibe, and the vocals (which feature Madonna giving little gasps and moans of pain) do their part to strengthen it. By including shots that show what is "really" happening, the sequence highlights the fact that many of its more fanciful visuals are a kind of translation of another set of events.

That further destabilizes things, because throughout the sequence objects of pain turn into objects of pleasure and vice versa: women into flames, ice into women (see Fig. 8.4). The question becomes: do fire, ice, and electricity represent the inflicting of pain or the pain itself? By turning

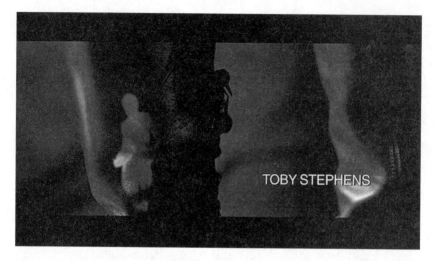

Figure 8.2 The gyrating silhouettes are integrated into the narrative, but how? From *Die Another Day.*

Figure 8.3 The visual elements of the traditional Bond-film title sequence are all transfigured in *Die Another Day.*

them into the good old gyrating silhouettes, does the sequence eroticize the means of inflicting pain (electrodes, pokers, and ice buckets)? Or does it eroticize the pain itself, the experience those means occasion? This is what necessitates "clos[ing] my body now": inside and outside become confused in this sequence. The song and the title sequence imagine a body the boundaries of which are breaking down.

Figure 8.4 Figures of pain, figures of the infliction of pain? From the title sequence of *Die Another Day*.

This emerges as a central question, because *if* the women represent pain, then for the first time a song would be explicit in saying that the women aren't things James Bond sees, imagines, or fantasizes, they instead represent *parts* of James Bond himself—in the context of this song the masochistic, feminized, submissive parts of his psyche. There is a strong undercurrent of sexual panic that runs through the song: can one be victimized by women and still be a man? The sequence finds the panic underneath 007's sexism and agitates it further. Each and every one of the visual tropes of the title sequence is recast as something representing violation.

But what recasts them? Who sees them this way? If they are fanciful depictions of torture, why the fancy? This was, as we saw, a question for the title sequences in general, but here the question becomes central. Perhaps the movie is using its fanciful visuals as a means of sugarcoating something that would be impossible to show for real. Perhaps the movie is depicting how the mind deals with trauma, how the extreme pressure of real events pushes our experience of them into the fantastical. Perhaps it is a depiction of how traumatic events are recollected.

"Die Another Day" seeks to throw itself into the depths of Bond's trauma. It's in the struggle to depict this unrepresentable experience that the song's fractured construction truly becomes effective. Madonna's record deliberately exposes its fault lines. It places highly processed but "real" voice, strings, and flamenco-clacks against "artificial" but sonically very present (and historically laden) synths. Its fragmented lyrics, which veer between ordinary and traumatic utterances, must do their work within a tense dance-versus-pop frame. In context of the credit sequence and the film as a whole, this all adds up to something volatile and unresolvable. The song depicts *both* traumatic experience *and* the impossibility of fully recollecting or expressing it.

And the rest of the movie, to its credit, does not disavow what the song tells us about Bond's condition. Nor does it disambiguate its title sequence. A lot of Bond movies do: oh, it's about a diamond mine, or a hollowed-out volcano, *now* the weird opening visuals make sense! No such luck in *Die Another Day*. The movie never acknowledges the events of the title sequence again, but they loom over the plot the way trauma tends to: totally removed from what's going on, and yet clearly motivating all the action. Impossible to understand, but equally impossible to let go of.

The very autonomy that made the opening sequences moments of safety and respite has now turned on Bond. The closed-off, even closed-in feel of the sequence reflects Bond's imprisonment, not his security. On the level of genre, the threat to Bond in this sequence is like an autoimmune disease. Genre conventions are supposed to make things stable—keep us safe—but not in this sequence. All that the Bond film and the Bond song have relied on to keep themselves safe has turned against the character.

"ANOTHER WAY"—REPETITION AS SYMPTOM

Trauma does strange things to time. It perforates its orderly sequence—long-past events start to matter in ways that they shouldn't, events that should matter immensely are blocked from memory. The act of recovering the traumatic event may be therapeutic, or it may just be an impotent pointing. Think of midcentury Hollywood movies and the way they treat unconscious memory: Marnie remembering the kill-ing of the soldier, Catherine remembering Sebastian's death in *Suddenly Last Summer*. This, this is what is causing everything. This is what "Die Another Day" attempts, but it can do little more than point.

Everything shatters in "Die Another Day," but everything looks and sounds like fake shattering. The first digital effect we hear in the song once the strings fall away is something that sounds like a cracked mir-ror, or maybe a gunshot, maybe Bond getting splashed into a bucket of icewater, but that doesn't sound much like anything. It's a dislocated sound, coming from no particular instrument, from no particular loca-tion, effect to no particular cause. Someone is getting wounded, but it's hard to spot the moment it's happening or the way it's happening. The song is obsessed with trying to isolate the moment of trauma, trying to reconstruct the temporal sequence, and has an incredibly hard time pin-ning that moment down at all. Trauma is all over it from the very first note—and from the first note the song is careful to show us that to search for its origins runs up against artificiality.

As so often, it's tempting to ascribe *Die Another Day*'s obsession with trauma to its world-historical context—it was filmed in early 2002 and released in the fall of that year and is thus the first post-9/11 Bond film. And the way the attacks on the World Trade Center were both overly present and overly mediated in the aftermath of 9/11 certainly seems to inform "Die Another Day" as well. But like the "new Bond" meme that keeps getting trotted out with each new release, the concept of trauma was neither entirely new to the series, nor has it abated since.

What is more: the elusiveness of authentic memory of 9/11 had to do with the intense mediation of the event as it was unfolding. Mediation was forced on the remembering public: most of us witnessed it through television. "Die Another Day" has a choice in the matter, but it chooses to frustrate us by having our search for authentic origins run up against fak-ery at every turn. While there may be something to the 9/11 connection, it alone doesn't explain why traumatic narratives and traumatic temporal-ity became mainstays of the Bond sound and the Bond-song aesthetic in the new millennium.

It's probably more accurate to say that the Bond series (and above all their songs) understood their own weird temporality as somehow analogous to that of trauma. *Skyfall* is the film (and the song) that makes this analogy most explicit, when it treats the title song's rummaging through fifty years of canon for the "essence" of the Bond song as pretty much the same thing as the film's psychoanalysis of Bond's childhood traumas. But traces of this idea were present in earlier outings already: Bond's quest for his own origins, the songs' quest for a sound receding into the past, and the films' treatment of Bond's subjectivity—all of them draw increasingly on the vocabulary of trauma and the recovery of traumatic experience.

Flippantly put, by the time the castañets got clacking on "Die Another Day," the Bond character wasn't suffering from flashbacks engendered by forty years of traumatic events, he was simply suffering from those forty years themselves. "The past isn't dead, it isn't even past," William Faulkner famously wrote. And it is the immense pastness that looms behind every new Bond outing, the accumulated weight of the forty years of franchise-dom, that lends itself to traumatic narratives. Not the peculiar qualities of the past mattered; its sheer quantity was enough.

The opening visuals returned to the idea of trauma in *Skyfall*, once again treating the weird iconographic tradition of the title sequences as a set of dream images to sift through, like a psychoanalyst does. But it's remarkable how differently these two sequences, *Die Another Day*'s and *Skyfall*'s, go about depicting trauma. *Skyfall* is all about burrowing, getting deeper and deeper, unearthing one layer and then the next. It's also monomaniacal in its focus—the camera tracks ever forward toward a particular point in the visual field, even if that point disperses the moment it is reached. The message is clear: maybe we can't find it, but we are looking for *one* origin, *one* point in time that would explain the trauma.

Die Another Day functions entirely differently: here trauma is about sheer excess, about dispersal. There is no focus, no origin. Fire, lightning, water, scorpions, boots—all of these have been part of Bond title sequences before, but *Die Another Day* combines them. Any of them would make plausible implements of torture, but for some baroque reason Bond's torturers decide to use them all. That muchness is probably behind the strangest choice in the iconography—the scorpions (see Fig. 8.5). There are parts of the sequence that are clearly meant to depict the products of a fevered imagination (the fiery women, for one), there are others that clearly represent the film's reality from Bond's perspective (the poker, the lady torturer), and there are things we see as an objective observer would see them. The scorpions are somewhere in between.

It appears they are used on Bond during his torture, which seems well enough. But the sequence throws dozens of the critters at the screen—did Bond stumble into the North Korean dungeon that abuts a wing of the National Zoo? One scorpion would do the job quite nicely, and really how many backup scorpions do you need? There is of course a genre where a hundred of a thing are better than just one of the same thing—the horror film. This is what the German philosopher Immanuel Kant called the "mathematical sublime"—it inspires feelings of overwhelmedness simply by dint of its extension or number. It seems like a weird thing for a spy film to rely on. What is more, the mass of scorpions looks incredibly fake.

Die Another Day wasn't blessed with the most credible special effects, but even by the film's low standards these scorpions look bad. Shimmery, metallic, very obviously digital. That may well be on purpose. For one

Figure 8.5 Even for 2002, these special effects look deliberately fake—scorpions in the title sequence for *Die Another Day.*

thing it places the scorpions somewhere between the real and the imaginary: perhaps there is one real scorpion and Bond adds the rest; perhaps they represent pain and there are no actual scorpions.

But their obvious CGI-shimmer accomplishes something else as well: the song talks about "closing my body," and in some way the visuals follow suit. The song peels back the layers behind Bond's façade with an almost surgical precision. But the visuals are busy trying to sustain the surface against any such surgical attempts on it. As Bond comes dangerously close to talking about his inner life ("Sigmund Freud, analyze this," Madonna says between verses), as he comes dangerously close to *enjoying* his torture, the title sequence obsessively restores surfaces—and makes clear that they are indeed surfaces.

This would prove to set the tone for the next four title sequences in the series: as the songs started digging deeper, the visuals became ostentatiously shallow. Like the scorpions, the visuals of the title sequence for *Casino Royale* became deliberately flat, two-dimensional, with pure icons. When a person dies in that sequence, they dissolve into a flurry of hearts or spades (see Fig. 8.6). *Quantum of Solace* rediscovers depth, but it's a depth very obviously created in a computer, as schematic avatars stride

Figure 8.6 Two-dimensionality and icons—the title sequence of *Casino Royale* (2006).

through a digital wasteland—a motif that the title sequence in *Skyfall* would likewise turn to three years later (see Fig. 8.7).

These are cartoon-like digital effects, effects that we are *meant* to recognize as such. Digitality in these sequences becomes a cypher for artificiality. This is a common aesthetic strategy in films of the mid-nineties and after, but in the Bond movies such artificiality increasingly becomes a place of refuge. As the songs start the long dig into Bond's psyche that reaches its apogee in Adele's "Skyfall," the title sequences are trying to keep up appearances. But they no longer have faith in those appearances: the visuals look like wallpaper, or a screensaver. They are appearances that barely try to fool us. It's the only way the Bond songs know to cover themselves, but they are aware it's no longer really working for them.

The songs that underscore these opening sequences combine the same compulsion to repeat with a pronounced fear of that compulsion. They understand that they have to sound a certain way and say certain things, but they no longer understand that "having to" as a matter of doing a job, as a matter of tradition, or as a part to play—they understanding that "having to" as a psychological compulsion. And they hate themselves for giving into it.

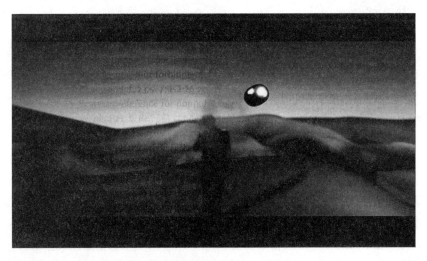

Figure 8.7 CGI in the title sequence of *Quantum of Solace* (2009).

Each of the two Bond songs that follow "Die Another Day" starts out by trying to break away from the entrenched Bond sound, but both of them swerve right back and give in. Both songs have intro sections in which aggressive guitar-playing creates a burst of anti-Bond-song energy: for different reasons each opening seems much too "rock" to fit into the canon. But both records quickly start to buckle under the weight of past Bond songs. By the end they meekly do their duties, and give off a sheepish air.

It's not hard to hear what they borrow from the Bond-song archive. "Another Way to Die," written by Jack White and sung by Alicia Keys and him, takes its acoustic-piano part—and its structural contrast between pop-oriented piano and hard-rock guitar—from "Live and Let Die." Chris Cornell's "You Know My Name" can be heard as *starting with* the guitar-driven intensity that "Live and Let Die" reaches in its chorus; it's as if "You Know My Name" wants us to forget that McCartney's record arrives at this intensity by way of a textbook-pop verse—which it stomps all over. The intro of Cornell's record thus prepares us for the corporate-rock vocal timbre of this former Soundgarden lead singer.

But the intro of "You Know My Name" also reuses a key Bond-sound artifact. Its crunchy power-chords pastiche the characteristic 3+3+2 rhythmic figure of Barry's "007," first heard in *From Russia with Love* and often appearing in later Bond songs and film scores. The heavy guitar-riff that opens "Another Way to Die" is equally compromised: its lo-fi fuzziness and blank sonic ambiance establish a world apart from the Bond sound—but only for two seconds, after which a cheesy Barry-derived horn arrangement enters the texture.

And after their aggressive guitar-driven openings, these two songs sink into late-Bond-song lugubriousness. "You Know My Name" quickly introduces flaccid string and horn arrangements. The long intro section of "Another Way to Die" works more analytically, cobbling together a mood-piece out of stuff found in Barry's garage. But it does so in an awkward and low-energy manner: for a very long forty seconds, a half-dozen slightly-misprized Bond-sound elements peek out one by one. It doesn't add up.

These songs gain little from their initial bursts of energy. In a way they reverse the strategy of Gladys Knight's "License to Kill," which begins with a direct borrowing of the "Goldfinger" intro but turns into a perfectly up-to-date late-80s R & B ballad. The "License to Kill" intro slows "Goldfinger" down, adds Knight's soulful ad-libbing, and ends up giving back more than it borrows. It gestures toward Bond-song tradition and moves on. By contrast "You Know My Name" and "Another Way to Die" show signs of exhaustion, wobble when they engage with Bond-song materials, and barely make it to the finish line.

"Another Way to Die" opened 2009's *Quantum of Solace*. While it wasn't as heterodox as "Die Another Day," it was an atypical Bond song in another important respect: it was the first duet in the long Bond canon, and it uses its duetting voices in ways that are highly unusual for a Bond song, indeed for any song. And yet from the first word the song's lyrics sound a note of fatigue. "Another Way to Die" presents itself as a long list of things that have happened before, "another" this, "another" that. And in the end each "another" turns out to be "just another way to die." Behind every detail ("a door left open / a woman walking by / a drop in the water / a look in your eyes") lies the same old, boring thing—death. There are echoes of Madonna's "Die Another Day" in this use of "another," where the lyrics forgo the far more idiomatic "die *some* other day" in favor of the rote and exhausted-sounding "I guess I'll die another day." In both songs repetition functions as a way to delay the inevitable, but given that inevitability a pronounced exhaustion hangs over the need to repeat.

> Another ringer with the slick trigger finger
> For Her Majesty
> Another one with the golden tongue
> Poisoning your fantasy
> Another bill from a killer turned a thriller
> To a tragedy.

The song's vocabulary is a trip through the Bond song's Rolodex, almost like Bond-song mad libs. Golden stuff? Check. Her majesty? Yep. Killers? Slickness? Present. "I'm gonna avoid the cliché," Madonna sings in "Die

Another Day"; this song goes the opposite route and piles cliché upon cliché until the whole construction creaks under their load. The internal rhymes give each line an almost overly thought-out quality. The way Keys and White lilt through them, they sound like tongue twisters, and their delivery seems far too polished. We've all been here before, we've rehearsed this a million times. We used to pretend it all amounted to more than just whiling away the hours before our death, but at least Keys and White have stopped pretending. However much manic intensity the duetting vocals and riff-driven instrumental arrangement bring to the proceedings, the lyrics express depressive sentiments.

The source of this depression is far more clearly laid out in "You Know My Name," Chris Cornell's song for the Daniel Craig reboot *Casino Royale*. The entire song is addressed to some phantomic "you" who, as the title goes, knows "my" name. The confident title not withstanding, it's actually quite hard to determine who the "I" and the "you" are in "You Know My Name." The title clearly suggests that we the audience know who James Bond is, even though he's being played by a guy who looks nothing like the last guy or the guy before that.

It's also a nod to what is missing from Cornell's song: "You Know My Name" stays in the Bond-song idiom, but like David Arnold's score it avoids allusions to the Monty Norman theme. That's reserved for the end credits that roll immediately after Daniel Craig finally utters the line, "The name's Bond, James Bond."

But if this is another Bond song speaking in Bond's own voice (which, as we saw, had become the preferred mode of address for the twenty-first-century Bonds), who exactly is "you"? Who is this person who is "just next in line" who will be betrayed by the odds, who has to arm him- or herself? It's unlikely to be Le Chiffre, who is already armed to the teeth and who probably doesn't think of himself as "divine." Take a look at the following lyrics:

> I've seen angels fall from blinding heights
> But you yourself are nothing so divine
> Just next in line

In lines like this one it seems as though whoever "I" is, he or she is addressing Bond—after all, the warnings the song imparts to its addressee could all apply to the very young, very inexperienced, very rough Bond we meet in the film itself. He is overconfident, inexperienced, and unprepared for the emotional toll a spy's job takes. In the song's chorus, it almost sounds as though the person speaking might be none other than M—it certainly echoes her sentiments during the various stern lectures she gives Bond throughout the film.

> Arm yourself because no one else here will save you,
> The odds will betray you,
> And I will replace you.

M of course is the person who presides over the franchiseness of the Bond franchise with a near-perfect poker face. M has no trouble addressing Pierce Brosnan as James Bond one day and Daniel Craig the next, and she's such a pro she doesn't even mention the fact that the two look nothing alike. That's something earlier Ms (Bernard Lee and Robert Brown, who presided over five different Bonds between them) also had to deal with. But what *Casino Royale* asks of Judi Dench is far more remarkable. Her character has aged forward, but the new Bond is younger and has no memory of their earlier adventures—in *GoldenEye* she is clearly new to the job. Much to Bond's dismay, now he is just starting out while she's been at it for a while. Given the song's insistence on replacing "you" with whoever is "next in line," perhaps it is indeed the wizened spymaster talking who has seen so many agents (and so many Bonds) come and go.

Still, why would M tell us that "you know my name"? We don't actually know her name at all—Bond readers know what "M" stands for, but there was never any mention of a real name for any of the Ms in the Bond canon. It would be odd for one of the world's most famous pseudonyms to insist that we know her name. No, it would seem that what is speaking in "You Know My Name" is something more rarified than a movie character, it is the spirit of the franchise itself. It is "James Bond" independent of the various Commonwealth subjects who amble into and out of the role—it is the legend that looms over Daniel Craig as he tries to step into Bond's shoes, it is the franchise that has betrayed, replaced, and passed the role to the next in line.

There's a good chance, then, that "You Know My Name" is something like a monologue, playing off *this* Bond (who is "just next in line") against the Bond persona *as such* (who will "replace you"), avatar against divine principle. Greater than any threat the villain can muster looms the traumatic history of the Bonds who have gone before, the mystical entity "James Bond" that preexists Daniel Craig and will outlive him. This entity the character doesn't recall, but the franchise incorporates it as a kind of unconscious. Adele's "Skyfall" puts James Bond on the couch, the person we see interacting with others on screen. "You Know My Name" does the same with "James Bond," a far more metaphysical figure who has transcended time, media, and many different incarnations.

Neither "You Know My Name" nor "Another Way to Die" deviates as far from Bond-song convention as Madonna's "Die Another Day." But neither of them is slavish in aping the sonic vocabulary of the earlier songs. This goes beyond their heavy-rock openings. "Another Way to Die" is the most uptempo Bond song since Monty Norman's original theme, just beating out Lulu's forgotten "The Man with the Golden Gun." "You Know My Name" is far more guitar-driven than any previous Bond song. That they don't buck tradition as obviously as "Die Another Day" has to do with the fact that by the early twenty-first century there were several Bond traditions to attach themselves to. They don't sound much like "Goldfinger," but that's okay as far as fans are concerned, because they sound sufficiently like "Live and Let Die." "Another Way to Die" draws on a Bond tradition of its own, that of the deliberate mismatch.

Just as "Live and Let Die" combines incompatible elements for the purpose of hearing itself come apart, so "Another Way to Die" puts together two universes and watches them never quite intersect. Even on paper this collaboration seems odd: both its artists were riding high in 2008, but why would you have a lo-fi faux-naïve neo-rock-and-roller like Jack White (of the White Stripes) write and produce a song for Alicia Keys, a highly professional R & B singer/songwriter? Why would you have the two artists sing as a duet, the first time the Bond songs had tried such a gambit? White gently undermines the white male privilege that got him the gig (while still benefiting from it, as ever), taking advantage of Keys's superior capabilities as a singer: Keys's voice has a polish that White's can't match, and whoever wrote the song knew that—because that person was Jack White. But he chose to accentuates this by making the chorus lie just out of his range. The result is an audible strain whenever the song reaches an emotional peak.

The song also counterposes two kinds of instrumentation, each associated with one of the two performers. While the song doesn't actually include Keys's piano-playing—a shame, since she's a better keyboardist than White—it still relies on the contrast between electric guitar (coded as "white," "rock," and "male") and acoustic piano (which reads in context as "black," "pop/soul," and "female"). The music video shows Keys at the piano and White on the guitar—the common iconography around these two musicians. But they duet with one another only in a very restricted sense—in the video they spend little time interacting and most of the song walking in different directions.

They're both exceptionally skilled performers, which covers over the mismatch somewhat, but what mismatch exists is deliberate and almost ostentatious. These are two people *trying* not to duet, *trying* not to come together. But that's probably where the song's sense of exhaustion and futility comes from: because the tweak White and Keys perform on the Bond formula is itself by now Bond formula. Not only have the signifiers they play with become part of the Bond-song tradition, so have the tricks you can use to negate them. They can do another black-music/white-music mashup; they can do another twist on the instrumental soundscape of the series. But it's not really a step out of the series' overlong shadow; it is just a step into another shadow.

The song of the Brosnan era had sounded traditional and had restricted its innovation to some electronic touch-ups, because it could tell itself, in that Blairite bon mot, that "it works"—why change it up if it's doing the job, and the alternative is too nerve-racking to contemplate? The song of the trauma era sounds traditional simply because it is scared to death of the alternative. It has no more swagger left; instead it's cowering in the cor-ner. It knows that whatever it's doing is no longer working, and it wants to let the audience know—but it's afraid of the pain, the terror, the confusion that would come with "breaking the cycle" or "shaking up the system." So after initial bursts of pain and newness, the Bond song closes its body.

NOT QUITE
THE END

WHO will "return"
as the next Bond singer?

Coda

James Bond Will Return in . . .

Fifty years is a long time. In pop culture it's an eternity. For a set of films to have held on to the same aesthetic features so tightly is unheard of. Why has James Bond kept going, why have the songs kept him company, and what does it mean to keep going now? As the franchise put one foot before the next, with a somnambulist's surety, but also with a somnambulist's level of reflection, the songs became repositories for all the series' anxieties. And prime among them is: Why take that next step? As we saw, it wasn't the question the songs started out with. From Matt Monro's "From Russia with Love," via "Goldfinger," to the *Thunderball* ballads, the songs went on because the series went on. They were responsible for telling us that the adventure you were about to watch was only one of many, and that the glories of capitalism would conjure up another madman in another two years' time. Luckily of course James Bond, his special effects department, his composer, and his costumer would ride to the rescue and defeat the excesses of capitalism with nothing so scary as a different social arrangement. Bond would do it by shooting, by screwing, by looking amazing in a tux, by lounging at a pool, and by striding into a casino with that classy theme jangling in the background. Bond's niftiest gadget was his style, and the music was a central part of it. The Russkies could steal nuke plans from us, but they would never attain Bond-style technology.

By the time they started to raise the question of what it actually *meant* to keep going, the Bond songs were almost a decade old. And that was when the fantasy became threadbare, when its contradictions began to show. "You Only Live Twice" blabbed on many of the secrets that had sustained the series thus far. Bond is magical because he allows two things to coincide that would normally be irreconcilable. When we watch him on screen, he is both a young up-and-comer and a beleaguered, middle-aged middle manager. His time is the immediate present, with the latest technological advances; but his time is also a recent, already mythic past, when people depended on the United Kingdom for world peace, when colonialism had some legitimacy left, and when whiteness wasn't "white" but simply "universal."

It was at this moment that the aesthetic fortunes of the Bond song and the Bond film diverged. Because the Bond films had no way of acknowledging that these moments, when two contradictory things could both be true, were becoming impossible. Instead, films like *You Only Live Twice* and *Diamonds Are Forever* kept reasserting them like a man afraid of forgetting his mantra. But the songs *didn't* keep going. They started to overthink and to reflect. They had done something successfully over and over again and suddenly self-sabotaged by wondering *how.* They started asking the hard questions, even if they often chickened out on answering them. So if you're looking for the Bond films to address the role of blackness in Bond's universe, the role of femininity, the role of history, you will find those moments in the songs. The directors could make films like it was 1965 for pretty much twenty years—let Corman, Scorsese, Godard revolutionize filmmaking, but *Thunderball* really doesn't look substantially different from *A View to a Kill*. Yet the musical world was changing too rapidly around James Bond for the Bond songs to not dive in. They were never eager to embrace the new, but unlike the characters they were always forced to live in it.

But given so much newness, and given their difficulty in assimilating it or even responding to it, why go on opening the films with Shirley Bassey knockoffs? The 70s Bonds had in many ways the most elegant answer, which was a shrug. This was their job, and just as James Bond didn't question his assignments, they wouldn't either. Their job description was: take (grudging, reluctant) notice of the musical world around you, then press it into a formula you know to be outdated. But still make it sound like *you*, since, you know, this is the 70s, and all crooners are now supposed to be artists and have highly personal visions. By the late 70s this led to a moment when singers refused that bargain. Buoyed by developments outside the Bond canon (disco, adult contemporary), they essentially turned the Bond song into an annex of broader pop phenomena. You couldn't hear Tom Jones's "Thunderball" on the radio and not be aware it was a Bond song. With a song like "All Time High," it was all too easy.

Weirdly enough, though they embraced a more modern sound by incorporating new wave in the mid-80s, the songs went back to sounding very much like Bond songs and unlike anything else on the radio. This put a lot of the 80s songs in a bind: they knew that listeners couldn't possibly forget the fact that they were Bond songs. But the singers also knew that those listeners would probably judge them against the Bond songs made by their parents' generation, and they seemed to expect that they'd find them wanting. Doing Bond was no longer simply a matter of showing up and doing a job—it had become a matter of faking it until you made it. Act as though you are making a Bond song, and if you're really lucky the rubes will let it pass.

The Bond songs of the 90s didn't have this problem because they sounded so much like Bassey songs. They didn't have to fake anything, they just repeated it. But that made the question of *why* Bond songs repeat themselves even more urgent. To make matters still more complicated, the 90s in Britain and elsewhere were obsessed with figuring out how their trends related to those of the 60s—and Bond had, both serendipitously and somewhat embarrassingly, stuck around long enough to have to self-cannibalize to find out. The past, the canon, was turning from something that stabilized the songs (by outlining their job, by providing the template they had to mimic in order to pass) into something that haunted them, something they secretly wished to work through, perhaps even be rid of. In closing this book we'll try to think through what it might look like if they had gotten their wish.

Why was it the *songs* that proved so attuned to changes in the broader culture, while the films they introduced blithely plowed on? Some of it surely has to do with the fact that filmmaking didn't shift as radically as pop-song production during the half-century since *Dr. No*—you could make movies in the 80s that had the optic of the 60s, and it would be okay; but making music as though it was still the 60s had long since become impossible. But if "Die Another Day," "You Know My Name," and "Another Way to Die" labor in the shadow of a half-century of Bond songs, they labor in a separate one as well. That shadow becomes noticeable in the songs' openings, which are all quite strange, and strange in very similar ways. When it comes to those openings, the songs are no longer just in dialogue with what it means to be a Bond song, but with what it means to be a pop song more broadly.

Pop songs are old and new. Assembled in the studio, pop songs are collages of discrete musical objects: place an instrument here, a sound effect there, throw in backing vocals, add reverb, and suddenly you've got a very different thing on your hands. This means that every pop song registers history in multiple ways, because each of these discrete musical objects can be new or old. What feels familiar or novel about a song is not usually a matter of an overall halo, but rather of distinct, identifiable elements. This feature or that feature functions as a callback, or a decisive tweak of the formula. The relationship between familiarity and novelty, and between part and whole, is seldom harmonious—a song almost always exists at the intersection of features that look backward and features that look forward, between elements that express the song's position vis-à-vis its forebears, and elements that are just owed to the whims and predilections of the many hands busy assembling it.

We started our book by considering how recent Bond songs looked backward in time. We will close out our book by wondering about the way the Bond songs look forward. Because we all know that this book will be outdated one day: there will be a Bond song we didn't write about, by a singer who in all likelihood was in middle school when we wrote this. We can't talk about that song, of course, but we can tell you about the future the Bond songs seem to imagine for themselves *now*. What do they want to sound like ten, fifteen, twenty years hence? Of course, when the Bond songs gesture toward the future they make no commitment—they invoke a vague future they won't ever have to deliver on. That's someone else's job, someone else's problem. But—pardon the crazy phrase—they do tell us what we *want* the Bond songs to want to sound like, the kind of future we want *them* to envision for themselves. What are the gestures that they think push the Bond song in new directions? What is the legacy they take themselves to be leaving for the next singer in the canon, and the one after that?

That's where the trio of songs that we looked at in the last chapter— "Die Another Day," "You Know My Name," and "Another Way to Die"— becomes instructive once more. All three songs open with a musical fake-out. They deploy all the elements of *one* kind of song, and then almost instantaneously revert to another kind. Why would a song begin by lying to us about where it's going, what kind of song it will be? How, and how much, does it matter that these three openings might well sound off-putting to Bond-song audiences? The first fifteen seconds of Chris Cornell's "You Know My Name" and the first few seconds of "Another Way to Die" trick us into thinking we're about to hear a true *rock* Bond song—finally, one is tempted to add.

Never mind that this happened in 2006 and 2008 respectively, long after a power-chord or an aggressive guitar-riff could be counted on to sig- nify rebellious rock sentiment. Only in a Bond song could a power-chord still have even the faintest whiff of heresy. Still, when the opening titles come on and Chris Cornell's guitar roars, it's easy to sit back and think, "Wow, the last guy on earth who really bought into the myth of rock as anti-establishment finally grew up—and only now do the producers feel comfortable doing their first rock song." But the gesture toward rock remains just that, a gesture: the rest of the song is far less rock and the opening chords are actually a dissimulation.

The first moments of Madonna's "Die Another Day," too, dissimulate about what the song will turn into. It begins Bond-appropriately, with strings and a gunshot, along with the sounds of flamenco dance. All these elements are heavily processed, so (like the electric guitars of the two songs that follow "Die Another Day"), the overall effect might chafe against audience expectations. But this opening discloses nothing about the central tension that animates the song. It signals neither pop nor electronic dance music, which are the two genres actually vying in the song; this opening gives no hint of the dance-versus-pop contrast that makes the song a special case in the Bond canon. Hearing Madonna's song, we may be lulled for the first few seconds into a sense that we know what's coming, namely what forty years' worth of predecessors have primed us to expect—orchestrated, classically inflected, simmering low-modernism—only to have that certainty brutally shattered, as the song veers as far away from the Bond tradition as it can imagine.

We can provide a quick answer to the question of why these openings try to fool us and what it means that they do: one could imagine hearing them as attempts to escape the repetition-compulsion the Bond songs have fallen prey to. They are an attempt at having one's cake and eating it too: repeat tradition, but repeat it in a new way. Acknowledge the weight of the past, but try to sidestep it at the same time. The two fake-rock songs fail in this attempt, turning in little more than a Bond song with some extra garnishes, while Madonna's contribution shows a lot more fight.

But this is really the shallow answer: the "deeper" meaning is to be found in the practices of the ordinary pop song, independent of James Bond. Pop records of the fifties and after place great weight on what happens in their first few seconds: as if aware that they could be talked over by a disc jockey, cross-faded with a previous song, or ignored until the lead vocalist enters the texture, they often try to distinguish themselves right away. An unwritten rule of pop-song production is that a record should contain some sort of compelling hook—a catchy melodic gesture,

a memorable phrase, an unusual sound—within its first few seconds
(about as far in as it takes you to say "where's the hook?"). And the record
should do so while also maintaining a balance between familiarity and
novelty, and within an understanding that pop records are supposed to
be intelligible even if they're heard only in part.

All three of these Bond songs fulfill this set of responsibilities, but they
fall into the special category of records that begin by introducing themselves as something they're not. They all begin, moreover, with what in
Bond-song terms is a burst of negative energy. The surge of the unexpected provided by those first few chords goes nowhere and evaporates
without so much as a trace. The songs start with a moment of defiance,
maybe petulance, of refusing to play along. Given that that they are so
eager to disappoint (at least for a moment) an audience expecting a traditional Bond song, they're profoundly antisocial, if what you're expecting
is a bloated horn arrangement or a staid piano accompaniment.

Even if what comes after seems to take back a lot of these initial bursts of
energy, it's an unusually confrontational stance for a Bond movie to take.
As in White and Keys's arrangement in "Another Way to Die," this stance
allows things to be noticeable and jarring that could easily be smoothed
over. But if there is no real need for the songs to make these jarring leaps,
it becomes interesting to wonder what exactly is forcing their hand. Is it
an acknowledgment of rupture, of the weird temporality that time, that
trauma has forced onto Bond and his music? Or is it just another example
of the Bond songs ticking off genres and styles (quite late in the day, as
usual), without taking the time to commit to them with any degree of
seriousness? Is it, in other words, a way of carrying on repetition, or a
valiant struggle to break free from it? And do we, the audience, in the end
want the songs to break free?

This last question may be the one these songs pose most openly. They
finally turn up the lights in the theater and put the spotlight on us, the
audience. Their lyrics—with their insistence on repetition, on exhaustion,
on replacements—basically rub our noses in it: fine, we've been repeating
ourselves for fifty years now. What's stranger—that we went back to the
well every two years, or that you took pleasure from us doing so? Do you

really want us to "shake up the system"? Do you want us to truly "break the cycle," as Madonna proposes in "Die Another Day"? Or are you happy to hear a fairly traditional song that *talks* about these things but that won't, in truth, ever be in danger of doing anything about that sentiment? Are you happy to be united in grousing over these songs online or in reviews, comparing them unfavorably to "Goldfinger," and in the bargain upholding aesthetic standards that, in your everyday listening, you'd recognize as horribly outmoded and retrograde?

Because whatever else these songs do in the brief moments of negative energy, they're opening fissures within the audience—those who think rock is dead, and those who welcome it as a much-needed shot in the arm; those who believe techno belongs on the dance floor, and those who think it can be in a movie; those who think black music and white indie rock are compatible, and those who think any points of contact will just be forms of appropriation. Those rifts close again when the songs settle into the kind of musical lingua franca the Bond song has developed over a half-century of middle-of-the-road pop, a language none of us are too invested in, but one that none of us are offended by either.

In that movement—from a seeming departure from convention to a safe return of the convention—the songs by Madonna, Chris Cornell, and Alicia Keys and Jack White challenge us by not challenging us. When we breathe our sigh of relief, we realize that, at least for the moment, the songs have stopped asking what a Bond song is (a question Adele eventually returned to in "Skyfall"), and instead start contemplating why we the audience would listen to a Bond song. They ask you: What is that you would like to hear? They say: Alright, I'm not the song you want. Well, what *is* the song you want?

It is a question that has eaten at us while penning all these loving critiques. Well, what *would* you have liked them to sound like? It's easy to nitpick and mock. How should they have been different? Sometimes we're lucky enough to have songs that might have been, or songs that existed and didn't get chosen—Alice Cooper's version of "The Man with the Golden Gun" is a pretty great track, far better than the atrocity that actually opens the movie.

But most of the time we didn't have the luxury of an alternative track, and even if we did, our certainty deserts us as soon as we approach the contemporary scene. We don't know who will write the song for the next Bond film, and we don't know what their song will sound like. We have some educated guesses, we have a few dream candidates, but in the final analysis we realize we don't know.

What is more, we're not sure what we want our dream candidate to do to the Bond-song formula. Would we want the Bond singer of our dreams to absolutely shred the conventions and formulae of the last fifty years? Probably not, having just spent 200 pages lovingly interrogating those conventions and formulae.

Conversely, ask yourself, would you want your favorite singer to put him- or herself entirely in the service of a preexisting, and ultimately not all that exciting, format? We certainly didn't. Writing a Bond song isn't something one tends to wish on one's darlings, and few of the people who have sung these songs were ever anyone's darlings. Maybe Paul McCartney is the exception, but then imagine Mick Jagger, John Lennon, or David Bowie doing a Bond song, and suddenly Sir Paul feels sort of safe. We all know we don't have to love everything he does; we admire him, but without fervor. And that seems to be required for a Bond singer.

So every time we whine about the fact that our favorite artist didn't get picked, and some talentless hack did, some part of us surely is happy that we won't have to navigate a complicated web of competing loyalties when the song comes out and sounds, well, okay, as okay as all Bond songs sound. Competent, inoffensive, a bit staid. And a similar thing happens when we rail against the many seminal musical styles the Bond songs have taken but minimal account of, if they've paid any mind at all. Would we *want* a Bond song that sounded truly contemporary, would we *want* a song that did more than just pay lip service to trap, techno, industrial, alt-country? Or are we content with a few nods to current trends, ready to mock the songs for not committing to being truly modern, but secretly relieved that they've remained anachronistic, predictable, safe?

Kibitzing about the uncoolness of James Bond songs is a ritual as old as the James Bond song. These songs have no target audience. They are meant for all of us, but they are not meant to belong to any of us. They wash into our lives and then disappear again. For precisely none of us do they become our favorite song of all time. They inspire precisely zero teenagers to form their own bands. No one picks them up and puts them on after a breakup, a death in the family, or the birth of their first child.

That isn't the job they have to do. They've known their job, and if they have at times chafed against it, they've shown up for work each time yet. They are the least megalomaniacal pop imaginable, and that is their great defect and their great charm. Feeling superior to them is part of succumbing to that charm. No one looks up to these songs—not that this keeps people from singing along to them when they come on the radio. Any loyalty to them is tinged with faint condescension, but any condescension is at least in part a kind of loyalty. There is something only they know how to do—nobody does it better.

Since we're being honest: loyalty and condescension have been our guides in navigating the Bond canon as well throughout this book. We started by following Adele back in time. She (and we) were trying to figure out what made a Bond song a Bond song. If Adele and her songwriter Paul Epworth had hopes that they'd mastered the quintessence of the Bond song, they were surely disappointed. Their song is not the summa of the Bond song. It is a Bond song. It was everywhere for a while, and it is nowhere now. In a few years' time, another song will take its place. Adele may not be okay with that, but some part of her song always knew.

And as we moved forward in time, from the first Bond songs to the moment when Adele and Epworth found themselves with fifty years of music to account for, we quickly realized that we had in a way made John Barry the villain of the piece. Perhaps somewhat unfairly. We've criticized him for being too pop and not pop enough, too "modern" and too "traditional." We say his songs sound too thin, and we say they sound too thick. We've razzed him for accepting film-scoring assignments his musical vocabulary couldn't do justice to, and we've razzed him for not scoring films during his self-imposed tax exile.

But we realize we've been asking Barry to do something nobody has ever achieved: we've wanted him to be a first-class composer of film scores, a first-class maker of post–rock and roll pop songs, and a first-class producer—Bernard Herrmann, Paul McCartney, and George Martin stuffed into one rumpled suit. Barry couldn't become that, any more than he could stop being English, having friends he wanted to hire, liking the sound of brass sections, or believing melodies should be long and lyrical. Even as we've grumbled about throwing ourselves into the worst of the Barry Bond songs, we've had to acknowledge that *any* of his Bond songs can get into your head and stay there for weeks. We've lamented the ways that Barry's songs have straitened the Bond song's career, but we've been compelled to admire how clearly he has stamped the post-Barry Bond songs. At the end of the day, Barry invented an old/new kind of pop song, and a traditional/modern way of integrating it within a film score. His songs managed to stop time—not just for the three minutes they play during the title sequence, but for more than half a century.

In writing this book, we have had to learn the same lesson as Adele and Paul Epworth. We won't master the code of the Bond song, and we won't be giving you a definitive statement of what they've meant to people over the last fifty years. We have no way of knowing what will happen next. We're not sure what *should* happen next. We hope they'll keep sounding the way they've sounded for many years to come. And we dread the possibility that they might keep sounding just the way they have. Pop is about the promise of youth and of the future: even if it's completely derivative it barges in with the cocksure stride of something unexpected, unheard-of, unprecedented. The Bond songs are pop for people afraid of the future. The two of us suspect that means it's pop for pretty much all of us.

ACKNOWLEDGMENTS

We are not—and we should have admitted as much at the outset—superfans of either James Bond or the songs that accompany the Bond films. But we grew up with the James Bond songs. They accompanied our childhood and adolescence with a sometimes amusing, sometimes puzzling, always reassuring regularity. This is a book that came out of listening deeply and intently to songs that had, when we first heard them, tended to fade into the wallpaper. We've loved drilling into them in all their weird splendor.

Others seem to have taken the same delight at giving this gaggle of pop-culture castaways a closer listen than they'd previously received (closer sometimes perhaps than some deserved). Carol Vernallis read the whole manuscript, offering insights, corrections, probing questions, and sympathetic shakings of the head; this book is better for her interventions. Our colleague Stephen Hinton followed along on our journey through the Bond canon, and read several chapters with great care and giddy enthusiasm. Other colleagues at Stanford too deserve thanks for tolerating our utterly irresponsible roving beyond all disciplinary decorum. Norm Hirschy at Oxford University Press was on board from the first and gave crucial suggestions throughout the process. The two anonymous readers for the Press spurred us to sharpen, clarify and temper many points (and saved us from several howlers). Kate Nunn and her colleagues on the production side helped make the process smoother and pleasanter than we imagined possible.

Adrian would like to thank David Copenhafer for sharpening his Wagner-tuned ear to pop's history, Mara Fortes for turning him onto the kinky loveliness of Madonna's "Die Another Day" all the way back in 2002, and Augustin Hung Le for watching the entirety of the Bond canon with him. He would like to dedicate this song to Dieter and Diemut Daub, who allowed him to watch *Moonraker* with them one Sunday night circa 1989.

And while Penny Kronengold and the late Jack Kronengold never warmed to the Bond films, Charlie thanks them all the same for helping him think about music and film in serious (and silly) ways. As ever, Charlie's brother Matthew lent his uncommonly long and accurate cultural memory, as well as his strong opinions about the Bond songs and the pop music that surrounds them.

NOTES

Introduction

15 "the modal structure or the chord": Epworth quoted in http://www. mtv.com/news/1698899/golden-globe-nomination-skyfall-paul-epworth/

22 The Bond music became important in promoting: Jeff Smith's well-researched article on the marketing of Bond songs describes the licensing arrangements that governed the music and merchandising. See "Creating a Bond Market: Selling John Barry's Soundtracks and Theme Songs" in Christopher Lindner, ed., *The James Bond Phenomenon: A Critical Reader,* 2nd ed. (Manchester and New York: Manchester University Press, 2009), 136–52.

22 "modern capitalism has no purpose": Joan Robinson, *Economic Heresies: Some Old-Fashioned Questions in Economic Theory* (New York: Basic, 1973), 143.

23 affective labor "produces ideas": Michael Hardt and Antonio Negri, *Multitude* (New York: Penguin, 2004), 108.

Chapter 1

28 Simon Winder: See his *The Man Who Saved Britain* (London: Picador, 2006) and, on James Bond's defense of Britishness in the novels, Tony Bennett and Janet Woollacott, *Bond and Beyond: The Political Career of a Popular Hero* (Houndmills, Basingstoke, Hampshire and London: Macmillan Education, 1987), 99–114.

28 "musical code": Epworth quoted in http://www.hollywood.com/
    movies/golden-globe-nominated-producer-says-adele-recorded-
    skyfall-vocals-in-10-minutes-57154792/

31 "compulsion to repeat": Sigmund Freud, *Beyond the Pleasure Principle*
    trans. C.J. M. Hubback (Vienna: International Psychoanalytic Press,
    1922), 21.

39 Camp "cannot be taken altogether seriously": Susan Sontag, "Notes
    on 'Camp'" [1964], in *Against Interpretation, and Other Essays* (New
    York: Macmillan, 2013), 284.

Chapter 2

51 the MacGuffin: Hitchcock interviewed in François Truffaut,
    Hitchcock, revised ed. (New York: Simon and Schuster, 1985), 137–39.

Chapter 3

78 the concept of the haiku and the person of Basho: Ian Fleming, *You
    Only Live Twice* (New York: Penguin, 2003), 109.

78 "As Basho said, or almost said": Fleming, *You Only Live Twice*, 135.

79 "the state of your health": Fleming, *You Only Live Twice*, 16.

Chapter 4

108 the "masculine organ": Ian Fleming, *The Man with the Golden Gun*
     (New York: Penguin, 2004), 34.

112 boa constrictors and a chicken: Jon Burlingame, *The Music of James
     Bond* (New York: Oxford University Press, 2012), 264.

Chapter 6

139 to actually sound nervous: We're informed here and throughout
     this chapter by the discussion of new wave's nervousness in Theo
     Cateforis's *Are We Not New Wave?: Modern Pop at the Turn of the
     1980s* (Ann Arbor: University of Michigan Press, 2011), especially
     86–94.

163 "the oldest person in the audience": Glen quoted in Burlingame, *The
     Music of James Bond*, 185.

Chapter 7

166   the "system of objects": Jean Baudrillard, trans. James Benedict (London and New York: Verso, 2005), 180. Baudrillard's point is that advertising may not succeed in persuading us to buy a particular object, but its goal is to make us subscribe to the imaginary contained by the totality of such objects.

169   "only a number": Ian Fleming, *Casino Royale* (New York: Penguin, 2002), 13.

169   "racially, subject is probably": Ian Fleming, *Casino Royale*, 14.

171   Barry heard some tracks: as reported in Burlingame, *The Music of James Bond*, 210.

177   "something you can enjoy on the surface": quoted in Burlingame, *The Music of James Bond*, 220.

178   the homosocial triangle: Eve Kosofsky Sedgwick, *Between Men: English Literature and Male Homosocial Desire* (New York: Columbia University Press, 1985), especially chapters 1–2.

181   "whether it works": Tony Blair, *A Journey: My Political Life* (New York: Vintage, 2011), xviii. The complete sentence runs as follows: "Not accountability, transparency or whether it is honest or not, but whether it works to deliver effective change in times that need radical change."

Chapter 8

186   "007's come a long way, baby": Kempley's review is archived at http://www.washingtonpost.com/wp-srv/style/longterm/movies/videos/thelivingdaylightspgkempley_a09f96.htm